ODS

Building the
Operational Data Store

W.H. Inmon

Claudia Imhoff

Greg Battas

John Wiley & Sons, Inc.

New York • Chichester • Brisbane • Toronto • Singapore

This book is dedicated to Ed Young,
a friend and an inspiration

Publisher: Katherine Schowalter
Editor: Robert Elliott
Managing Editor: Micheline Frederick
Text Design & Composition: Integre Technical Publishing Co., Inc.

This text is printed on acid-free paper.

Library of Congress Cataloging-in-Publication Data:

Inmon, William H.
    Building the operational data store / W.H. Inmon, Claudia Imhoff, Greg Battas.
      p. cm.
    Includes index.
    ISBN 0-471-12822-8 (acid-free paper)
    1. Database management. 2. Management information systems.
  I. Imhoff, Claudia. II. Battas, Greg. III. Title.
  QA76.9.D3I5374 1996   95-16914
  658.4'038'028574–dc20   CIP

Printed in the United States of America

10 9 8 7 6 5 4

Preface

When the New World was as yet without human population there were first the deer trails. Then early man came along and there were native American trails that followed the deer trails. In later years, the native Americans showed the trails to the mountain men and trappers. Soon, the wagons of the homesteaders and ranchers followed where the mountain men had once trod. The ruts formed by the wagon wheels made by the homesteaders began to connect newly sprouting towns. And in time, the traffic to these towns blossomed as farmers and ranchers brought their goods to market. Soon the farm-to-market roads were graded, then paved. With the advent of the automobile, two-lane roads covered the paved roads, which then were subsumed by four-lane roads, which ultimately gave way to interstate highways.

Along the way, throughout the progression from deer trail to interstate, new growth, new opportunity, new functionality, and new demands caused the familiar pathway of today to be uprooted, refined, and improved into a gateway for tomorrow. With each improvement there was both a cost and a new functionality or benefit. Each improvement built on the foundation of the past, driven by requirements and opportunity. And today, in a world of mature networks of transportation, in the appropriate place there is a wide mixture of graded roads, deer trails, and interstates, according to the natural laws of economics, demand, and functionality that have evolved over the years.

A similar manifest progression can be witnessed with the evolution of information systems. First there were simple accounting applications that ran on punched cards and paper tape. Then magnetic tape appeared and a whole new class of applications became possible. Tape gave way to disk storage and database management systems, and another whole new environment of computing developed. With online processing the technician and the businessperson became intertwined as never before. Soon there was relational database and database on personal computers.

But each new improvement in technology often failed to displace the older application systems that were built with earlier technology. The newer systems built around or extended the older legacy systems. The result was a lack of integration across the many aging application systems and older technologies that remained in place as the technological evolution marched onward. The lack of integration of older applications led to integrated databases, which gave way to historical integrated databases that included both detailed and summarized information. And finally there were online integrated databases. Each step in the progression of databases and their accompanying systems was marked by the recognition of the limitations of the existing technology and the need to expand the opportunities for information processing. Each step along the evolution of information systems provided great new opportunities that were not possible with the existing technology of the day and the then current way of doing business. Each step in the progression of information systems had an expense associated with the opportunity. And at each step along the way there were detractors proclaiming that the current way of building systems was adequate if we would just "do things right" or just have the right level of "commitment" to today's technology.

From the humble beginnings of punched card applications and magnetic tape master files there has evolved a world of old unintegrated legacy application systems, of every shape and variety.

Somewhere in the late 1980s or early 1990s the realization came about that a higher-level architecture was required in order to make sense of information systems. There simply was a finite limit to what was attainable with unintegrated legacy application systems. The first major architectural entity that was discovered in this evolution of information systems architecture was the data warehouse. The data warehouse was an integrated, historical repository of data that supported almost exclusively the world of DSS processing. It was the data warehouse that provided the foundation for the fulfillment of the promises of earlier technologies such as DSS and EIS. Data warehouse provided the path through which organizations began to do a whole new style of processing.

The new style of processing proved to be very valuable to the competitive world in which organizations were attempting to gain and protect marketshare and to maximize both short-term and long-term profits. In short, for very good reasons, data warehouse attracted and kept a large portion of the attention of serious system developers and the business community.

The key driver for decision-support systems was the opportunity presented by improving iterative business processes—not the functions of the clerk but the functions of the knowledge worker. To improve iteratively belied the architectures of serial computers, nonrelational databases, functional applications, and repetitive functions.

But data warehouse was only one interesting (and important) construct of the evolving architecture, although a very powerful and useful construct. As people were building the data warehouse, the discovery was made that there was another architectural entity that was beginning to be as well defined and understood as the data warehouse. That construct was called the *operational data store* (ODS). The ODS had some characteristics very similar to the data warehouse. Indeed, in the early days, the operational data store was sometimes confused for the data warehouse. But the operational data store also had some very distinct differences from the data warehouse.

In many ways, the combination of the operational data store along with the data warehouse "fleshed out" the modern information architecture of systems. Together these two architectural constructs complement each other and combine (along with legacy systems and DSS/EIS systems) to form a complete picture of modern systems architecture.

Data warehouse has been adequately described in other books, which are mentioned in the references. It is assumed that the reader has at least a passing acquaintanceship with data warehouse. This book is about the operational data store—what it is, how it is built, how it fits into a modern systems architecture.

The operational data store in many ways is the embodiment of what once was called "subject databases." In years past, as organizations struggled with the lack of integration of their legacy applications environment, there arose the notion that the legacy systems needed to be reshaped into these subject databases. The appeal of subject databases was undeniable. But the realization of their implementation was another matter altogether. For many reasons, building and implementing subject databases turned out to be very difficult. For example:

- Whatever their deficiencies, legacy systems, once entrenched, proved very difficult to replace.
- The technology required for the full implementation of subject databases as originally envisioned never materialized.
- The demand for information was more immediate than what could be accommodated by a subject database.
- The plan for building subject databases required data models that in many cases took as long as five years to complete (and even then often were not complete).

Ironically, the operational data store has a strong kinship with many of the objectives of the subject database of yesteryear. One important difference between the operational data store and subject databases is that the ODS is able to be implemented without years of design and modeling, and does not require superhuman technology for implementation.

Some of the more important subjects to be covered in this book are:

- What is an operational data store?
- How does an operational data store compare/contrast to a data warehouse?
- What does the modern systems architecture look like and how does the operational data store fit within that architecture?
- What is the system of record and how does it relate to the operational data store?
- What are the design considerations of the operational data store?
- What are the steps in the design of the operational data store?
- What administration considerations are there?
- What does the operational data store workload look like?
- What about hardware platforms and the operational data store?
- What about DBMS technology and the operational data store?
- What about CASE technology and the operational data store?
- What methodological considerations are there?
- Which should be built first—the operational data store or the data warehouse?

This book is for the systems designer, the systems architect, the database administrator, the data administrator, computer science students, management that needs to build an operational data store, and the vendor of products that fit within the realm of architecture. This book defines what an operational data store will do for a company and what it will not do. The reader will be equipped to build an ODS and to properly place it in the context of a larger architecture.

Thanks to the following people for various kinds of support and encouragement:

Jim Ashbrook, Prism Solutions
Arnie Barnett, Barnett Data Systems
Doug Cheney, AT&T GIS
Richard Cohen, Prism Solutions
Paul Cooper, Tandem Computers
Cheryl Estep, Chevron

Jeanne Friedman, screenwriter
Jon Geiger, Florida Power/Light
Kevin Gould, SYBASE
Suzy Green, Bell South
Lowell Fryman, Intelligent Solutions
Carol Haywood, RAM Mobile Data
Rob Holbrook, Tandem Computers
Dave Imhoff, Valleylab
Melba Inmon, Forest Rim Technology
Ed Kerr, QED
Jim Kerr, Kerr Systems International
Peter LaPorte, Prism Solutions
Hung Le, Prism Solutions
Dave Liles, Tandem Computers
Gary Melnik, Tandem Computers
Brenda Moncla, US WEST Communications
Jim Ogle, Bell South
Sue Osterfelt, NationsBank
Bill Pomeroy, Keane, Inc.
Cynthia Schmidt, Prism Solutions
Gary Scott, Bell South
Betty Spinelli, Xerox Corp
Cass Squire, Prism Solutions
J. D. Welch, Prism Solutions
Ed Young, Prism Solutions
John Zachman, Zachman International

Bill/Claudia/Greg

Contents

Evolving to the Operational Data Store

In the beginning of the information systems profession were applications. The design of these early applications was shaped by the understanding of the requirements of the business at the time the applications were designed. For the most part, the early applications focused on the day-to-day clerical needs of the organization. The applications were built, or otherwise acquired, one application at a time, in a piecemeal, unintegrated fashion. Figure 1.1 shows day 1 of the genesis of the information systems that exist today.

Soon the business needs of the corporation changed and the corporation started to do maintenance on the applications, as seen in day 2 of the progression (Figure 1.1). The applications required a lot of changes for a variety of reasons, among them:

- New requirements that were only recently recognized
- Changing business requirements
- New opportunities that only became apparent with the advent of the implementation of the application

At the same time that the original applications were being maintained, there arose a request to get more information from the applications. The significance of this request for information from an existing base of information systems was not recognized

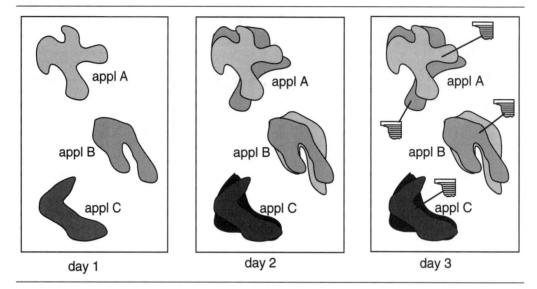

Figure 1.1   There is a predictable progression in the way systems and technology are implemented.

at the time it was made. But history has shown that, indeed, the desire to obtain further information from an existing base of information systems was a very profound request.

The first attempt to satisfy the request for more information resulted in the writing of programs that created reports, as seen in day 3 (Figure 1.1). These reports were typically written in COBOL, and were written in a customized fashion. The theory was that getting more information out of an existing base of information systems was as simple as writing reports. Unfortunately, there were some major limitations with writing reports as the means to satisfy the information needs of the organization.

The first limitation was that when a report was written it was limited to the data that resided in any one given application. If there was a desire to get further information from other applications for the report, then merely writing a report would not suffice. A second limitation was that once the reports were written, they were constantly being changed and maintained. A considerable effort was required in order for the end user analyst's changes to be accommodated. A third and very obvious limitation with using reports to try to get information out of a base of existing information systems was that the reports themselves required a large customized, and often complex effort to be written in the first place. A fourth limitation was that when similar data was retrieved from different sources, the data was inconsistent. In short, the practice of writing customized reports as the only means of satisfying the information needs of the corporation passed quickly.

The next step in the progression of satisfying the information needs of the corporation was to "interface" the applications together, as seen in day 4 of the progression, shown in Figure 1.2.

Figure 1.2 shows that in day 4 applications are "interfaced" together. This means that when one application needs data from another application for the purpose of reporting, the requesting application sends a transaction or notification to the application holding the data. Once the holding application receives the request for data, the data is located and is passed back to the requesting application.

While interfacing data works well in theory, there are some major drawbacks. The first is that the application holding the

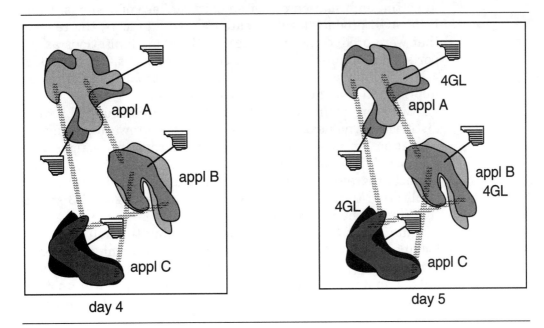

day 4   day 5

Figure 1.2   The thirst for information drives the progression.

data that is being requested may not welcome interruptions in its processing pattern. For example, if the application holding the data that has been requested is a high-performance application that is processing many transactions per second, a request for 100,000 records in the middle of the high-performance processing window will not be welcome. A second drawback to interfacing applications is that even if the data is received back at the requesting application with no fuss, there is the task of integrating the requested information with the information that already resides at the application. Such integration is traditionally very difficult to do.

The next step in the progression of the thirst for information was to use 4GL products, as seen in day 5 (Figure 1.2). The notion behind 4GL products was that information was difficult to acquire because reports could not be written fast enough. There were claims that 4GL products would increase the productivity of an organization by as much as 1,000 percent. There was no question that 4GLs provided a significant gain in the writing of code over COBOL. But the speed of production of code was not the main reason why organizations had such a difficult time in getting information out of an existing base of systems. Even if the 4GL products could create code very quickly, the reports that were produced were subject to the same limitations as reports that were produced on a customized basis. Very quickly, 4GLs were unveiled as the panacea to the problem of gathering information from an existing base of systems.

But soon, reality dawned and the limitations of 4GLs were discovered. The next step in the progression toward getting information out of an existing base of information systems was the introduction of the extract program, as seen in day 6. The extract program is one in which a program moves data from one application to the next on a wholesale basis. Figure 1.3 shows this step in the progression.

An extract file is created by rummaging through data and looking for units of data that meet some predetermined criteria. Once having found data that meets the criteria, the qualified data is moved off onto an extract file and shipped to another application. In some ways, extract files represented an advance over interfaces, in that there is a minimal disruption to the processing window of the application holding that data that has

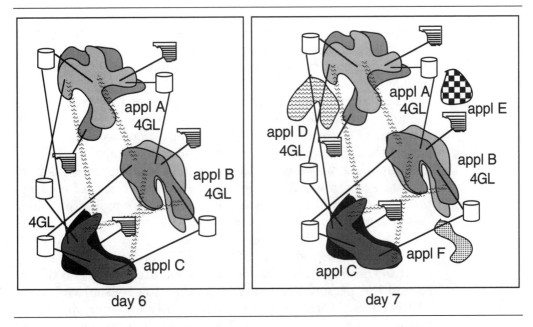

Figure 1.3 The progression continues as new applications are built and extract processing becomes a reality.

been requested. But there were some major problems associated with extract files. The first problem with extraction is that the data put into the extract file is never more current than as of the moment when it is extracted. As soon as the extraction process completes, the extracted file starts aging. A second problem with extraction is the machine resources required for doing the extraction. A third problem is that once the data is extracted, it has to be integrated with the data that already resides in the application where the extracted data is being sent. This integration process is a very complex activity. Either the data that is extracted retains its definition and context from the originating application or the extract process must transform the data to the definition and context required by the requesting application. And finally, in the face of many extraction files, there soon was a massive proliferation of redundant data.

For these reasons, the extract approach was not a good long-term solution. The progression toward accessing information from a base of existing information systems continued.

At this time in the progression there had grown to be a large number of older applications, and the difficulties manifest in these applications became apparent. New theoreticians sprang up and declared the development techniques of the past to be ineffective.

The theoreticians of the day declared that new applications should be written in a new and improved manner. Once written, the natural superiority of the new applications would be so apparent that they would displace the older, "bad" applications. So fresh applications were written in a new and improved fashion, and soon they were implemented. But for a variety of reasons, these newer applications had a difficult time supplanting older legacy applications, whatever difficulties and whatever shortcomings the older legacy applications had. Day 7 in Figure 1.3 illustrates the introduction of new and improved applications.

Into the fray came the personal computer (PC). The theory behind the personal computer was that the reason why there had been a general failure to successfully pull information in a timely, usable form out of the existing information environment was that the wrong organization had been in control of information processing all along. The Information Technologies (IT) organization had been making promises for the delivery of information for many years and had not delivered. Figure 1.4 shows day 8, where the personal computer is brought into the information processing organization and is given to the end user community so that the end user community can take control of their own destiny.

With the arrival of the personal computer the end user was freed from the tight control of the IT organization. The personal computer proved to be immensely popular. But merely bringing the personal computer into the organization hardly sufficed to satisfy the hunger of the end user for information. Very quickly the end user found that, with no data to operate on, having the PC on the desk was an exercise in futility.

The next step in the progression was to allow the end user to hook the personal computer up to the systems of the corporation. This hookup to the "official" corporate systems was accomplished through gateways and simple networks, as seen in day 9 (Figure 1.4). But soon the end user discovered that it was one thing to have access to official data and it was quite another to make

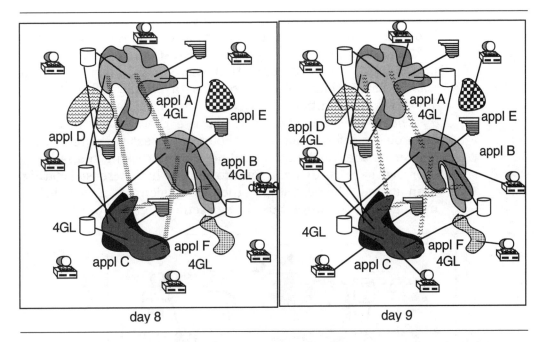

day 8   day 9

Figure 1.4   The end user takes control with the PC and by adding gateways to the corporate computing environment.

sense of that data. Once allowed into the corporate systems, the end user was subject to the same lack of integration, the same lack of consistency, and the same limitations that everyone else was subject to prior to the advent of the personal computer. A few end users persevered and were able to succeed in accessing and analyzing data. But technology itself stymied many users. The result was a stratification of users into a new business social order—information-starved users or information-rich users. The illusion that getting information was as simple as buying a personal computer and turning the end user loose with the equipment faded quickly.

The next step in the progression of trying to get information out of existing information systems was to buy ever more powerful personal computers, which were quickly called "workstations." The workstations at first ran on a 286, then a 386, and then a 486 chip. Soon there were Pentium chips. Powerful spreadsheets were added as well as desktop database management systems. Soon there were gigabytes of data that were economical to store and manipulate on the work station, as shown in day 10 (Figure 1.5). But for all the power that was being added to the desktop, there was general frustration with information processing because the data that was going into the desktop was no better than the data that was available before. Figure 1.5 shows the addition of powerful tools to the desktop.

The progression continued because there was still a real demand for information even though the past track record for delivering that information had been unsuccessful. If anything, over the years the demand for information had increased, rather than abated. The next step in the progression was toward interlinking all of the workstations, as seen in Figure 1.6.

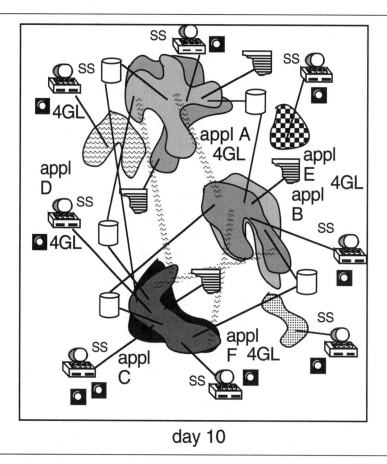

day 10

Figure 1.5   Spreadsheets and powerful workstation technology are added.

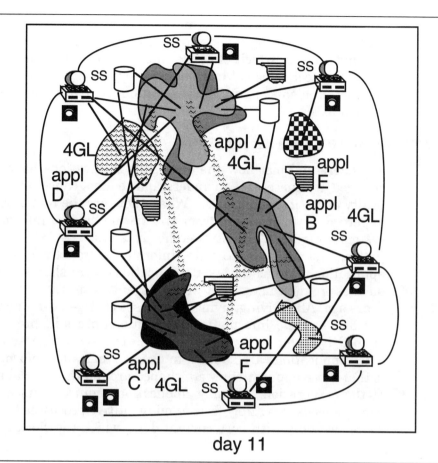

day 11

Figure 1.6   Networking is added to the equation.

Figure 1.6 shows that workstations and personal computers were interlinked in a network, as seen in day 11. While there were certainly some advantages toward establishing a network of this variety, making communications easier did nothing to improve the quality of data that was available for analysis.

Over the years there has been a wide variety of technological band-aids placed over a very serious wound. All the technological band-aids in the world will do nothing to address the fundamental problems at the root of the inability to access information. Adding more technological band-aids to the chaos shown in day 11 does nothing for an organization other than to heighten the desire for information. Nothing short of a fundamental restructuring of the base applications will suffice to form a foundation on which effective information processing can be done. The technological band-aids have patently not addressed the root problems of getting information from an existing information base.

AT THE HEART OF THE MATTER

To understand just how the old legacy applications have to be changed, it is necessary to understand the root causes of the difficulty in getting information. What, then, are the root problems of getting at information from an existing base of information systems? Figure 1.7 illustrates the obstacles.

The first difficulty in getting information from the base of old applications is that those old applications were shaped around business requirements that were relevant as long as twenty-five years ago. All thriving, living businesses change over a quarter-century, but the information applications are still profoundly shaped by their early requirements. The second reason why older applications are so hard to use as a basis for information is that those applications were shaped around the clerical needs of the corporation. Shaping application requirements around clerical needs inevitably focuses on repetitive processes that are concerned only with very current data, which the clerical com-

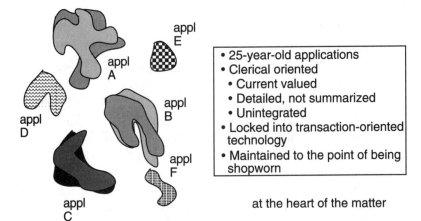

- 25-year-old applications
- Clerical oriented
  - Current valued
  - Detailed, not summarized
  - Unintegrated
- Locked into transaction-oriented technology
- Maintained to the point of being shopworn

at the heart of the matter

Figure 1.7   Rethinking the architecture of applications.

munity needs in order to run today's business. By focusing on today's data, the opportunity to store and use archival data preempts management of the opportunity to examine data over the spectrum of time. In many cases, management would like to compare today's results with last month's, or last quarter's, or even last year's similar results. But a clerically focused application of necessity does not have the historical foundation required to support a long-term view.

The second reason why the clerical perspective does not support management's needs for information is that the clerical community focuses on detailed data. While detailed data is fine for the day-to-day clerical needs of the organization, management needs to see summary data in order to identify trends, challenges, and opportunities. And summary data was never designed as an integral part of the legacy application environment. Of course, detailed data is required in order to calculate and reshape summarizations. While management needs to look at things on a summarized basis, the detail that supports the summary allows the data to be looked at with flexibility.

The third reason why the clerical perspective does not suffice for management's need for information is that the clerically oriented applications were built one application at a time, and there was little or no integration from one application to the next. The result is that the old legacy applications cannot easily and reliably be combined to produce a unified perspective of data.

The fourth reason why the older legacy applications are not viable as a foundation for informational processing is that the older applications were built on a foundation of older transaction-oriented technology. While it was fine for the purposes for which it was originally intended, older transaction technology is not appropriate for today's informational processing.

A further reason why older legacy applications are not appropriate as a foundation for informational processing is that in many cases the older legacy applications have been maintained to the point that they are fragile. Many organizations are reluctant to do any large or complex amount of maintenance to applications that have been altered to the point of being threadbare.

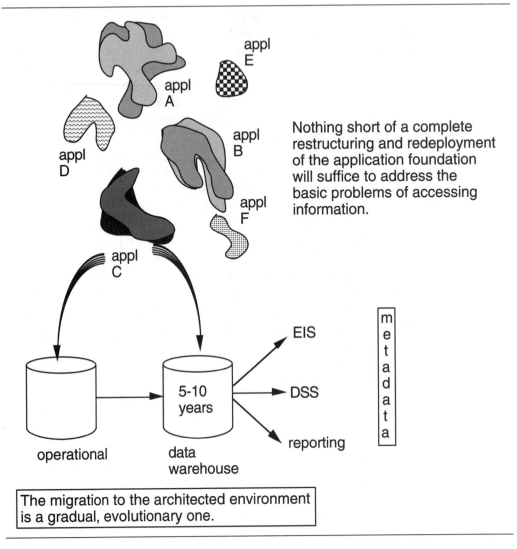

Nothing short of a complete restructuring and redeployment of the application foundation will suffice to address the basic problems of accessing information.

The migration to the architected environment is a gradual, evolutionary one.

Figure 1.8   Further rethinking the architecture of applications.

A CHANGE IN ARCHITECTURE

For these and other reasons, the older foundation of applications will not suffice as a basis for the important informational processing that organizations need to do in order to become efficient, competitive corporations. Nothing short of an entire change in architecture and a fundamental restructuring of the applications foundation will suffice. Fortunately, there is an alternative architecture, which consists of a separation of processing into two broad categories—operational processing and Decision Support System (DSS) processing. Figure 1.8 depicts the classic architecture that companies discover they need in order to bring about fundamental changes to their legacy systems environment.

The architecture outlined in Figure 1.8 is one that has been well described in other books and articles. See the references for a complete description of the literature that describes the architecture.

THE DATA WAREHOUSE

The centerpiece of the architecture is the data warehouse, which positions an organization for informational processing. Furthermore, a data warehouse can be built quickly and tangible results can be achieved and demonstrated to the sponsor of the data warehouse effort. There are many very positive aspects to the data warehouse environment. A simple view of the data warehouse concentric architecture is shown in Figure 1.9.

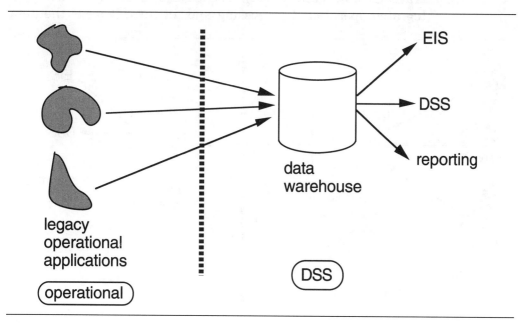

Figure 1.9   For all the advantages of the data warehouse, it did nothing for the integration of the operational environment.

Figure 1.9 shows that older, disparate applications feed the data warehouse, where data is integrated and stored over a lengthy period of time. There are many advantages to the data warehouse. But for all of the advantages, there are some disadvantages, or limitations that deserve to be mentioned. The major drawback to the data warehouse concentric architecture is that it does nothing for the organization seeking *operational* integration. As long as the organization is seeking integration for informational processing, then the data warehouse is ideal. But when the organization requires operational integration, the data warehouse *is not* the proper architectural construct.

Figure 1.10 shows that there is an alternate configuration or architecture that does take into consideration the need for operational integration.

THE OPERATIONAL DATA STORE (ODS)

Figure 1.10 shows that the unintegrated applications of the legacy systems environment feed what can be termed an operational data store (ODS). The ODS is a basis for doing integrated operational processing and, in turn, it feeds the data

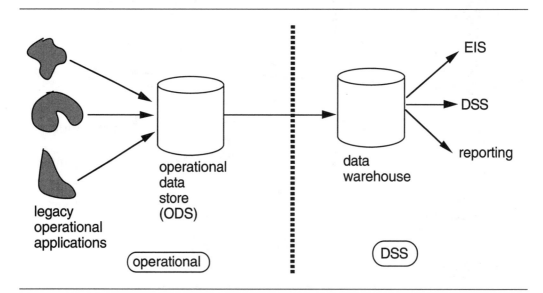

Figure 1.10   An alternative to the classical integrated informational architecture is one in which there is an architectural construct—the operational data store.

warehouse. There is still a clear line between operational processing and informational processing. The ODS is a separate architectural entity from the data warehouse.

The operational data store serves the needs of the operational environment while the data warehouse serves the needs of the informational community. For those organizations requiring operational integration, the ODS is the architectural entity that fulfills their needs.

WHAT IS AN OPERATIONAL DATA STORE?

An operational data store is an architectural construct that in some ways looks very much like a data warehouse. But in other important ways the ODS is very different from a data warehouse. Figure 1.11 illustrates the definition of an operational data store.

An ODS is an architectural construct that is:

- Subject oriented
- Integrated (i.e., collectively integrated)
- Volatile
- Current valued
- Contains only corporate detailed data

Each of these aspects of an operational data store deserves an explanation.

Subject Oriented

The operational data store is designed and organized around the major subjects of the corporation. The major subjects of the corporation are typically such things as CUSTOMER, PRODUCT, ACTIVITY, POLICY, CLAIM, and SHIPMENT. The operational data store is *not* organized around any specific application or function. The subject orientation of the operational data store is one of the ways in which it represents a collectively integrated image of data across the corporation.

Integrated

The data found in the operational data store is an aggregation of detailed data found in the legacy systems that feed it. As

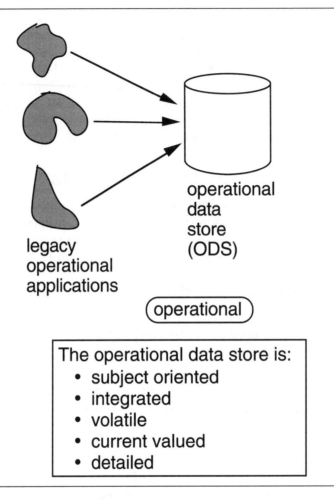

legacy
operational
applications

operational
data
store
(ODS)

operational

The operational data store is:
- subject oriented
- integrated
- volatile
- current valued
- detailed

Figure 1.11   Operational data store characteristics.

the data is pulled into the ODS from the legacy systems, the data is fundamentally transformed into a consistent, unified whole. The transformation and integration of detailed legacy data results in a truly integrated, corporatewide understanding of data as it resides in the ODS. The transformation of data into the operational data store is very similar to the transformation and integration of data that occurs as legacy data flows into the data warehouse. As the older legacy application environment becomes integrated over time, the interface to the operational data store becomes cleaner and more straightforward. Indeed, over time some data may be entered into the ODS directly.

Volatile

Data in the operational data store is updated on a regular basis. Every time the data in the foundation source systems—the legacy systems—changes, the operational data store needs to be updated. In some cases, the update of the operational data store occurs on a very quick basis—second by second and transaction by transaction. In other cases, the update of the ODS occurs only periodically—every hour or every day. In still other cases, the update of ODS data is casual, happening on a twenty-four-hour basis or even longer. In any case, however quickly the operational data store is updated, the data in it is very much subject to change.

Current Valued

Data in the ODS is quite up-to-date; there is very little, if any, archival data found in it. If, for whatever application need, archival data is found in the operational data store, it is never more than a few days old (or at most, an accounting cycle's worth of data). If the designer finds that data older than a few days is being placed in the operational data store, the question needs to be asked—why?

Detailed

Data in the operational data store serves the operational community and as such is kept at a detailed level. In most cases, storing detailed data is straightforward and easy. But in other cases, what constitutes detailed data is not clear. For example, suppose that a corporate executive wants to look at the collective account status of an international customer that is found in the ODS. The collective account balance of the corporate customer is calculated as a result of many individual account balances (which are constantly changing).

In that sense, the operational data store collective account balance is very much a calculated piece of information. However, in the eyes of the corporate executive, the collective account balance is still a single piece of information that is constantly subject to change. From the perspective of the end user—the corporate executive—the collective account balance of the international company is very much a detailed piece of data. (Said another way, what may be detailed to one community may well be summary to another community.) Furthermore, even though the decisions that result from the data in the ODS are being made at the executive level, they are nonetheless operational decisions. The operational data store then represents a uniform collective view of data.

COMPARING THE DATA WAREHOUSE AND THE OPERATIONAL DATA STORE

The operational data store is similar to the data warehouse in some respects, but is very different from it in other respects. The operational data store and the data warehouse are *identical* when it comes to being subject oriented and integrated. There are no discernible differences between the two constructs with regard to those characteristics. However, when it comes to volatility, currency of information, and detail, the operational data store and the data warehouse are very different. Data in the ODS is subject to change every time one of its underlying details changes. If an operational data store represents a collective bank account for a large international customer, then every time *any* of the customer's individual bank accounts change, the collective account changes as well. In the case of a data warehouse, changes are created by taking a snapshot. Each snapshot is placed in line with other snapshots, creating a historical record of data.

The second way that the operational data store and the data warehouse diametrically differ is in the currency of data. The ODS contains very fresh and current data. In most cases, there is *no* archival data whatsoever in the ODS. If archival data must be placed in the operational data store, it still is very current. For example, an ODS designer may place data that is no older than twenty-four hours in an operational data store for reasons known only to the designer. But nowhere would data of any significant age be found in an operational data store. The data warehouse, on the other hand, contains data that is rich in history. The data warehouse contains data that may be as much as ten years old.

The third major difference between the operational data store and the data warehouse lies in the summary data that is found in each. The operational data store contains data that is detailed, while the data warehouse contains much summary data. (For an in-depth discussion of the different kinds of summary data refer to the Prism Solutions Tech Topic on summary data listed in the Reference section of this book.) Of course, data in the operational data store can be summarized, and a summarized value can be calculated. But because the summarized value is subject to immediate change, it has a short effective life. Such summary data is called "dynamic summary data."

Summary data that is found in the data warehouse, on the other hand, is data that is static. Because it is static, it can be (and often is) stored for long periods of time. This difference in the types of summary data found in the data warehouse and the operational data store, then, forms the third major difference between the two environments.

SUMMARY

There has been a predictable progression from the early applications that were developed up to the point of the building of the operational data store. Driving the progression is the desire to get information out of an existing older legacy base of information. In the early days, reports were written. Then, interfaces between applications were created. Next, extracts were created along with the usage of 4GLs. PCs were added as well as communications and sophisticated software. The net result was a technological mess. Organizations discovered that a fundamental change in architectures was the only effective way to address the problem. Soon, the data warehouse was created; but it was good for only the informational aspects of processing. For organizations desiring to achieve operational integration, the data warehouse did nothing. Thus was born the architectural entity known as the operational data store. The ODS is subject oriented, integrated, volatile, current valued, and detailed.

There are some notable similarities and dissimilarities that characterize the operational data store and the data warehouse.

2

The Corporate
Information Factory

The operational data store, data warehouse, and the older legacy applications combine to create a common architecture that can be called a "corporate information factory." Figure 2.1 shows the most common form of the corporate information factory.

CORPORATE INFORMATION FACTORY

Figure 2.1 shows that raw, detailed data is put into the corporate information factory by means of data capture, entry, and transaction interaction with the older legacy applications. The raw, detailed data is integrated and transformed and then passed into the operational data store or the current detail level of the data warehouse. As the refined data passes out of the operational data store it goes into the current level of the data warehouse. Once the refined data is summarized, it passes from the current detail level of the data warehouse into the summarized level of data in the data warehouse. Informational processing can be done throughout—at the operational data store level, at the current level of detail, or at the summarized level of detail. The corporate information factory provides the context and infrastructure in which the operational data store resides and interacts with the other components of the architecture. As will be discussed in this chapter, there are variations in the corporate

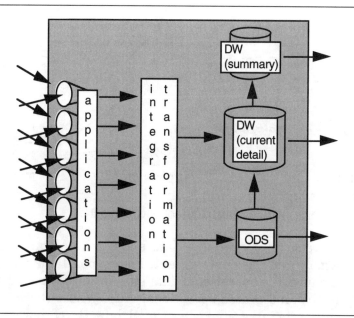

Figure 2.1 The corporate "information factory" of which the ODS and data warehouse are a prominent part.

information factory. The corporate information factory that has been described is in its most general state, as shown in Figure 2.1.

In some cases, the corporate information factory has an operational data store and a data warehouse. In other cases, the corporate information factory has only a data warehouse. When there is an operational data store there is always a data warehouse, but the converse is not true. The flow of data from the older legacy systems environment within the context of the corporate information factory is illustrated in Figure 2.2.

In one case, data flows from the applications into the data warehouse. In the other case, data flows from the applications into the operational data store. Then, once into the ODS, the refined data flows into the data warehouse. Both flows of data are normal and acceptable. Based on the simple lines of flow that have been described, the two most common forms of the corporate information factory are shown in Figure 2.3.

Figure 2.3 shows that in one case there is only the data warehouse and the legacy systems environment and in the other case

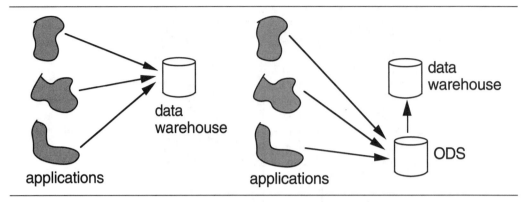

Figure 2.2   The flow of data in the different environments.

there is an operational data store, a data warehouse, and the legacy systems environment. The corporate information factory includes the operational data store where there is a need for collective, integrated operational data. Where there is no need for corporate integrated operational data, the corporate information factory does not include the ODS. It is noteworthy that many corporations run quite successfully with no need for corporate integrated operational data. In that vein, it is noted that there is a high cost associated with the building and ongoing operation of the ODS. The underlying technology—hardware, DBMS,

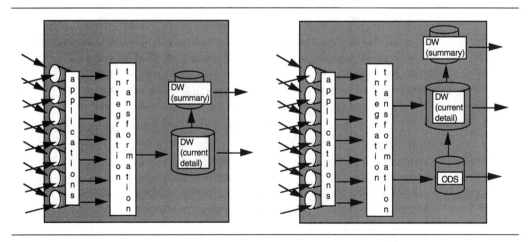

Figure 2.3   Two variations on the same theme—both are valid architectures.

etc.—of the ODS is typically expensive. In addition, the work required to integrate the legacy application systems data into a cohesive, collective integrated form is never easy or cheap, even in the face of automated tools that are designed specifically for the purpose of building the operational data store.

DIFFERENT FUNCTIONS AT DIFFERENT LEVELS

There are different functions that are performed at the different architectural constructs within the corporate information factory. Figure 2.4 shows the different functions that are found within the different levels of data and processing. The applica-

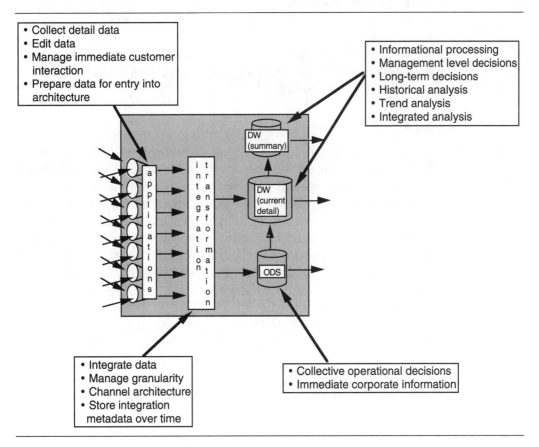

Figure 2.4   The different kinds of functions that are fulfilled by the various components of the architecture.

tion layer of the corporate information factory serves the purpose of collecting raw data, editing that data, and performing the basic and routine function of interacting with the customer. Once the raw detailed data has been edited and collected, it is then prepared for entry into the operational data store and/or the data warehouse (depending on the type of corporate information factory). The entry and integration of data into the operational data store and/or the data warehouse is done by means of going through the transformation and integration layer. As data passes through the transformation and integration layer, a variety of transformations occur, such as the following:

- Reformatting data
- Changing the key structure of data
- Converting data
- Recalculating data
- Choosing between multiple sources of data
- Changing technologies
- Summarizing data
- Filtering data

After the raw detailed data is transformed and integrated, it then passes to either the operational data store and/or the data warehouse. As data passes to the operational data store, the corporation is able to use the data in an operationally integrated, collective manner. The operational data store is the architectural construct that enables operational, integrated corporate informational processing to occur. Refined, integrated data passes into the data warehouse from both the operational data store and the integration/transformation layer. Once the integrated data enters the data warehouse, classical informational processing is enabled. At the higher levels of summarization of the data warehouse, management-level analysis and reporting occurs.

DIFFERENT FUNCTIONS IN DIFFERENT COMPONENTS

Different functions then occur at different places within the corporate information factory. Another way to understand the fundamental differences between the data and the processing that occur at each architectural construct of the corporate information factory is in terms of typical transactions and activities that are executed at each level. Figure 2.5 depicts the different types of activities that occur throughout the information factory.

At the direct customer interaction level, individual customers engage in detailed and up-to-the-second transactions with the bank using online applications. During the direct customer interaction, it is determined whether a check can be cashed for an individual customer—Judy Jones.

At the operational data store level, an entirely different kind of interaction occurs. Here, the online operational collective account for a large customer—AT&T—is managed. A corporate officer decides on the interest rate to be given to AT&T based on the collective balance and status of *all* of AT&T's accounts as of the instant the decision is made. The analyses and decisions made here are up to the second, operational in nature, and collective.

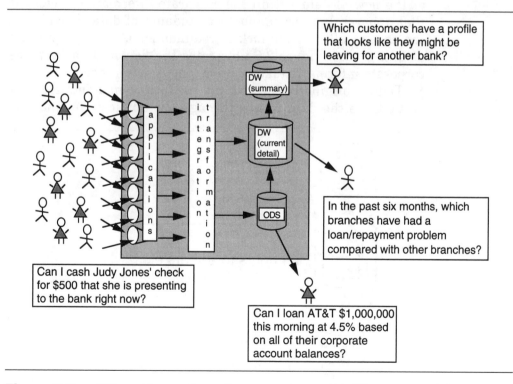

Figure 2.5 Different types of questions are answered at different parts of the architecture.

The current detailed data of the data warehouse is used for yet another purpose, that of ad hoc analysis of the branch banks. The analyses and the decisions made here are long term and strategic in nature.

At the historical summary level of the corporate information factory, data is used for even higher, longer-term functions. Identifying and analyzing patterns of data are typical analyses done here, such as the determination of the common profile that emerges among customers that leave the bank.

There are, then, very different functions and communities of interest being satisfied at the various levels of the corporate information factory.

REDUNDANCY OF DATA

One of the comments typically made when a person first looks at the flow of data within the corporate information factory is that apparently there is much redundancy of data. Such is not the case at all, but the lack of redundancy is hardly apparent at first glance. Figure 2.6 illustrates the flow of data from one corporate information factory component to another.

Data is originally entered into the factory in a detailed, raw state. Once the data passes through the applications and into

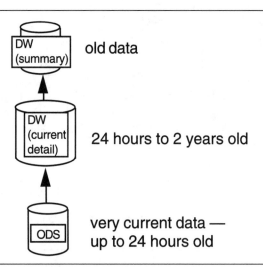

Figure 2.6   From the standpoint of timeliness of data, there is little or no overlap among the different architectural constructs.

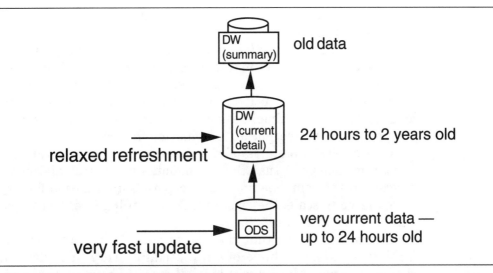

old data

24 hours to 2 years old

relaxed refreshment

very current data —
up to 24 hours old

very fast update

Figure 2.7   The speed of update reflects the timeliness of data within the different constructs of the architecture.

the integration/transformation layer (where a significant transformation of data occurs), the data enters the ODS. Figure 2.6 shows that only very fresh data finds its way into the operational data store. Once the data ages more than a few days in the ODS, the data is moved to the data warehouse current level of detail. The data ages for a long while in the current level of detail—up to two years.[1]

After the data is no longer needed in the current level of detail, it is moved to archival storage and/or the summarized levels of storage, as indicated in the diagram. The movement of data based on the timeliness of data then points out that indeed there is an absolute minimal amount of redundancy of data within the corporate information factory. In line with the age of data within the components of the corporate information factory is the reconstitution and replenishment cycle of the data. Figure 2.7 shows the rate of reconstitution and replenishment

---

[1]Note: the length of time the detailed data ages in the current level of detail of the data warehouse is a function of the business of the enterprise. Some businesses need current detailed data to contain data no more than six months old. Other businesses need the current level of detail to contain data as old as ten years. The value of two years is offered only as a mean across many lines of business.

for the operational data store and the current level of detail of the data warehouse.

Data is moved into the operational data store very quickly in most cases, but it is moved into the current level of detail of the data warehouse on a relaxed basis. The movement of data and the reconstitution and replenishment of the different levels relate to the timeliness of the data found in the various components of the corporate information factory.

One of the anomalies of the diagram of the corporate information factory is that the components are not at all drawn to scale. If the components of the corporate information factory were drawn to scale, they would look something like the components shown in Figure 2.8.

Figure 2.8 shows that the operational data store contains a relatively small volume of data, certainly very little data in comparison with the current level of detail. The summary data is smaller than the current level of detail but larger than the operational data store. And the current level of detail contains a huge amount of data.

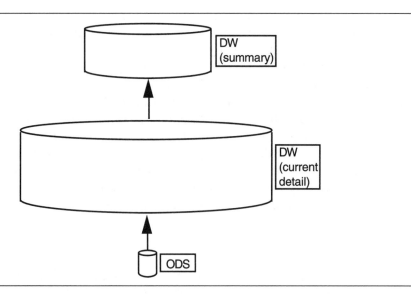

Figure 2.8   The different architectural constructs drawn to scale.

THE INTEGRATION/TRANSFORMATION LAYER

One of the interesting aspects of the corporate information factory is that of the integration/transformation layer. The integration/transformation layer is the mechanism that allows the detailed applications to communicate with the operational data store and the data warehouse. The integration/transformation layer consists of code, data, procedures, and metadata. When the ODS and the data warehouse are being supported by the world of old, unintegrated systems, the integration/transformation layer is complex, as seen in Figure 2.9.

The sheer number of interfaces going into and out of the integration/transformation layer presents its own problems and adds to the complexity of that layer. The age of the older legacy applications and the fact that the applications were never de-

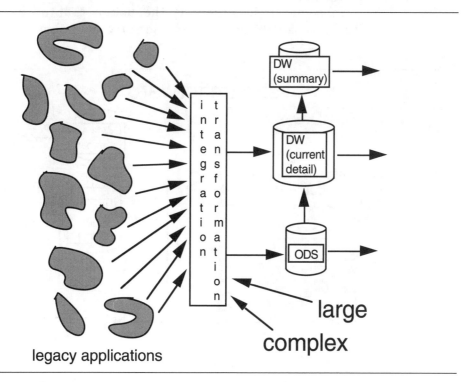

Figure 2.9　In the face of many old, unintegrated applications, the integration and transformation process is large and complex.

signed with integration as a priority also contribute mightily to the complexity of the interface. Yet another complicating factor is the mixture of software packages along with custom-written in-house applications. All of these factors add up to a very complex interface between the old legacy systems and the other two (operational data store and data warehouse).

But when the application component of the corporate information factory is highly integrated (an infrequent occurrence at best!), where the applications are subject oriented and highly integrated, then the integration/transformation layer is straightforward and relatively simple, as shown in Figure 2.10.

Of course, where integration is achieved, there is the issue of maintaining integration over time as well. Even where the complexity of the application interface is not an issue, there is the issue of the volume and speed of movement of data through the integration/transformation mechanism.

In some circles, there is the notion that if the application layer is subject oriented and integrated then the integra-

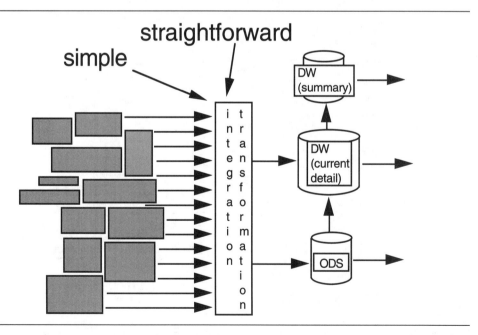

Figure 2.10 Where the application foundation is tightly integrated and well designed, the integration and transformation component is much simpler.

tion/transformation layer is not needed. Such is not the case at all. The integration/transformation layer is needed even if the application layer is perfectly integrated. Much more occurs in the integration/transformation layer than straightforward integration, for instance:

- The changing of technology
- The summarization of data
- The routing of data for movement to the operational data store or the data warehouse
- The creation of the metadata infrastructure

DIFFERENCES IN TECHNOLOGY

Using conventional technology when the different components of the corporate information factory are built, different platforms are used for each of the different components. In such a manner, the very different operating characteristics of the various components can be accommodated. Any given component can be optimized for the type of processing that occurs on it.

However, on occasion, the operational data store and the data warehouse may be built on the same technological platform. When the ODS and the data warehouse are built on the same platform, the technology that houses them is internally separated by what can be termed "firewalls." The data that is physically housed on one side of the firewall serves one environment and the data that sits on the other side of the firewall serves the other environment. As long as there is the firewall separation of the data, then it is possible for a single technology to serve both ODS and data warehouse purposes. Using conventional technology, it is not normally a good idea to physically combine the operational data store and the data warehouse on the same platform.

One reason why the operational data store and the data warehouse do not combine well on conventional technology is the significant difference in the requirements for underlying technology needed to support the ODS and the data warehouse. A conventional technological platform is able to optimize one set of tasks. When a platform attempts to optimize on diametrically opposed sets of tasks at the same time, it ends up being nonoptimal for any task.

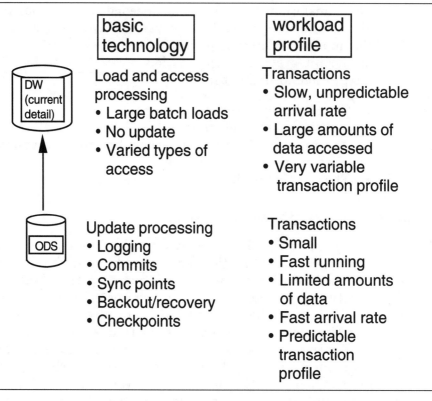

	basic technology	workload profile
DW (current detail)	Load and access processing • Large batch loads • No update • Varied types of access	Transactions • Slow, unpredictable arrival rate • Large amounts of data accessed • Very variable transaction profile
ODS	Update processing • Logging • Commits • Sync points • Backout/recovery • Checkpoints	Transactions • Small • Fast running • Limited amounts of data • Fast arrival rate • Predictable transaction profile

Figure 2.11   The technological requirements for the various environments are very different.

Figure 2.11 illustrates some of the basic differences in the requirements for technology that underlie each of the various environments found in the corporate information factory.

Figure 2.11 shows that the world of the data warehouse is a world of load and access technology. Data is periodically loaded into the data warehouse. Once loaded there, it is accessed. General-purpose record-level update is not normally done within the confines of the technology that houses the data warehouse. The absence of general-purpose record-level update processing makes data warehouse load-and-access processing efficient. There is no need for log tapes or journaling in a data warehouse. There is no need for record locking or COMMITs. In short, the processing on the data warehouse platform is very simple, straightforward, and efficient. But the simplicity of processing within the data warehouse does not end with the absence of a need for a high-level of integrity of database processing. Other important differences between data warehouse processing and ODS processing are that the physical blocks of data can be loaded so that there is no freespace in the data warehouse. (Since no update will occur, no space needs to be reserved for future space management.) And data in the data warehouse can be heavily indexed since no individual transaction update will occur that will cause the indexes to be rewritten.

In addition, the data in the data warehouse can be organized to accommodate the large transactions that will be used to read and analyze it. It is normal for a single data warehouse transaction to issue tens of thousands of calls (or more!), something that would never be accommodated in an operational data store. The workload that is formed by transactions also constitutes a major difference between the technological requirements in the operational data store and the data warehouse. The data warehouse typically has a very variable workload run against it. The transactions that run against the data warehouse are of the very large variety. It is normal for as many as 10,000,000 records to be read during a data warehouse transaction. In addition, the transactions vary in size radically within the data warehouse. The variability of the size of the transactions and the variability of the rate at which the transactions arrive at the processor form another difference between the technological requirements of the data warehouse and the operational data store.

Still another (and perhaps most important) reason why the data warehouse and the operational data store requirements don't mix well technologically speaking is that the operational data store requires a physical organization optimal to the flexible update processing of data and the data warehouse requires a physical organization optimal to the flexible access of data.

Normally optimizing flexibility of the physical organization of data implies that data of like varieties is physically aggregated. (In other words, the data is normalized.) Data in the operational data store—where transaction access efficiency is optimized—is organized quite differently physically. In the operational data store, data is organized so that efficient access may be made on an individual transaction basis. This entails bringing together an eclectic collection of data in a single physical unit, the exact opposite physical organization of data that is optimal for the data warehouse. (In this case, the data is physically denormalized.) And at the end of the day, data can physically be organized in only one of two ways—either optimally for the data warehouse or optimally for the operational data store.

For these reasons (and plenty more that are not mentioned here), the underlying technology that is optimal in the support of the data warehouse is very different from the underlying technology required to support the operational data store. Of course, if firewalls are used in the same technology, then ODS data and data warehouse data can reside on the same platform.

The operational data store is typified by general-purpose record-level update processing, where many transactions have a need to access the ODS and update records in it with no chance of an integrity conflict. For this reason, ODS processing must be managed with a high degree of locking, COMMITs, and checkpointing. The transaction profile in the operational data store during the peak period day is very stable. The peak period transaction accesses a small number of units of data—typically from two to ten units of data. Furthermore, the pattern of arrival in the operational data store environment during peak period is reasonably uniform, with predictable peaks and valleys. From the standpoint of internal physical data organization, the operational data store requires that different types of data commonly related by a single key value be physically stored in a single physical location in order to make performance acceptable.

BULK STORAGE

There is another important component of the data warehouse/ODS corporate information factory environment—that of bulk storage. Bulk storage is the place where old archival data is located, and is almost always some form of electronic storage media. Bulk storage is less expensive than classical disk storage. Bulk storage is accessed less frequently than disk stor-

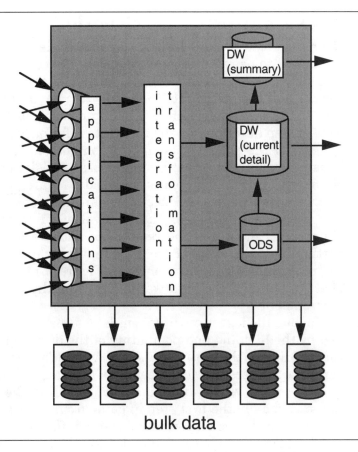

bulk data

Figure 2.12 Bulk data is an important but passive part of the corporate information factory.

age, and is accessed more slowly. Almost always, bulk storage is accessed en masse, where many records are simultaneously accessed. It is unusual to have to access bulk storage for the purpose of retrieving a few records. Figure 2.12 shows how bulk storage fits in the ODS/data warehouse corporate information factory.

Bulk storage is an important part of the corporate information factory because, economically, the amount of data that resides in the corporate information factory must reside on multiple media over the long haul. The bulk storage medium is one that best not be treated as an afterthought.

WHAT HAPPENS TO LEGACY APPLICATIONS?

Over time it is natural for the complicated legacy systems environment to be rewritten and replaced. The corporate information factory is the architecture that results from the eventual rewrite and replacement of the production environment. Figure 2.13 shows the legacy systems environment being replaced over time, a step at a time, by the corporate information factory.

Part of the older legacy application goes to the data warehouse. Typically, data that is summarized and data that is old—six months or more—is placed in the data warehouse. In addition, reports that are produced for management find their way into the data warehouse. The removal of summary data and old archival data, and the removal of massive amounts of reporting have the effect of greatly simplifying and streamlining the production/legacy environment. Figure 2.14 illustrates the effect of building the data warehouse from the legacy systems environment.

In fact, the legacy environment is so streamlined and simplified by the building and populating of the data warehouse that the building of the data warehouse is considered to be the precursor to successful reengineering of the legacy environment. Because of its very salubrious effect, building the data warehouse is usually the first step in going from the legacy systems environment to the corporate information factory.

The second step in the dismantling of the legacy environment is the building of the operational data store, if an operational data store is to be built at all. The operational data store will contain collective integrated data and will be used for corporate integrated decisions. In almost all cases, the operational data store will *not* contain the edit, capture, and direct end user interface. (This topic will be discussed later in this book.) The operational data store is usually built after the data warehouse is well under way. As in the case of the data warehouse, the building of the ODS has the effect of greatly simplifying the legacy environment. After the operational data store is designed and populated (assuming that the ODS is built at all), the front-end collection and editing application systems are now in a position to be integrated. The progression of development of the data warehouse and the operational data store is seen in Figure 2.15.

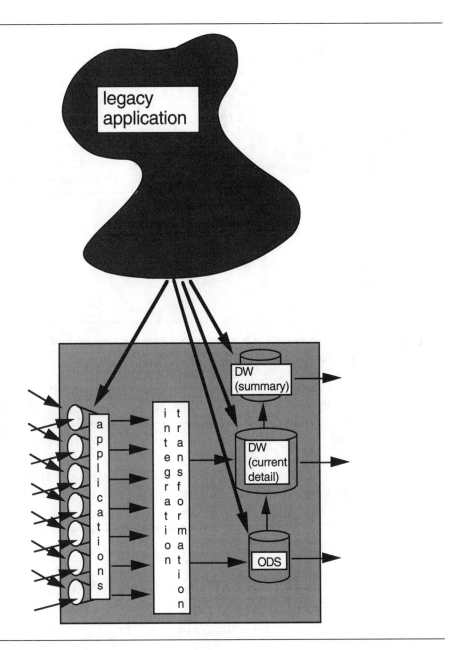

Figure 2.13   Dismantling an old legacy application.

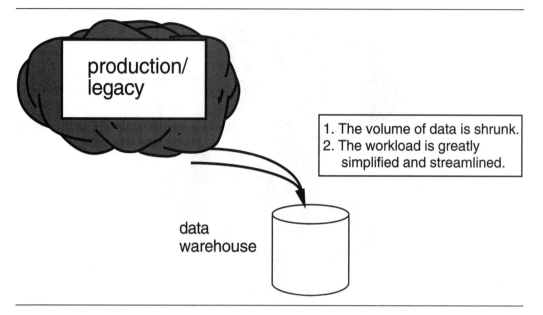

Figure 2.14   Building the data warehouse first has a very beneficial effect on the legacy environment.

Figure 2.15 shows that each construction of the different components of the corporate information factory has a profound and healthy effect on the management of the production/legacy systems environment.

Not until the data warehouse and the operational data store have been built will the legacy systems environment be reduced to a point of smallness and simplicity of data and processing that the production environment will be able to be effectively integrated.

CORPORATE INFORMATION FACTORY AND METADATA/METAPROCESS

One of the interesting aspects of the corporate information factory is that the entire environment is intellectually unified by a single data model. Figure 2.16 shows the unifying effect of the enterprise data model with regard to the corporate information factory.

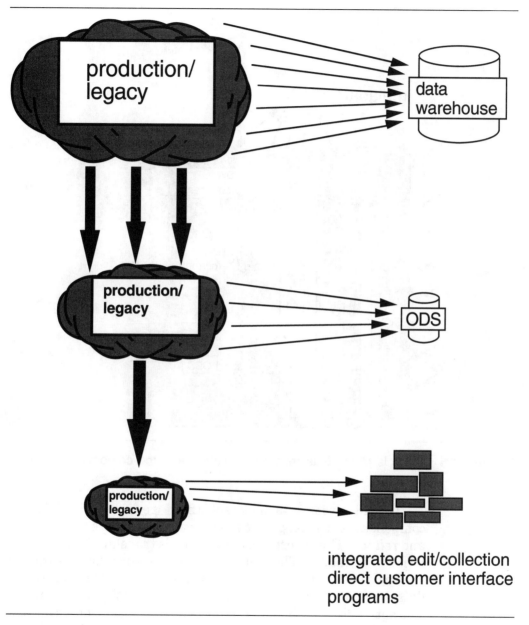

Figure 2.15   The recommended sequence of building for the different components of the corporate information factory environment.

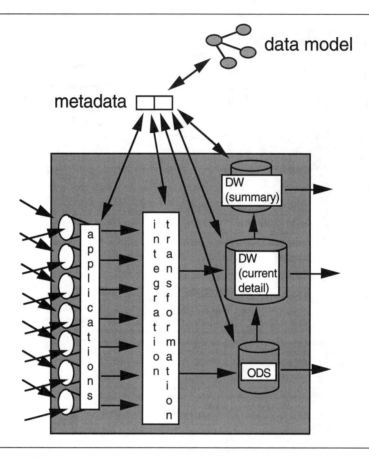

Figure 2.16   The role of the data model and metadata in the corporate information factory.

The enterprise data model sets the stage for how the different components of the corporate information factory are to be shaped and related. The enterprise data model is translated into several forms of metadata. The metadata—in its several forms—then is used as a basis for design for the data warehouse, the operational data store, and the integrated edit and collection applications. The enterprise data model then provides the basis for a cohesive and unified view of the components of the corporate information factory.

In addition to the corporate information factory requiring metadata, the corporate information factory also requires metaprocess information. Metaprocess information applies to the processing that is done in the operational data store and the legacy systems (or capture and edit) processing. The metaprocess information identifies and codifies the repetitive activities that surround the corporate information factory. The metaprocess model in conjunction with the metadata model defines the unified information paradigm that serves as a roadmap for the data and system architect.

SUMMARY

The corporate information factory is made up of several components—the operational data store, the data warehouse, the integration/transformation layer, and the edit and collection applications. There is a different flow of data throughout the corporate information factory depending on the application and the contents of the information factory. The corporate information factory may or may not contain an operational data store, depending on whether there is a need for collective operational, integrated information. The different components of the corporate information factory serve to fulfill the different information needs of various communities.

Because of the transformation of data that occurs as data passes to the operational data store or the data warehouse and because of the aging of data as it passes from the ODS to the data warehouse, it is said that there is little or no redundancy of data between the data warehouse and the ODS. There is a real difference in the reconstitution and replenishment time for the operational data store and the data warehouse.

If the legacy environment is large and unintegrated, then the integration/transformation component will be large and complex. But if the edit and collection environment is integrated, then the integration/transformation component will be very straightforward.

3

Class I, Class II, Class III
Operational Data Store

There is an architecturally recognizable entity known as the operational data store. But within that entity are some distinct classes of operational data store. In addition, the ODS has some operating characteristics that are unique. This chapter explores some of the more interesting aspects of the architectural characteristics of the operational data store.

THE OPERATIONAL DATA STORE WITHIN THE INFORMATION FACTORY

The corporate information factory may or may not have an operational data store, as mentioned in the previous chapter. Figure 3.1 illustrates what the corporate information factory looks like when there is and when there isn't an operational data store.

If an operational data store is optional, then what characterizes a corporation that needs one, as opposed to one that does not?

Operational Data Store Discriminators

The first discriminator between corporations that do and do not need an operational data store is that of size. The larger the corporation, the greater the chance there will be a need for an operational data store. The smaller the corporation, the

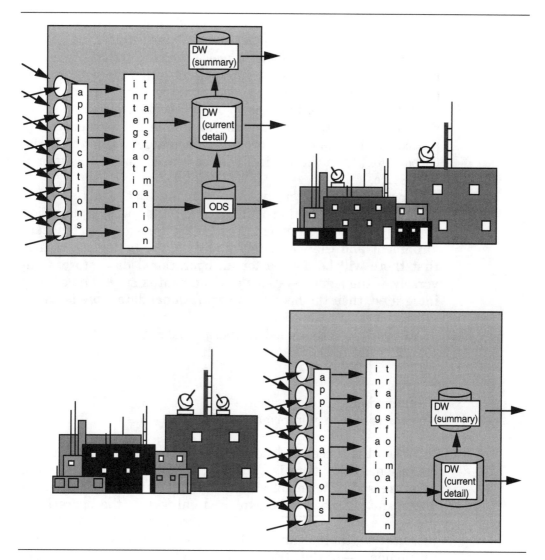

Figure 3.1   Some companies need an architecture that includes an operational data store; other companies need an architecture that only has a data warehouse.

smaller the chance it will be needed. Size plays an important role when it comes to integration, among other things. Very small organizations rarely experience any great distress because of a lack of integration. But the larger the corporation, the greater the chance that a lack of integration has caused or will cause problems.

The second factor leading to the need for an operational data store is the nature of the business of the corporation. If the corporation has an immediate need for information—typically because of direct customer interaction—then there is a good chance that an ODS will be needed. Some corporations may have little direct customer interaction but will still have an immediate need for information, such as information in the manufacturing process. If there is a need for very immediate information in the corporation, then there will likely be a need for an operational data store.

The third characteristic of a company that needs an operational data store is that it has a large and messy application legacy systems environment. The larger the legacy systems environment and the less integrated it is, the better the chance that there will be a need for an operational data store. Conversely, if the legacy systems environment is small and/or very integrated, then the need for an operational data store is not as great.

Corporations that need an operational data store share three common characteristics:

- Size
- Immediacy of information
- Status of legacy information systems

When the three conditions intersect in a corporation and an operational data store is indicated, the need for one can often be expressed in terms of a business opportunity. The business opportunity is able to be exploited only when the operational data store is built. While the ODS certainly has a technological justification, there is an equal business justification for it. (This phenomenon—of the ODS having equal value in both the technological and the business community—has long been observed in the data warehouse environment.)

THREE CLASSES OF ODS

For those corporations for whom an ODS makes sense, there are three classes of ODS (Figure 3.2). One class of ODS is updated synchronously (Class I). Class I ODSs have updates entered into them within two to three seconds after the update has entered

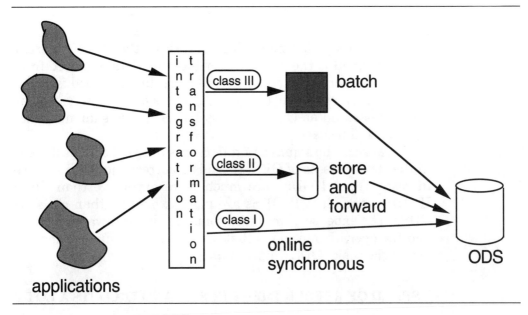

Figure 3.2   The three common types of update into the ODS.

and transacted with the operational world. In many cases in Class I ODS, very little if any transformation occurs as the data passes from the operational environment into the operational data store. In extreme cases (and there are some real dangers to this case), the data flows into the operational data store *at the same time that the transaction flows into the operational environment*. In this extreme case, there is no synchronization of data after operational update as there is throughout all other components of the environment. Class I ODS are used for extremely high-performance transaction-dominated environments.

In the second class of ODS (Class II), data is stored and forwarded into the ODS. The flow of the store and forward is done on an hourly or even half-hourly basis. There is not nearly the immediacy of the data as is found in Class I ODS systems. Usually a fair amount of integration and transformation is accomplished as the data flows into the Class II ODS.

The third class of ODS (Class III) is the asynchronous class, where data is trapped in the operational environment and is loaded into the operational data store on a twenty-four-hour-or-more basis. In almost every case, a significant amount of integration and transformation is done as the data passes into the Class III ODS.

The primary distinguishing feature of the three different classes of ODS is the speed with which the data is moved from one environment to another. Class I refreshment speed is blinding. Class II refreshment speed is not slow, but it is not as up-to-the-second as Class I. Class III ODS refreshment occurs on a relaxed basis.

Because of the significant differences in speed of refreshment in the three classes of ODS, there is a corresponding difference in costs. Class I ODSs are much more expensive than Class II ODSs, and class II ODSs are more expensive than class III ODSs. The expense differential comes in the hardware platform and the operating systems that are required to support the different classes of ODS. Simply stated:

SPEED OF REFRESHMENT COSTS, AND IT COSTS A LOT

in the world of the operational data store. When the decision is made as to what class of ODS is required, there need to be compelling business and economic reasons why Class I is chosen over Class II or Class III. Indeed, there are some cases where the speed of Class I produces a competitive advantage such that the business case can be made to justify the expenditures. But because speed costs (not just a little—it costs a lot!), it should not be assumed that the operational data store will be Class I without a stringent investigation into both the business advantage that will be gained and the possibility of doing business with a Class II or a Class III ODS.

Class I—An Example

As an example of a Class I ODS, Figure 3.3 depicts a banking environment where a bank has many individual accounts for a large multinational customer. As each of the individual accounts change, the corporate operational data store is updated. Or, periodically—every minute or so—the individual accounts are swept and an update as to the status of the account is sent to the operational data store. However the update mechanism

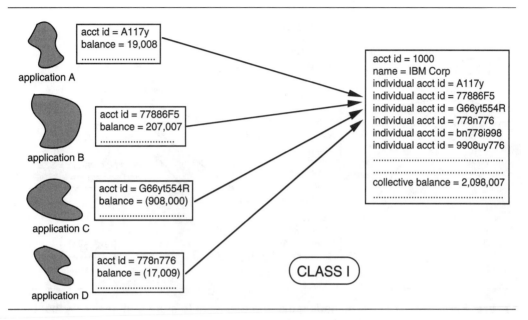

Figure 3.3   A fast form of update—synchronous update.

is triggered, the update quickly finds its way into the operational data store. Once it's there, the corporate manager is able
to manage the customer on a collective, up-to-the-second basis.

Note that in the Class I example described in Figure 3.3
there is a back reference to the account number as the account
number is known in the legacy application. This is one way of
handling disparate keys.

Class II—An Example

When the update of the operational data store is handled by
store and forward techniques, the data in the ODS is not quite
as fresh as it is in a Class I ODS, but it still can be reasonably
fresh. The individual banking example in Figure 3.4 shows that
data is stored and forwarded to the operational data store.

In Figure 3.4, an integrated individual bank account is kept
on a weekly basis. The daily transactions that occur during the
week are stored and forwarded to the operational data store on
an hourly basis. Once in the operational data store, a composite
picture of the customers' weekly activities is formed. The indi-

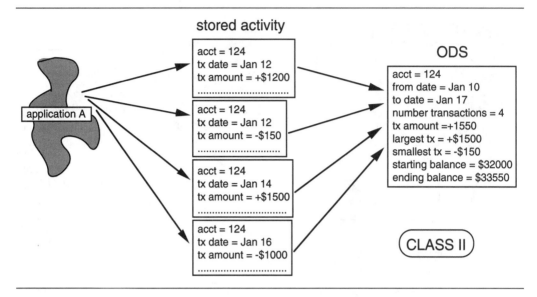

Figure 3.4   An example of loading the operational data store from activities that have been stored and forwarded.

vidual transactions and activities are not reflected separately. Instead, the individual activities are transacted against the operational data store record in such a way that a composite record of the account is formed throughout the week as the detailed data is collected.

The technique shown in Figure 3.4 for the Class II ODS is a common way of aggregating and "profiling" an account. The technique shown has the advantage that many individual transactions can be represented in the operational data store without taking up an enormous amount of storage. However, in order to create a useful profile, the designer must have a good feel for the usage of the data. Creating the profile without understanding the audience and the ultimate usage of the operational data store is like flying a plane in a fog bank with no radar.

Class III—An Example

The third class of ODS is one in which the refreshment from the operational environment occurs in a relaxed manner, typically every twenty-four hours or so. Consider the customer profile created in an operational data store shown in Figure 3.5.

Figure 3.5 shows that a customer record is created in the operational data store. Data from different applications are merged in order to create a composite customer record. Note that there are back references that enable the user to go from the operational data store record back to the legacy application if necessary.

The data that is in this class of ODS is updated in a casual fashion. For one thing, the customer data changes very slowly. When the data does change, the immediacy of the data is not paramount. There just is no business case for the immediate update of the operational data store in the example shown. Therefore, a relaxed (and inexpensive!) refreshment strategy can be employed for this class of ODS. The choice, then, of Class I, II,

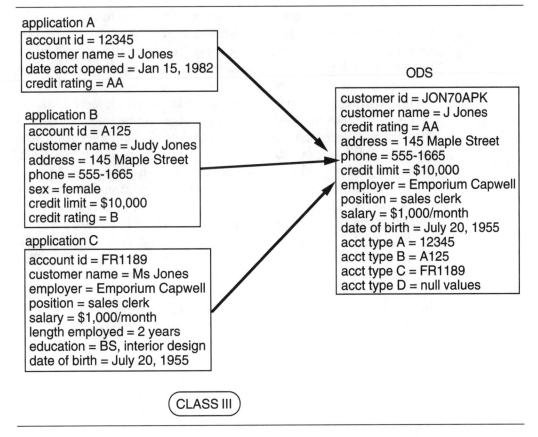

Figure 3.5   Creating the integrated record from the various applications—a form of asynchronous batch update.

or III ODS depends in no small part on the data that will be contained in the operational data store and the usage of that data. The class is chosen to fit the data.

TRAPPING THE INCREMENTAL OPERATIONAL DATA

The refreshment of the operational data store from the operational environment is a very important topic because it is an act that every ODS designer must consider and because, if not done properly, it can cost an inordinate amount of money. There are considerable technical and economic considerations to the refreshment of the operational data store from the operational environment.

The operational data store is fed from the results of transactions being executed in the operational environment. Only very rarely is the operational database read directly, then used as input to the refreshment process. Instead, the refreshment process is fed by the trapping of the results of updates that have occurred in the operational environment. Note that operational transactions are trapped *after* they have been executed. It normally does no good to trap operational transactions *before* they have executed because the results of their execution are unknown. What may happen is that the transaction may not pass edit and may abort in the operational environment. In that case, erroneous results occur when the operational data store traps the transaction before it has executed. The techniques for trapping the results of an execution are shown in Figure 3.6.

Figure 3.6 shows that databases can be read if necessary to feed the operational data store refreshment process. The (rarely occurring) instance of reading operational databases is done when transactions are stored in the operational databases. In most other cases, this is a very ineffective and expensive strategy for refreshment of the operational data store.

The second strategy is to use delta files for the purpose of trapping the changes that have occurred. Delta files are sometimes written at the application level, usually for the purposes of auditing. On occasion, these delta files will contain the data and the element of time necessary to feed the operational data store environment. When a delta file exists, it usually is an efficient and effective source of data for ODS refreshment. Unfortunately, the creation of delta files is not a normal application practice.

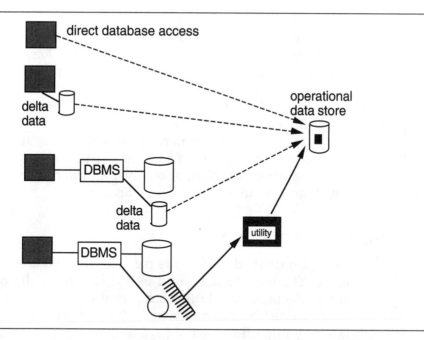

Figure 3.6   Common ways that legacy data is trapped prior to refreshing the ODS.

The third strategy for trapping data for the purpose of refreshing the operational data store is to trap database changes
at the DBMS level. Some DBMSs are very amenable to this
trapping and provide easy to use EXITs. Other DBMSs are very
difficult to tailor for this purpose. In any case, when this approach is used, there should be an awareness that there will
be an I/O impact on the online environment when the data is
trapped. In some cases, this I/O interference may cause *severe*
performance interruptions.

A nice aspect of trapping changes to an operational database
at the DBMS level is that there is no interruption to application
programs or transactions. The trapping occurs entirely independently of the legacy code and for this reason alone is a popular
option when the DBMS is amenable.

The last option is the usage of the online application log
tape (or journal) for the purpose of trapping changes that have
occurred in the operational environment. When the log tape is
used, in almost every case a utility is run that selects the data
off of the log tape and prepares the data for inclusion into the
operational data store refreshment job stream.

The usage of a log tape is desirable because it is entirely independent of application code and because there is no I/O impact on the system. In addition, once the log tape has been written, it can be processed off-line, on a processor far away from the operational platform. Removing log tape processing to a platform other than the one doing operational processing is usually a cost-effective strategy.

In whatever way the changes to the operational environment are trapped, they are then batched together and transmitted to the integration/transformation layer in order to be prepared for entry into the operational data store.

THE SOURCE RECORD

The operational data store is fed from the operational environment. The data that is used as the source in the operational environment is called the "source record."

Defining the source record for the operational data store is a very important part of its development process. The source record is the definition of exactly what operational data is needed in order to support the operational data store environment. Figure 3.7 illustrates the source record environment. (In the data warehouse environment, the source record was referred to as the "system of record.")

There are many considerations in choosing the correct source. Some of these are as follows:

- If there is more than one source, under what conditions is one source better than another?
- What reformatting/conversion must be done to prepare the source for entry into the operational data store?
- What if the key structure of the source data is incompatible with the key structure of the data in the ODS?
- What if the source data has too many occurrences for inclusion in the operational data store (such as transaction files often have)?
- How accurate is the source?
- How up-to-date is the source?
- How old is the source data?
- How complete is the source data?

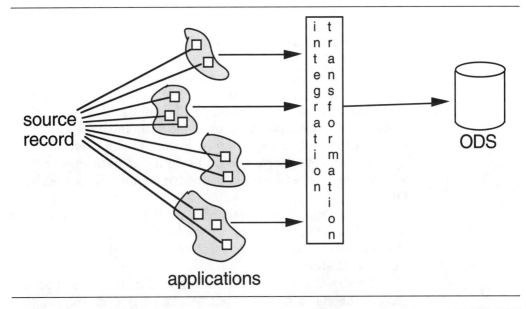

Figure 3.7   The source record is an important definitional aspect of the ODS.

- How compatible is the source structure of data with the operational data store structure of data?
- What will be required to integrate the source data into the mainstream?
- What technology is the source data in?
- How efficiently can the source data be accessed?
- How does the source data compare with the enterprise data model?

There are a multitude of considerations in selecting the best source of legacy data with which to populate the operational data store. Given that there are a multitude of considerations, the designer will not make the correct choice in every case. And in other cases, the correct choice as to the best source of data will change over time. Fortunately, the establishment of the operational data store is an iterative process, much like the development of the data warehouse. The operational data store is built in small, fast increments where periodic corrections to the design are made. One of the corrections that is commonly made is in the definition of the source record for the operational data store.

AUDITABILITY OF THE OPERATIONAL DATA STORE

The operational data store contains much valuable information. It forms a foundation on which to make important corporate decisions. But the operational data store is *not* the place for corporate auditability. Figure 3.8 makes this important point.

Figure 3.8 shows that corporate auditability—detailed adjustments to operational records—is done in the legacy applications, at the source record level. For all of the usefulness of the operational data store, the auditability of data does not move with the legacy data as it is transformed and integrated into the ODS.

Adjustments, billing records, audit trails, detailed accounting, and other such functions remain at the legacy environment. It is patently a mistake to try to shift auditability to the operational data store.

Of course, if incorrect data is found in the operational data store it needs to be corrected. A company certainly ought not to be making important corporate decisions based on poor data. There is, however, a correct procedure for the correction of bad operational data store data. Figure 3.9 outlines that procedure.

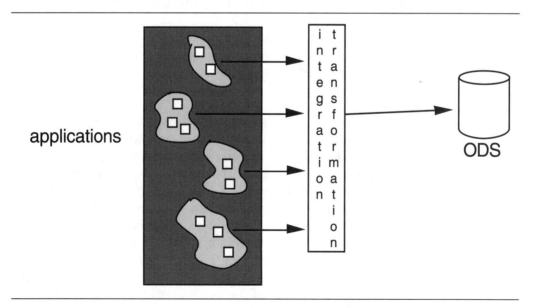

Figure 3.8   Auditability is a function of source record processing.

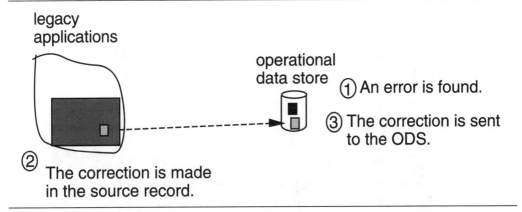

Figure 3.9 The mechanics of making corrections and adjustments.

An error is found in the operational data store. The source of the data that feeds that part of the ODS is located. Then the transformation and integration logic that governs the movement of data from the legacy systems environment to the operational data store is examined. The correction is then made in the legacy source environment and the data is moved into the operational data store. In such a manner are corrections made in the ODS environment; it is improper to make the corrections in the ODS without first correcting the data in the source record environment. If, by chance, corrections are made independently in the operational data store, then the integrity of the relationship between the source systems and the operational data store is compromised and reconcilability of data is lost.

There are many different ways in which data is moved from the source environment to the operational data store. Figure 3.10 identifies five different common ways in which data is moved into and manipulated within the operational data store. The simplest way in which the data is moved and manipulated is in terms of a simple record insertion. The source data record is moved to the operational data store and simply inserted, verbatim. A variation of simple record insertion is record insertion/replacement. In the record insert/replace mode, data is moved to the ODS. If data with the same key is found in there, it is replaced by the new value that has just been brought over. On the other hand, if there is no key of identical value in the operational data store, the record is inserted into it.

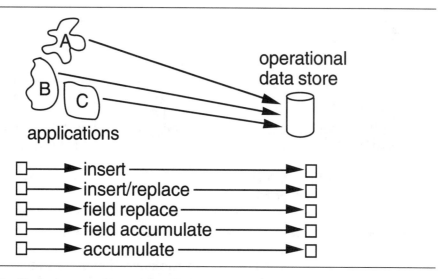

Figure 3.10   Typical types of inserts/updates into the ODS.

The field replace mode is similar to the record replace mode that has been discussed except that only a field is replaced instead of an entire record. The field accumulate mode is one in which the data from a single field going into the operational data store is accumulated. In the accumulate mode, more than one field is accumulated.

Another possibility is the field count mode, where the number of records being moved to the operational data store is tallied. The field count mode can be modified so that only fields within a certain domain are counted, and so forth. There are countless variations on the different ways in which data can be moved from the source environment into the operational data store environment.

THE OPERATIONAL DATA STORE WORKLOAD

The operational data store workload is important because its demeanor has a great effect on the type and the size of the platform on which the ODS is housed. And, of course, the size and type of the platform that houses the operational data store has a great effect on the budget required for it. For that reason alone it is necessary to understand at least the rudiments of the platform the operational data store resides on.

Of the different classes of ODS, the most workload-sensitive environment is that of Class I. Class II and Class III operational data stores have an interesting workload, and certainly their platform is important. But there is much less latitude for error when dealing with Class I ODS. For that reason, the discussion will center around the Class I ODS insofar as the profiling of the operational data store workload is concerned.

Figure 3.11 shows some of the aspects of Class I workload on ODS platforms. There are at least three main concerns of the capacity planner when dealing with the Class I ODS workload. Those concerns are:

- the rate at which legacy transactions flow into the operational data store, and the nature of the transformation that occurs once in the ODS environment,
- the amount and rate of the 2- to 3-second transactions that are sent by the end users into the operational data store, and
- the rate and the nature of the massive analytical processing that sometimes occurs in the operational data store.

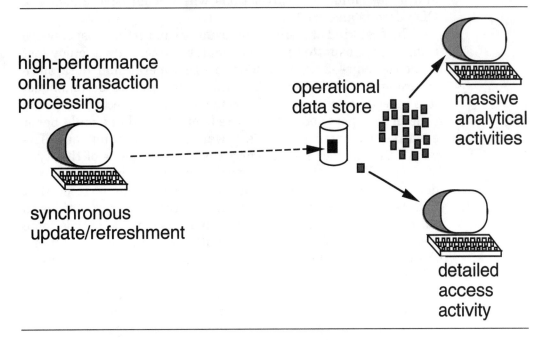

high-performance online transaction processing

operational data store

massive analytical activities

synchronous update/refreshment

detailed access activity

Figure 3.11   A typical workload profile for an operational data store that does synchronous processing.

The first factor affecting the operational data store workload is that of the rate of entry of the activities from the source systems. When many small transactions are being entered, where those small transactions are causing inserts or other space management activities, the workload is very sensitive to the resources being consumed. If only a few transactions are being entered, and if those transactions are causing only minimal space management activities, then the effect on the workload is minimal. Of course, since update is occurring, the entry of these transactions is magnified. If the transactions can be batched and summarized before arriving at the operational data store, for example, the performance impact is minimal. But batching and summarizing are normally not the nature of Class I transactions.

The second workload factor is the access of the operational data store data by the analytical community once the data has arrived. There are essentially two kinds of analysis that occur here—very fast, detailed analysis where many transactions are entered, each transaction accessing only a small amount of data, and a few "lunking" transactions where a massive amount of ODS data is analyzed.

The first kind of transaction usually causes the most concern because it is expected that the small transaction will enjoy fast response time—2 to 3 seconds—in the operational data store environment. As long as all workload factors can be managed, it is indeed possible to provide consistent 2-to 3-second response time in the operational data store (something that should never even be attempted in the data warehouse environment!). The workload manager has to worry about two aspects of this type of query: What is the rate of arrival and what kind of resources does each of these transactions consume? It is understood that update is not done by these small, fast-running transactions in the operational data store environment. As long as there is some degree of predictability to these small, fast-running transactions then the workload can be sized and the proper platform can be selected.

The second class of end-user transaction that is run in the operational data store environment is that of the large "lunking" transaction. The resources consumed by these large transactions can be minimized by doing two things:

- Limiting the number of them to be run
- Limiting the time of day they can be run

Usually these limitations are not too restrictive to the end user. But if they *are* too restrictive, then the end user requirements should be considered carefully and the operational data store should be designed to accommodate the end users' needs. However, the nature of these requests is such that they are defined heuristically so that it is very difficult for the end user to know what is needed until he or she discovers what is possible. For this reason, heuristic, massive analysis of the operational data store is best relegated to the wee hours of the morning when the machine has spare cycles and no one is impacted by one transaction sucking up huge amounts of resources.

Segmenting the Operational Data Store Day

Because there is a need to balance the resource utilization in the operational data store environment between predictable high-performance processing and heuristic analytical processing, the operational data store day is typically broken into different "time zones" of operation. Figure 3.12 illustrates what those typical time zones might look like.

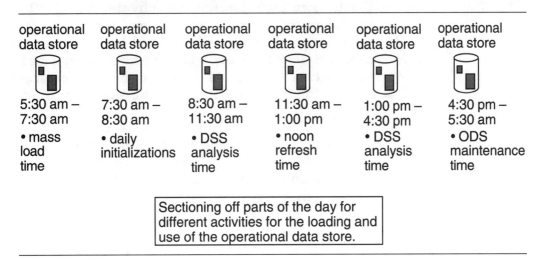

operational data store — 5:30 am – 7:30 am — • mass load time

operational data store — 7:30 am – 8:30 am — • daily initializations

operational data store — 8:30 am – 11:30 am — • DSS analysis time

operational data store — 11:30 am – 1:00 pm — • noon refresh time

operational data store — 1:00 pm – 4:30 pm — • DSS analysis time

operational data store — 4:30 pm – 5:30 am — • ODS maintenance time

Sectioning off parts of the day for different activities for the loading and use of the operational data store.

Figure 3.12   One approach to managing the loading of the operational data store and the need for high performance—an asynchronous approach.

Figure 3.12 shows that early in the morning the platform and the data that reside in the operational data store are dedicated to mass loads of data from the legacy system environment. This is true of even Class I ODS where more than one source feeds the operational data store environment. Later in the day (but still early!) the daily initializations and other utilities are run. Once the day starts only DSS analysis is done, and if the operational data store is a Class I environment, transactions are accepted from the source systems. At noontime, end-user access drops off and the spare machine cycles are used to run small utility and batch analysis jobs. After lunch, end-user utilization picks up again and the system is dedicated to end-user analysis. At the end of the day, as direct transactional end-user access plummets, the heavy-duty sequential DSS analysis starts. Later in the evening, ODS maintenance and batch processing commence until the early hours of the morning, at which point the cycle begins anew. The use of "time zones" allows the operational data store to be used for multiple purposes without undue interruption or disturbance to any one community.

Managing Resources

In light of the fact that resources are a precious commodity in the operational data store environment (especially the Class I ODS environment), there are several microstrategies that can be employed to improve the general profile of resource consumption. Figure 3.13 outlines some of the more important design and development practices that can be employed. For the massive heuristic queries (the "lunkers"), the following is good practice:

- *Checkpoint the transaction frequently.* This means that if restart is needed, massive amounts of work will not have to be repeated. In addition, frequent checkpointing has the effect of freeing up internal resources to the DBMS and operating system that may be needed by other programs and transactions.
- *Run at off-peak periods*, such as at 2:00 A.M. or on Sundays. Moving these programs to off-peak processing flattens the pattern of resource utilization over the life of the platform and extends the range of the platform and DBMS technology that houses the ODS.

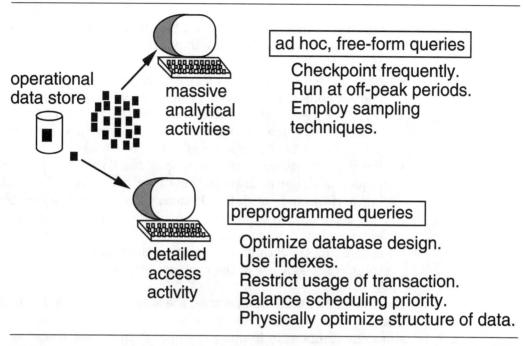

Figure 3.13   The different kinds of queries/access to the ODS.

- *Use sampling techniques*, especially where heuristic analysis is being done. Instead of discovering what the parameters of success are for an analysis by initially operating on massive amounts of data, start the heuristic process by operating on only a small amount of data, until the final heuristic analysis is ready to be run.

Optimizing the performance of the high-performance, transaction end-user analysis can be done in the following way:

- *Optimize database design*, so that the normal request for data can be accommodated with a very small amount of I/O. Normally, this entails creating a database design at the physical level so that different kinds of data are mixed together and are optimally located for speedy access.
- *Make sure indexes exist and that they are used properly*. Using indexes (or hashing) properly ensures that the primary access of data is done efficiently.
- *Restrict transaction processing during peak period times of day*, if necessary. For example, a department may be told that

they can run transaction type A, B, and C during the morning and transaction type A, D, and E during the afternoon. Such restrictions are not popular but can greatly extend the life of a platform.

- *Balance scheduling priority.* At the system level certain transactions can be given priority over other transactions when they enter the system. Those with low priority do not enjoy this scheme, but such a ploy can create overall system performance at the expense of only a few users.
- *Physically optimize the structure of the data.* Employ techniques of denormalization that have the effect of optimizing performance of data. Of course, to successfully employ this technique you have to know what transactions will be enhanced and what transactions will be deoptimized. Deoptimizing the wrong set of transactions can be a hazardous thing (to the career of the system designer!).

From a strategic perspective, the single most effective thing that can be done to improve performance in the operational data store environment is to move the operational data store from a Class I environment to a Class II or Class III environment. Figure 3.14 illustrates the difference that changing classes makes.

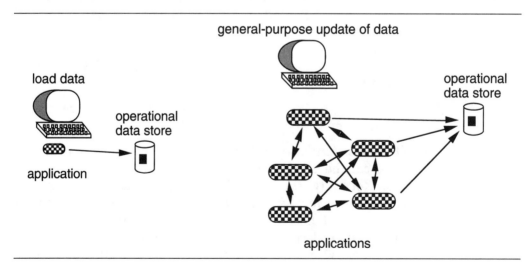

Figure 3.14   In the face of general-purpose update of the ODS, the application becomes more complex than if asynchronous update of data is done.

Where there is online general-purpose update of data, the system and the DBMS run under a tremendous amount of overhead. Where the general-purpose update is restricted to a load process rather than an update process, and especially where the load process can be run after hours, performance can be emancipated.

The dramatic effect of the emancipation is shown in Figure 3.15, where, from a systems perspective, one can see the difference that is made by not doing general-purpose update during the online day. There are *many* reasons why performance suffers when there is an insistence on doing peak-period online update.

The end result is that when update is done synchronously in the operational data store and where there is much access of data, there is the very real possibility that the operational data store and its platform will become a tremendous performance bottleneck. Figure 3.16 shows this possibility.

One technique that can help alleviate the operational data store from becoming a performance bottleneck is that of understanding where it is being accessed during its peak period. By understanding where the operational data store is being accessed, the systems designer can spread data out and/or add indexes where appropriate to enhance performance. Figure 3.17 shows the monitoring of the operational data store to determine where the performance bottleneck is.

METADATA AND THE OPERATIONAL DATA STORE

Metadata in the operational data store environment plays as important a role as it does in the data warehouse environment. Figure 3.18 symbolically illustrates the role of metadata in the operational data store environment.

The primary reason why metadata plays the role that it does in the operational data store environment is that informational processing occurs. Informational processing begins with the discovery process. In the discovery process, the end user begins to formulate what is required. The discovery process begins with a survey of what the possibilities for analysis are. And it is in this capacity that metadata plays a vital role. Metadata allows the end user to understand what data is available for analysis. In addition, the operational data store metadata allows the end

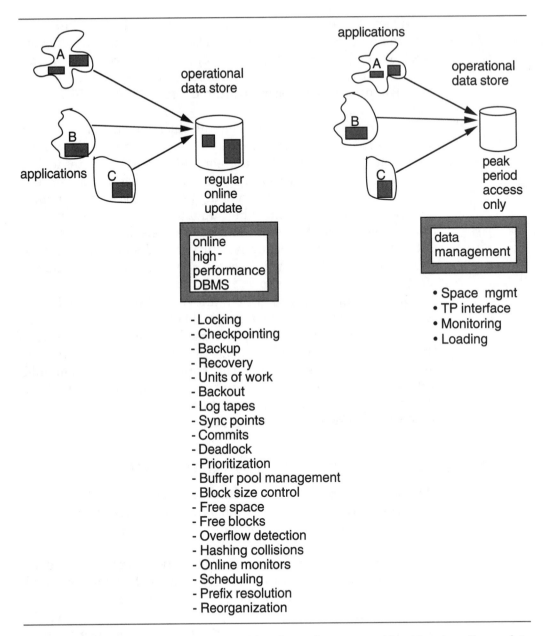

Figure 3.15 The technological considerations change considerably when the update feature is added to the ODS.

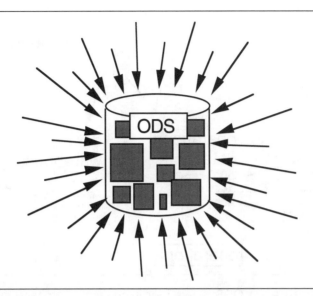

Figure 3.16 When update is done synchronously in the operational data store and where there is much access of the data, there is the very real possibility that the ODS will become a performance bottleneck.

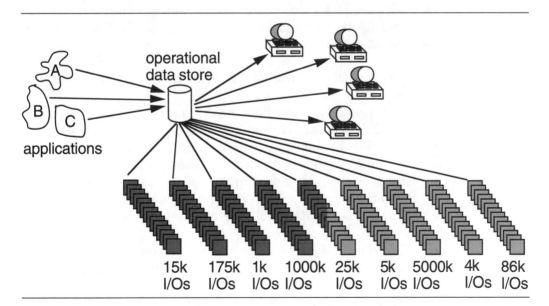

Figure 3.17 Monitoring operational data store utilization helps determine what ought to be stored in it and what ought to be stored in the data warehouse.

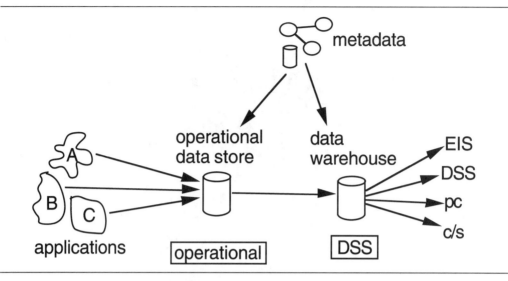

Figure 3.18 Because the ODS is used for informational processing, metadata is as important there as it is in the data warehouse.

user to make distinctions between different types of data found there. The end user can find out not only what data is available, but what is the *best* data available for analysis. The end user can look at such things as:

- What was the source of the data in the operational data store?
- What was the integration/transformation processing that occurred as the data passed into the operational data store?
- When did the data pass into the operational data store?
- How much of the data is there in the operational data store?
- How does one unit of data in the operational data store relate to another unit of data in the operational data store?
- Where does the data go after it leaves the operational data store?
- What business names does the data in the operational data store have?

Metadata, then, is a great enabler for the benefit of effective analysis of data in the operational data store. As time passes and the contents of the operational data store become more varied and voluminous, the role of metadata increases. Indeed, as long as the operational data store contains only a modest amount of data, the role of metadata is not obvious.

EXECUTIVE INFORMATION SYSTEMS AND THE OPERATIONAL DATA STORE

Executive information systems (EIS) have an important role to play in the larger picture of DSS. EIS is the executive's window into the operation of the corporation. The role of EIS in the data warehouse has long been recognized and discussed. What remains largely unexplored is the role of executive information systems in the ODS environment. EIS, in fact, has an important role to play with regard to the operational data store, however different that role is from the role that EIS plays in the world of data warehousing. Figure 3.19 identifies the role of EIS in the operational data store environment.

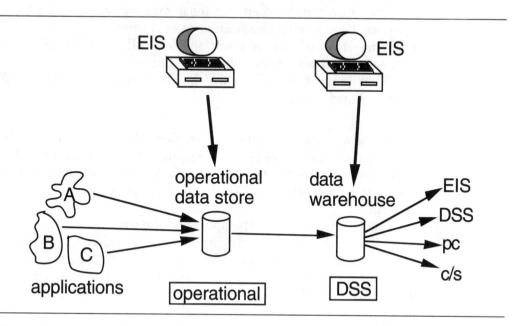

Figure 3.19 EIS has applicability to both the operational data store and the data warehouse. But the use of EIS is quite different in each environment.

EIS in the operational data store environment plays an executive-level operational role. The decisions that are looked at through EIS in the operational data store environment are up-to-the-second, summary-level, corporate-level decisions. Contrast these decisions with the ones made through EIS in the data warehouse environment. In the data warehouse environment the executive information systems assisted in making long-term, strategic decisions. There was little or no immediacy of decision in the data warehouse EIS environment. However, in the operational data store EIS environment, there is a very real immediacy of decision. The following are some examples of corporate executive-level immediate decisions:

- At what rate should we loan money to a large multinational customer?
- Should we place a group order for a new product line right now, based on how well the products are selling across our chain of stores?
- How should we react to a competing airline's lowering of fares in order to keep the most market share and at the same time lose the least amount of revenue?
- What lines of products are selling well in this Christmas season and which ones should be put on sale?
- What insurance policies will be affected by a hurricane off the Florida coast?

These are the kinds of considerations that are both immediate and at the executive level. The operational data store coupled with executive information systems form a foundation appropriate to the answering and analysis of these temporal business conditions.

It is noteworthy that the operational data store forms a very solid foundation for EIS. Trying to do EIS processing without the data that resides in the ODS is an exercise in futility. There simply is no way that legacy data can be organized, transformed, and analyzed quickly enough to support the fast-changing needs of top management. The operational data store allows the EIS to do what it does best—analyze and present information, without having to worry about the underlying foundation of data.

THE OPERATIONAL DATA STORE AND PARALLEL TECHNOLOGY

There is an excellent fit between the needs of ODS processing and parallel technology (Figure 3.20).

The parallel architecture of data and processing (sometimes called an "mpp"—massively parallel processing—approach) is one that is able (among other things) to:

- Manage large amounts of data
- Break processing up into units that can be operated on independently
- Provide scalable processing
- Provide good response time across massive amounts of data
- Allow individual units of data to be accessed very quickly and randomly

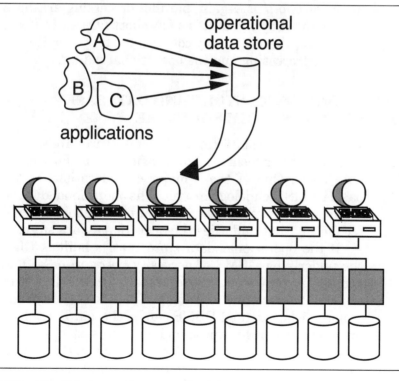

Figure 3.20 The fit between the operational data store and parallel technology is a very good one.

In truth, there are some other interesting properties of parallel processing that make it attractive for other kinds of processing. But for the purposes of ODS processing, the characteristics listed above are the ones that are of greatest interest to the operational data store architect.

The operational data store typically has a fair amount of data stored in it. Parallel architecture is good at managing lots of data. The operational data store environment often has massive requests that scan lots of data. Breaking a request up into independent units allows even very large requests to be handled efficiently. Programs and transactions that are written for one level of data work as well at another level of data in the operational data store environment. The ODS requires good response time, and parallel processing can be made to realize speed of access and processing. And the operational data store requires that massive amounts of individual units of data be accessible in one or two I/Os. Again, parallel processing arranges units of data so that any one unit is a few short I/Os away. For these reasons, then, there is a very comfortable technological fit between parallel processing and the operational data store.

OPERATIONAL DATA STORE AND DATABASE MANAGEMENT SYSTEM SOFTWARE

While hardware platforms and architectures are very important, there are other technological considerations for the operational data store. One of those major considerations is that of the basic DBMS technology in which the operational data store runs. Figure 3.21 makes some important points about the basic DBMS technology that underlies the operational data store.

If the operational data store that is built is Class I, then the underlying DBMS of necessity needs to be a full-function, general-purpose, record-level update DBMS. But if the operational data store that is being built is Class II or Class III, then a more niche-oriented DBMS can be chosen. There is no need to do online, general-purpose update in this case, so a much more efficient DBMS can be considered. Indeed, in this case the DBMS that is selected may look like the one that serves the data warehouse world. Of course, a DBMS that is load-and-access oriented will operate much more efficiently than one that is dragged down by the need for data and transaction update integrity.

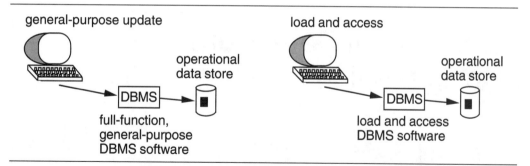

Figure 3.21   The functionality of the operational data store has a big impact on the type of DBMS software that can be employed.

SUMMARY

The ODS is an optional feature in the corporate information factory. Some companies have business conditions that demand it; other businesses do not. There are three classes of ODS—Class I is where online update is done synchronously, Class II is where refreshment of the operational data store occurs in a store and forward mode, and Class III is where the operational data store is refreshed asynchronously. The refreshment process is accomplished by means of accessing a log tape or trapping calls within the DBMS. Occasionally, a delta file is used. Even less frequently, access is made to the actual legacy data.

Defining the source of data in the legacy environment is a major design step. This is done iteratively, where changes and refinements occur over time. When changes need to be made to the operational data store, they need to be made at the source record, not within the ODS itself. There are many different ways legacy data is reflected in the operational data store. Some of the ways are insertion of records, replacement/insertion of records, field replacement, field accumulation, and record-level accumulation.

Normally, the ODS operating day is divided into "time zones." The time zones free up the ODS platform to become optimal for different types of processing that occur throughout the day. Collectively, the time zones provide all the windows needed for the different ODS activities.

4

Operational Data Store Design—High Level

The structure of the contents of the operational data store are shaped around the major subject areas ("entities") of the corporation. The major subject areas of the corporation are defined in the corporate data model. Figure 4.1 shows a simple corporate data model with its entities.

STRUCTURING THE OPERATIONAL DATA STORE

The major subject areas of the corporation are usually at a high level of abstraction, and typically include:

- Customer
- Product
- Order
- Shipment
- Payment, and so forth.

It is normal for an operational data store data model to be created from the corporate data model. The operational data store data model starts with the corporate data model as a point of departure. But there are some notable differences between the corporate data model and the operational data store data model.

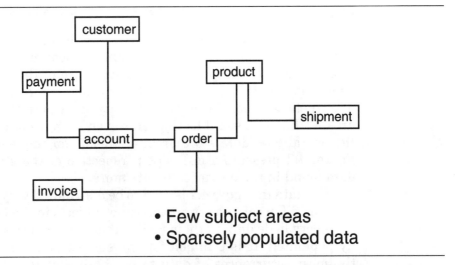

- Few subject areas
- Sparsely populated data

Figure 4.1 The major subject areas typically found in an operational data store.

While the corporate data model is inclusive of *all* the data the corporation needs for its information, the operational data store data model includes only the data that is needed for operational online integrated processing. Traditionally, the amount of data needed for online integrated processing is less than the entirety of corporate data. The exclusion of nonoperational, non-integrated, non-online data usually means the removal from the corporate data model of such information as:

- Historical information
- Summary information
- Management browsing information
- Information not directly related to the requirements of the processing at hand

In short, anything not directly related to the integrated online processing that is not supported by the operational data store is jettisoned from the corporate data model as the ODS model is built. The result of these modifications to the corporate data model is that the ODS data model is "sparsely populated," or "minimalist." Only the data elements needed for ODS processing are carried in the operational data store data model.

THE OPERATIONAL DATA STORE AND THE DATA MODEL

Looking at the ODS data model as the basis for the design of the ODS often gives a warped and misleading perspective. The data model perspective of the structure of the data in the operational data store is one that is flat, where each entity appears to be equal to every other entity and where all attributes are on a likewise equal footing. However, such is not the case as the operational data store architect heads for implementation. Figure 4.2 presents a different perspective of the structure of data found in the operational data store.

The data in Figure 4.2 is seen to be distributed very unevenly over the different subject areas. Some subjects in the ODS areas have very little data in them while other subject areas are heavily populated. It is common for the subject areas that contain the most occurrences of data to be those that relate to transactions or other important details. In the case of retailing, the majority of the occurrences of data in the operational data store relate to stocked items or sales. In a marketing and sales firm, the bulk of the occurrences in the operational data store relate to customers, and so forth. Each business has its one or two

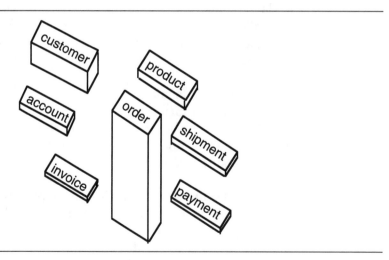

Figure 4.2   All entities are hardly created equal—in terms of volume, some entities tower above the others, and it is in these massive entities that the most interesting information hides.

most populous entities. And it is these "most populous entities" that often have the most potential in providing a real business advantage in the ODS online operational environment.

STAR JOINS

The most populous entities often represent data that is at the heart of the business. Because of their great importance in the operational data store environment, these most populous entities are designed to be in a construct unique to data warehouses and the operational data store—that of a "star join." Figure 4.3 illustrates a simple star join.

The notion of a star join in a DSS context was pioneered by Ralph Kimball in his work with large-scale data warehouse and ODS systems. The star join fits the data warehouse as handily as it does the operational data store. The star join data construct is one in which the primary data is held and stored in the one or two large tables of the operational data store (which usually represent transactions). Foreign key relationships are included with the primary data to reference smaller tables, which oc-

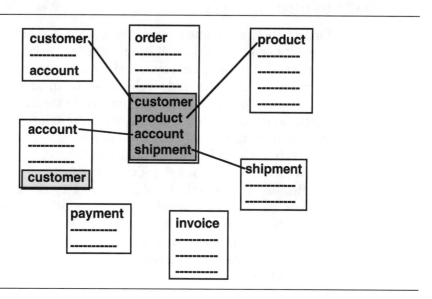

Figure 4.3   A typical structuring of operational data store data, sometimes called a "star join."

casionally need to be accessed after having accessed the large, primary table. These smaller tables are said to be prejoined to the larger, primary table. The incidental, secondary tables in the operational data store—when drawn around the large primary table—*join* to form a starlike structure, hence the name.

One of the interesting features of a star join is the simplicity of its structure and the data contained in it. Given the volumes of data that are being contemplated, there is simply no place for complex, slow-to-traverse structures in an operational data store. The star join, then, becomes the most fundamental description of the design of the data found in the operational data store.

With the star join, data relationships can be explored quickly. In addition, whole sets of data can be identified and ferreted out in the primary grouping of data. The ability to easily and efficiently identify subsets of data using a star join greatly facilitates the ability for the DSS community to use the operational data store effectively.

DATA RELATIONSHIPS IN THE OPERATIONAL DATA STORE

One of the important features of the data found in the ODS is the data relationships that are contained therein. As in all other forms of database, data relationships are vital in the operational data store. However, data relationships in an operational data store are implemented in a structure known as an "artifact" of a relationship. (Note: Artifacts of relationships are found in the data warehouse as well as the operational data store. Refer to the Tech Topic by Prism Solutions, vol. 1, no. 5, on data relationships for an in-depth discussion of artifacts of relationships.)

Standard data relationships that are commonly found in a DBMS, such as referential integrity or logical relationships, are applicable to operational systems. In a world of DSS analysis and integrated, online processing, many data relationships take on a new meaning. Most relationships that are found in the operational data store environment are a result of a transaction that has transpired. As a result, the only relationship that is accurate and relevant is the relationship that was in force at the time of the transaction. A "snapshot" is made at the moment of the transaction and the relationships relevant to the transaction at that instant are captured. Figure 4.4 shows an example of an artifact of a relationship in the operational data store environment.

The creation of a relationship is started by some "event" occurring. An event can be a discrete happening, such as the placement of an order, the completion of a sale, or the payment of an invoice. Or an event can be the marking of the regular passage of time, such as the end of the day, the end of the week, the end of the month, and so forth.

An event signals that a snapshot of some primary unit of data is to be taken. The snapshot focuses on something such as the placement of an order or the completion of a transaction. Once the snapshot of the order or the transaction is taken, other incidental relationship information that is relevant to the order or transaction at the instant of the snapshot is captured.

This incidental relationship information that is captured as part of the snapshot process is the relationship artifact information. Suppose a snapshot is made of an order. Other incidental

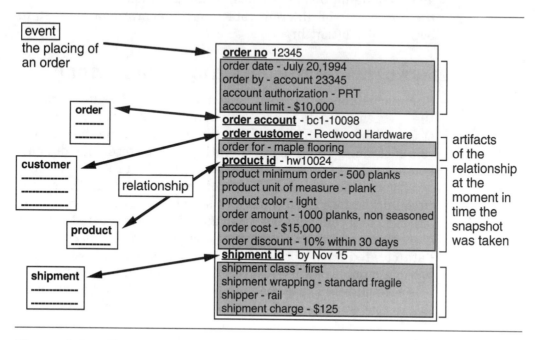

Figure 4.4   Elements of data relationships in the operational data store environment.

information that might be captured with the order might include:

- The identification of the clerk who handled the order
- The product unit of measurement being ordered
- The priority of shipment
- The type of shipment requested
- The credit rating of the customer as of the moment of the order

The incidental information stored along with the order is called *relationship artifact information*, and is accurate only as of the moment the snapshot was taken. Any inference of the relationship before or after the moment of the snapshot is purely coincidental and random.

Creating relationships in the operational data store by means of snapshots makes the operational data store a structurally streamlined environment. There are no cumbersome ties of data from one table to the next. There is no concern about changing business rules, or about having to synchronize the purge date of different tables in the operational data store because of relationships.

SUMMARY DATA AND THE OPERATIONAL DATA STORE

Summary data can be created from the detailed values found in the operational data store. But summary data is seldom if ever stored within the ODS itself. In order to understand the unusual role of summary data in the operational data store, consider how summary data is created, as illustrated in Figure 4.5.

The creation and calculation of summary data in the operational data store environment is simple. Detailed ODS data is accessed and refined, then a calculated value is created. At first glance, there is nothing unusual occurring here. But summary data created from detailed ODS data has a curious property. When a summarization is created in the operational data store, it is accurate *only* as of the instant it is created. In the very next instant the summary data may well be inaccurate.

For example, suppose a bank officer uses the operational data store to calculate the corporate balance for a large multina-

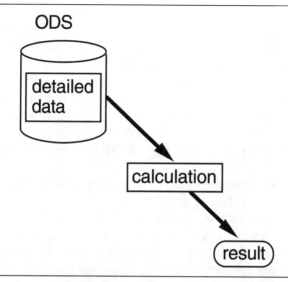

ODS

detailed
data

calculation

result

Figure 4.5   Summary data can be calculated from the operational data store, but the value that is calculated is accurate only as of the instant the data is calculated. Furthermore, a recalculation of the same data will yield different results.

tional corporation. Suppose the calculation is made at 10:35 A.M. At 10:40 A.M. the calculation is rerun and a different summarized result is achieved. Does this mean that the value calculated as of 10:35 A.M. was incorrect? Not at all; detailed ODS data is constantly changing (especially Class I ODS data). The value that was calculated at 10:35 A.M. was accurate at the instant it was calculated. At 10:40 A.M. another value was calculated (that in turn was accurate only as of that instant in time). The difference between the values obtained at 10:35 A.M. and 10:40 A.M. says nothing about the accuracy of the results.

When summarization is done on constantly changing details, the summary data that is created can be called *dynamic* summary data. Although dynamic summary can be very useful for many different kinds of business decisions, it is not appropriate for every kind of business decision. Dynamic summary data has several properties:

- Dynamic summary data is accurate only as of the instant of calculation, therefore storing dynamic summary usually does not make sense. Indeed, storing dynamic summary data and using the data for a decision at a later point in time may prove to be the cause of erroneous decisions.

- Dynamic summary data is almost impossible to audit. In order to audit dynamic summary data, the details that go into the calculation have to be returned to a set of values as of the instant in time when the summary was made. Resetting massive numbers of variables back to an instant in time is usually very difficult if not impossible to do.

For these reasons then, dynamic summary data is not stored in the operational data store.

Contrast the dynamic summary data that is found in the operational data store with the type of summary data that is found in the data warehouse (Figure 4.6). There is a whole host of summary data found in the data warehouse. In fact, there is even a hierarchy of summary data that is found there—lightly summarized data, highly summarized data, and so forth. But the summary data found in the data warehouse is very different from that which can be created in the operational data store.

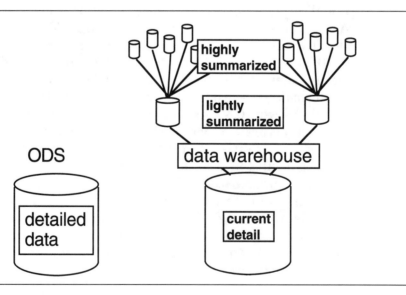

Figure 4.6   Unlike the data warehouse, the operational data store contains only detailed data.

Data warehouse summary data is static summary data. Static summary data is data that can be created and stored. Static summary data can be recalculated at any point in time in the future and the result will always be the same. For example, suppose at the end of the month a corporation's revenues are calculated. If the corporation should desire to go back and recalculate those revenues later (say, at the behest of the IRS), the calculation would come out the same. In addition, if there is a need to audit a calculation in the data warehouse, it could easily be audited. There is, then, a fundamental difference between the dynamic summary data found in the operational data store and the static summary data found in the data warehouse.

BROADLY DEFINED KEYS

One of the issues faced in the structuring of ODS data is that of the scope of the key. Each table in the ODS has a primary key. Some primary keys are intuitively and easily defined; other keys are not. As an example of a key that is open to interpretation, consider CUSTOMER, as seen in Figure 4.7. Who is a customer? Is a customer someone who currently is a customer? someone who once was a customer? someone who might be a customer? Is a company that has both a local office and an international

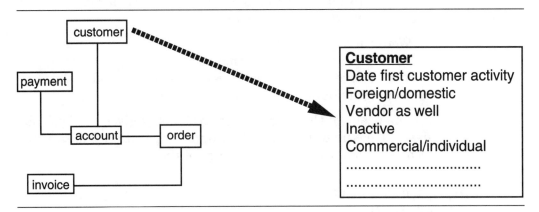

Figure 4.7　Attributes that serve to discriminate one type of customer from another are added to the data found in the operational data store, leading to what can be called the "broadly interpreted key."

office a customer? Is the local office a customer in the same way that an international office is a customer?

The architect of the operational data store can struggle with these issues and attempt to rationally sort through the problems and predetermine the best answer. The problem is that whatever interpretation the architect puts on the definition of the data in the operational data store, it will be wrong! Inevitably, the operational data store architect will exclude one or more classes of data that rightfully belong in it.

There is a technique for organizing and defining data that addresses many of the problems of the ODS architect. That technique entails making use of a "broadly interpreted key."

A broadly interpreted key is one that encompasses as many possibilities as feasible. The definition of the key the operational data store architect uses is one that encompasses as many subsets as can be reasonably encompassed. The data is loaded into the operational data store so that many subsets of the data are included. Attributes of data are included to allow one subset to be separated from another subset. Then the usage of the operational data store data is up to the DSS analyst. Upon accessing the operational data store data, the DSS analyst specifies discerning criteria to distinguish one subset of data from another.

As an example of the selectivity possible with a broadly interpreted key, consider the data shown in Figure 4.7. Using the attributes to qualify what data was required, a DSS analyst could look at all customers who:

- Were currently active
- Were foreign, inactive commercial
- Were active customers who were vendors as well
- Were individual inactive domestic customers

The usage of the broadly interpreted key gives the DSS analyst all possible flexibility, freeing the operational data store architect from prejudging the usage of the ODS.

THE OPERATIONAL DATA STORE—CENTRALIZED OR DISTRIBUTED?

One of the major structural and architectural decisions that must be made by the ODS architect is whether the operational data store should be distributed or centralized. Figure

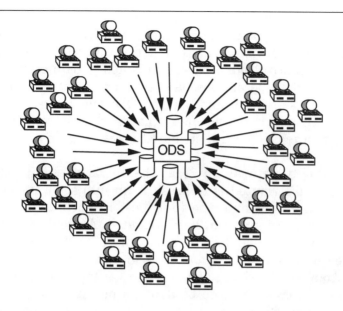

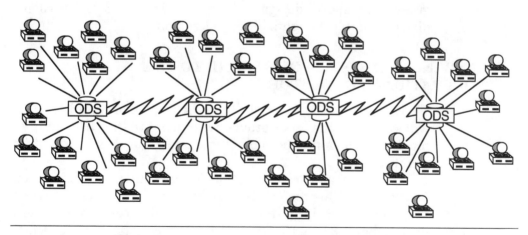

Figure 4.8 Should the operational data store be centralized or distributed?

4.8 depicts this basic choice. Unless there are mitigating circumstances, the operational data store functions better as a
centralized structure than as a decentralized one. There will be
a lot of data in the operational data store and it will have to
serve many communities with a wide variety of interests.

Creating a centralized ODS allows the maximum number of people with the maximum number of agendas to access the same operational data store data. When the operational data store data is decentralized, the data is divided into different domains. Once the data becomes separated over multiple domains, the DSS analysts who would use the ODS data must arrange for their own access to the many places to which the ODS data is distributed. Such a distributed access may not be a simple matter.

The only natural way that the operational data store can be easily distributed is to break it up into separate functional arenas and distribute the functions. In such a manner, ODS data and processing can be distributed. A problem arises with this structure when data from one unit of ODS data needs to be mixed with data from another ODS unit. Crossing the boundary from one distributed ODS node to another, if any significant amount of crossing is to be done, is not an enticing prospect. In addition, when the operational data store is designed and managed centrally, there is the possibility of a much tighter degree of control over design and content. Once ODS data becomes distributed, all thoughts of control vanish.

MOVING THE SYSTEM OF RECORD TO THE OPERATIONAL DATA STORE

There is the notion that over time the system of record for data will shift from the application environment to the ODS environment. Such a shift is possible (Figure 4.9), but is not without its ramifications.

There are many considerations to the shift. One ramification (discussed in Chapter 7) is the implications for technology. When the operational data store is a load and access environment during the daytime, the underlying DBMS technology needed to service it is simple and efficient. But when the system of record is shifted to the operational data store, the DBMS technology underlying the update processing is necessarily complex and inefficient. Because of the inefficiencies introduced by the advent of general-purpose, record-level update processing, moving the system of record to the operational data store calls for a serious consideration of performance.

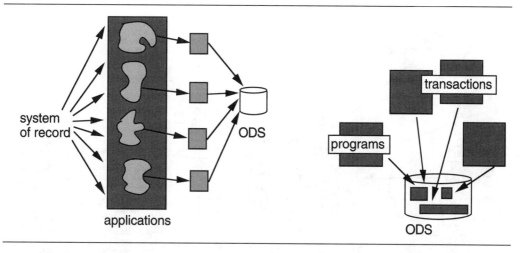

Figure 4.9   Moving the system of record to the operational data store—which can be done—entails moving an entire infrastructure of application code to the ODS.

There are other implications for moving the system of record to the operational data store. One is that much application processing must be moved there. When the system of record (or part of it) is moved to the operational data store, the operational data store takes on the responsibility for capturing, editing, and application execution, which heretofore had been done in the legacy applications. The movement of application code to the operational data store environment complicates the environment.

In addition, moving part of the application data to the ODS and keeping another part of the data back in the legacy applications may not be desirable. So, moving only part of the system of record to the operational data store may not be an option. Having an *all-or-nothing* circumstance when it comes to the moving of the system of record to the ODS probably is not optimal for the application designer or the maintenance programmer.

THE OPERATIONAL DATA STORE AND OBJECT-ORIENTED TECHNOLOGY

There is a very comfortable fit between object-oriented technology and the operational data store, at least at a high level of

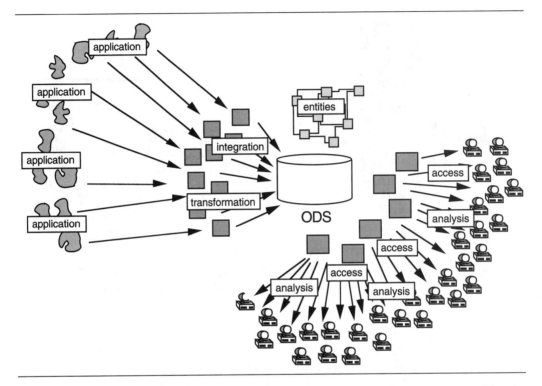

Figure 4.10   The operational data store and object orientation at the conceptual level.

conceptualization. Figure 4.10 illustrates the relationship between object orientation and the operational data store.

The basic orientation and design of the operational data store is around the major subjects of the corporation. The major subjects of the corporation form the basis for organizing data into objects. Code surrounds the ODS in two ways:

- The integration and transformation layer that shields the ODS from the legacy production applications.
- The application code that the DSS analyst uses in order to access and analyze the operational data store data. The basis of the integration and transformation algorithms is derived from the business rules of the organization.

There is, then, a very close fit between the notions of object orientation and the implementation of ODS.

HOW BIG SHOULD THE OPERATIONAL DATA STORE BE?

The size of the operational data store—the volume of data to be found within it—is one of the most important design and implementation issues facing the ODS architect, as seen in Figure 4.11.

There are several issues that relate to the size of the operational data store. The operational data store is rarely even close to the size of the data warehouse. The operational data store does not contain a great amount of historical data, and does not contain summary data, at least, no static summary data. For these reasons alone, the operational data store is smaller than the data warehouse.

However, the operational data store can still end up containing a huge amount of data. Given that the technology housing it is expensive, that it entails update, and that update implies a complex underlying technological infrastructure, the volume of data managed in the operational data store becomes an issue. One reason is that every unit of data in an operational data store is one or two I/Os away from direct access. There is a significant cost associated with keeping massive amounts of detailed data immediately accessible and updatable. For this reason alone, the operational data store volume should be scrutinized carefully.

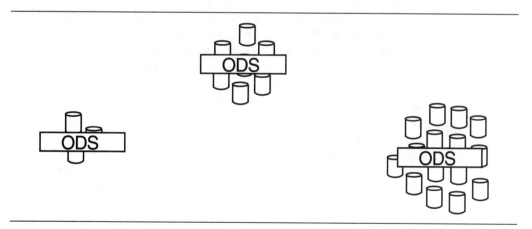

Figure 4.11   How big should the operational data store be?

As a rule, an operational data store should contain *only* data that is needed on hand for collective integration. There will be many details that are important to the corporation but that will never find their way into the operational data store. The operational data store will contain three types of values:

- Back reference data that allows the end user the ability to go from the operational data store back to the system of record in the legacy applications environment
- Discriminator data that allows the end user to distinguish between different classes of ODS data
- Up-to-the-second collective integrated values needed for corporate-integrated decisions

Any other types of data should be scrutinized carefully as to whether they belong in the operational data store.

The structure and contents of the operational data store can best be described as a minimalist structure. In at least the first few iterations of the development of the ODS, the ODS architect should avoid the temptation to place in it much unjustified data.

SUMMARY

The foundation of the design of the operational data store is the corporate data model, where major subjects (entities) are identified. The entities are not equal in terms of volume of data. Some major subjects will have many occurrences of data. Other entities will contain relatively few occurrences of data.

Some data is organized around the "star join" structure. The star join structure allows the very large tables in the operational data store to participate in a prejoined foreign key relationship with the smaller tables. The star join contains a simple amount of minimalist data.

Summary data in the operational data store is different from most other data because the values of summary data are accurate only at the instant they are calculated. This type of summary data is called "dynamic summary data." Because dynamic summary data is accurate only as of one instant in time, it is not stored in the operational data store.

Data architects in the operational data store environment employ the design technique referred to as the "broadly interpreted key." This allows the DSS analyst using the operational data store to specify whatever subset of data is desired for analysis.

One of the most important strategic decisions the data architect must make is whether the operational data store is to be centralized or decentralized. As a rule, the operational data store is best built and operated in a centralized mode.

5

Operational Data Store Design—Low Level

In the late 1960s and early 1970s Ed Yourdon, Tom DeMarco, Chris Ganes, and Trish Sarson (among others) described a standard application development process.

DEVELOPMENT LIFE CYCLES

The classical system development life cycle (SDLC) that was described is one that begins with the gathering of end-user requirements and the assimilation and organization of those requirements for the purpose of creating a system design. Requirements are analyzed, synthesized, and shaped into a system design. The system design is translated into a series of programs, which are then written, tested, and debugged. Once the programs reach a state of reliability and stability, they are implemented.

The SDLC has been recognized and discussed since the early days of structured analysis and design. The classical SDLC applies to operational application systems where clerical activities are being done at a detailed level, where collection/edit/update are occurring, and where the same activities are repeated throughout the day. Figure 5.1 depicts the steps of SDLC at a high level.

SDLC	CLDS
• Gather requirements. • Analyze, synthesize. • Design system. • Program system. • Test, debug. • Implement system.	• Start with implemented data, usually transaction. • Probe, test to see what is available. • Develop exploratory programs. • Based on results of exploratory programs, create a design. • Take results of design, analyze and synthesize. • Understand requirements.
classical application requirements-driven development	DSS discovery-driven development

analytical community/
heuristic, analytical processing

clerical community/
repetitive processing

Figure 5.1   Some approaches to system development.

The SDLC serves the world of operational processing well. But there is another legitimate system development life cycle that is the antithesis of the SDLC—the CLDS (so named because in most ways it is the opposite or mirror-image of the SDLC). The CLDS applies to DSS analysis where the end user discovers—as the last step in the process—what the requirements for processing are through a heuristic development process. The CLDS begins with the ability to get at some data that has been implemented (usually detailed transaction data). Once the implemented data becomes available, a certain amount of probing and testing is done to the old transaction data to determine exactly what data is available and the status of that data. After the initial probes and tests of the implemented data are done, some exploratory programs are developed.

These exploratory programs access and analyze the implemented data. The programs are developed iteratively, where each successive step of development refines and builds on the results attained in the previous step. After the heuristic programs have been built and patterns of data and processing start to emerge, a more formal design is done and more programs are written based on the design. Results are obtained and analyzed.

Finally, the requirements to satisfy the needs of the DSS analyst are isolated and understood.

The CLDS best applies to DSS systems where there is very little repetitiveness of processing and much analysis. The CLDS applies to a very different audience than does the SDLC. The CLDS applies to an analytical-oriented management community, where long-term decisions are being made.

A Spectrum of Development Life Cycles

The SDLC and the CLDS are both perfectly valid development life cycles and can be considered to be at opposite ends of a spectrum of development approaches. As with any spectrum, there are many gradations and variations between the extremities. ODS development involves some of *both* SDLC and CLDS development. In fact, if we depict the SDLC and CLDS spectrum, ODS development appears in the middle of it, as seen in Figure 5.2.

There are very positive elements of *both* the SDLC and CLDS in the development of the operational data store. On the one hand, the repetitive requirements of the end user shape the operational data store insofar as repeated access to data is concerned. On the other hand, the operational data store needs to be able to accommodate the changing heuristic needs of the DSS analyst who uses it for informational processing.

THE DATA MODEL/THE PROCESS MODEL

Another way to view the spectrum of development is not through the perspective of SDLC and CLDS development but through the relationship of the development life cycle to the data and process models. The data model consists of the identification and organization of the entities, keys, definitions, and attributes of

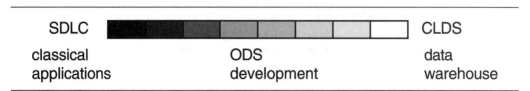

Figure 5.2   Where operational data store development fits on the development scale.

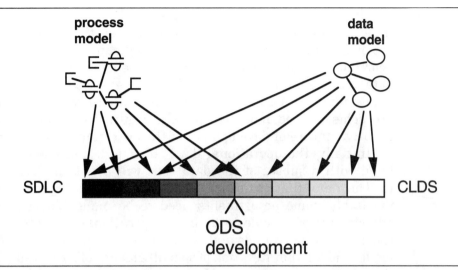

Figure 5.3   Applicability of process and data modeling on operational data store development.

information of the corporation. The process model consists of the identification and organization of the functions and processes of the corporation. Figure 5.3 shows how the data model and the process model can be arranged in a spectrum in order to reflect the different needs of development.

As in the case of the SDLC and the CLDS, ODS development is a mixture of both data modeling and process modeling, sitting somewhere in the middle of the spectrum. There is an equal measure of influence of the process model and the data model in the development of the operational data store. The operational data store must accommodate repetitive processing, and as such must make use of the process model. The same operational transaction is run repetitively by the end-user analyst throughout the day, so the ODS must reflect those needs.

By the same token, the DSS analyst uses the operational data store in an iterative fashion, as a vehicle for discovery. Because of the need to use the operational data store for informational processing, the data model needs to be included. The interests of these two very different communities and their very different patterns of usage dictate that the design and development of the ODS be influenced in equal measure by the process model and the data model.

Using both the data and process models in equal measure, the operational data store is developed iteratively. Developing the operational data store under the "big bang" theory is a very poor idea. Under almost *no* conditions should the operational data store be built on a onetime-only, all-at-once basis. Instead, it is built in a series of fast "pulses," where tangible results are achieved and modified quickly. Figure 5.4 illustrates the iterative nature of development of the operational data store.

Initially, the operational data store is designed and populated with a subset of the data that will eventually reside in it. The data that is initially loaded into it is explored and, inevitably, some adjustments need to be made. The iterative adjustments are made to both the operational data store and the code that surrounds and shapes it. Adjustments are quickly made, and another iteration of a small amount of data is added to the operational data store. More adjustments are quickly made, and the iterative development process continues.

Physical Tables and Logical Entities

Each of the major subject areas—or entities—found in the corporate data model turns into a physical table in the operational data store. Figure 5.5 shows the relationship of the corporate data model to the physical tables found in the ODS. The major subject areas found in the corporate data model form the foundation of design for the tables of the operational data store. The key structure of the entities in the data model becomes the key structure of the tables found in the operational data store. The

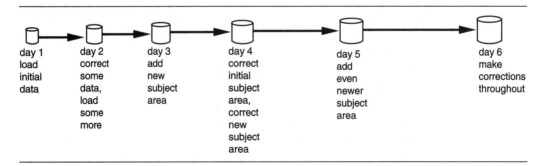

day 1
load
initial
data

day 2
correct
some
data,
load
some
more

day 3
add
new
subject
area

day 4
correct
initial
subject
area,
correct
new
subject
area

day 5
add
even
newer
subject
area

day 6
make
corrections
throughout

Figure 5.4   Iterative nature of development for the operational data store.

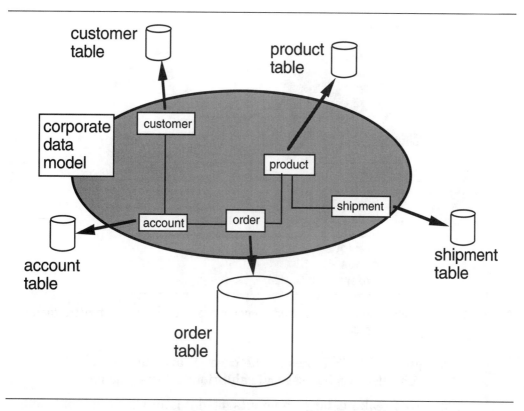

Figure 5.5   Each of the entities in the operational data store data model produces a physical table that is part of the operational data store.

attributes identified in the data model become the basis of the attributes that go into the operational data store. The corporate data model attributes are "filtered" so that only those attributes that are appropriate to the ODS are brought forward into it.

Of course, for large tables (i.e., tables that will contain a massive number of occurrences), the data model entity can be implemented as a series of related tables in the operational data store. There is no need to have a single physical ODS table correspond to a single entity. Figure 5.6 shows such an example, where the data model has specified ORDER as an entity. But there will be many orders that will populate the operational data store. So the entity ORDER is implemented as multiple physical ODS tables—foreign orders, back orders, current orders, and precious goods orders. Implementing several

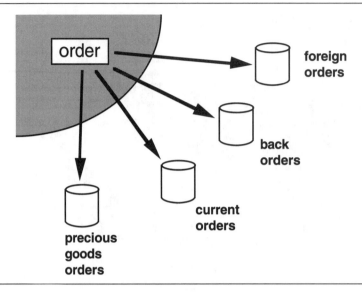

Figure 5.6   Entities that are large and complex are often broken into more than one physical table.

physical ODS tables in the case of large and/or complex major subject areas has several salubrious effects, such as:

- Breaking large amounts of data into a series of smaller amounts
- Creating environments where uniqueness of tables can be accommodated
- Breaking the work load into separate streams, where each stream is oriented to different styles and kinds of processing

Of course, the different physical ODS tables that are created can be related through common keys and through data values. While the same *type* of data may appear across multiple related tables, the same *occurrence* of data will not appear across multiple physical tables in the operational data store.

THE OPERATIONAL DATA STORE AND THE PROCESS MODEL

The operational data store is shaped by the process model in the same way it is shaped by the data model. Figure 5.7 shows the relationship of the ODS to the process model. Different pro-

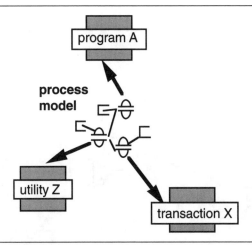

Figure 5.7   The process model shapes the programs and transactions that will be written to access the operational data store.

cesses and activities are identified in the process model. These processes become the basis of the design of the programs and transactions that are found in the ODS operating environment. The process model is useful for identifying such things as:

- Input/output to the process
- Sequence of execution of the process
- Algorithmic content of the process
- Transformations/conversions made during the process
- Conditions relevant to the process
- Flow of the process

From the process model comes the identification of the programs that will execute in the operational data store operating environment. (Note: Those programs that will execute repetitively are identified and analyzed here. Of course, the heuristic processes that will be run are not part of the process model that is built for the operational data store.) Once the programs are identified, how they will operate on the tables that are to be part of the operational data store is specified, as seen in Figure 5.8.

Figure 5.8 shows that the interaction of the programs in the ODS operating environment is scrutinized very carefully. ODS program-to-data interactions that are analyzed include:

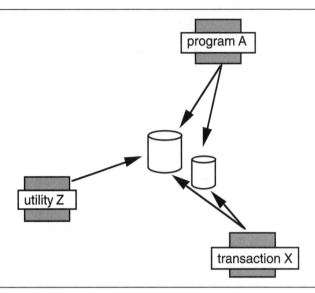

Figure 5.8 The programs and transactions that constitute the processing that will be done against the operational data store shape its content and structure.

- How many times a day the program will execute.
- How many resources will be used during an execution.
- The arrival rate of the programs.
- The time of day when peak interaction will occur.
- The sequence of programs' execution.
- Whether update will occur.
- The expected response time.
- The impact of a system outage on execution.
- The need to periodically restructure/reorganize data.

Based upon the profile of execution of the programs that have been identified, the operational data store architect can predict which parts of the system will be performance sensitive, and adjust the design of the ODS environment accordingly.

The process model for the operational data store environment is constrained along the same lines as the data model. Figure 5.9 shows that the operational data store process model is—like the operational data store data model—a minimalist one.

The operational data store process model contains only the barebones requirements for ODS usage. Because general-

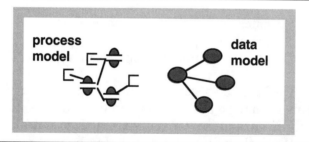

Figure 5.9   Both the process model and data model are constrained by the analytical activities that will occur within the operational data store—they are not general purpose at all.

purpose applications are not normally built in the ODS, the process model is small (compared with a general-purpose, applications process model).

CASE AND OPERATIONAL DATA STORE PROCESS MODEL DEVELOPMENT

CASE tools make a very good foundation on which to house and build the ODS process model. Figure 5.10 shows the relation of CASE tools to the ODS. In an operational data store environment, CASE tools are good for such procedures as:

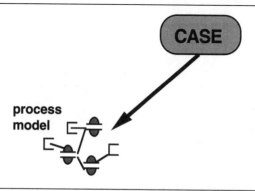

Figure 5.10   CASE technology is quite appropriate to the building of the process model.

- Collection and organization of requirements
- Specification of different levels of process
- Sequencing of process
- Detailed reformatting/conversion specification

CASE is also good for gathering the requirements for the transformation and integration of data as it flows into the operational data store. Of course, CASE is not an appropriate tool for the gathering and synthesizing heuristic requirements.

Mixing the Requirements

Once the program requirements are specified, they are used as input into the design process for the actual physical data structures of the operational data store. While the requirements of each process must be considered, processes are not equal participants. Some sets of requirements are much more important than others. Figure 5.11 shows the blending of the requirements based on different levels of participation and priorities of different programs. Some transactions run much more frequently than others. In addition, some transactions have a much higher

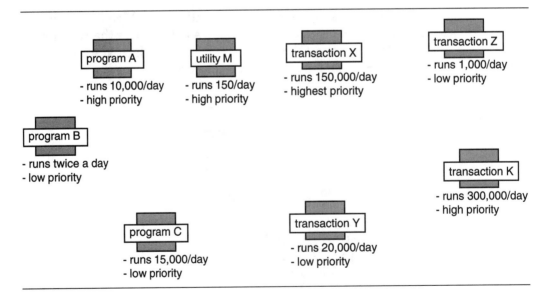

Figure 5.11   All of the processing that goes into the daily workload mix is considered in the design of the operational data store.

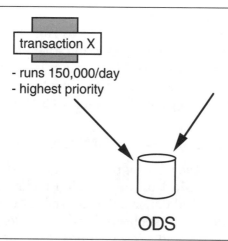

Figure 5.12 The operational data store is designed to optimize the performance of the most important activities.

priority than others. The design of the operational data store is weighted to accommodate those frequently executed, high-priority programs and transactions. In every database system ever written, design tradeoffs have been made. In the case of the ODS, the tradeoffs are made in favor of the "heavy hitters" (Figure 5.12).

ACCOMMODATING THE MOST IMPORTANT PROCESSES

The accommodation of the most important processes begins with the consideration of the I/O used by the most important transactions. I/O—input/output operations—is the center of attention because it is the largest performance bottleneck in a fast-response, transaction-oriented environment. I/O refers to the act of placing data onto and retrieving data from a disk device. Data that resides on a disk device is stored and accessed in terms of mechanical speeds. Inside the computer, the code executes at electronic speeds. Electronic speeds are typically three to four orders of magnitude faster than mechanical speeds. For that reason, when a programmer issues a simple READ... statement and the READ... statement needs data residing outside the computer, there is a severe slowdown in the execution of the program.

The job of the operational data store architect is to minimize the total system I/O required to run the ODS environment. In minimizing the total system I/O, there will be an overall performance gain. The way I/O is minimized across the system is by looking at the most important, most frequently run transactions and minimizing the I/O required for their execution.

DESIGN TECHNIQUES—MINIMIZING INPUT/OUTPUT

There are several design techniques that minimize the amount of I/O used. Most of these design techniques fall into the category of physical denormalization of data. The subject of physical denormalization has been discussed at length in the trade press and in books and presentations. See the references section at the back of the book for in-depth discussions of denormalization.

In order to optimize the access of data and minimize the usage of I/O, first the transactions and programs must be organized according to their importance and frequency of execution. The most important and most frequently executed programs and transactions are then selected and the way they access data is analyzed. Figure 5.13 shows the identification of the pattern of access of these transactions and programs.

When the process of physical optimization of the placement of data commences, the tables of data that will reside in the

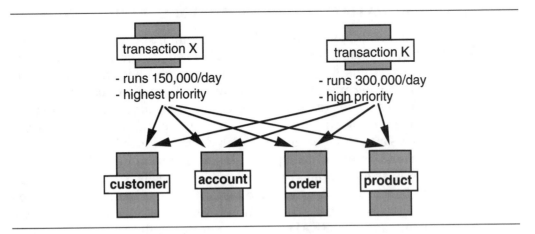

Figure 5.13 Optimizing the design begins with looking at the most important transactions and determining how they access data.

operational data store are generally highly normalized. Because of this, they do not contain redundant data, they are structured so that there are no repeating groups of data, and each unit of data stands on its own merit, independent of any other group of data. In addition, there is no summarized data and data is connected logically by means of foreign keys.

The access patterns of the most important programs and transactions are gathered and analyzed to determine whether there is a repeating pattern of access. In most cases, there is a predominant pattern of access of data that is repeated by many programs and transactions. The predominant pattern or patterns of access are identified and the data is physically rearranged in order to accommodate them. In doing so, the programs accomplish exactly the same functions they were designed to do but use less total I/O in order to do those functions. Some of the techniques of physically rearranging data will be discussed in the following section.

Physically Merging Tables

The most powerful design technique to enhance the reduction of the total amount of I/O used is that of merging two or more tables together. Figure 5.14 shows an example of this technique, where customer data, account data, and product data have been merged with basic order data. Fortunately, this technique fits very nicely with the notion of star joins. By merging the data into a single location, the end user can conveniently and efficiently access data without having to go to different physical tables. The merger of data into a common physical location greatly reduces I/O. In addition, when this technique is employed properly, the data can be arranged so that the end user sees the data "naturally," as he or she is used to seeing the data in the everyday workplace.

The design tradeoff of the technique of merging tables is that redundancy of data will creep into the design. In addition, while this technique makes access and processing efficient for some programs and transactions, it is inefficient for others. That is why the first question that must be asked is what are the most important programs and transactions.

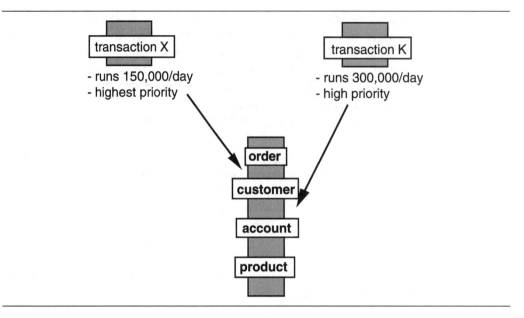

Figure 5.14   Merging data allows it to be accessed efficiently.

Indexing Data

A very simple way to reduce the total amount of I/O is to judiciously employ indexes. Figure 5.15 shows the introduction and usage of indexes. An index is an independent collection of data that contains at least two essential pieces of data—the key value (or other identifier) of an occurrence of data and the physical address of the data. The index is arranged according to the sequence of the key and is very efficiently accessed. Once the index is searched, it is simple to go directly to the location where the data is. When it comes to searching for data, the index can be a great saver of I/O; in many cases, the alternative would be a full scan of the table, which entails many, many I/Os.

The pattern of access of data is the best indicator as to how indexes should be created. Indexes should be built to accommodate the most frequently used patterns of access.

Purge Criteria

An important facet of operational data store design is that of the specification of its purge criteria. Figure 5.16 shows this

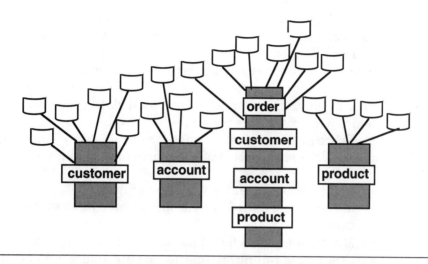

Figure 5.15   Indexing should be liberally used in accordance with the usage of the data in both sparse and fully populated mode.

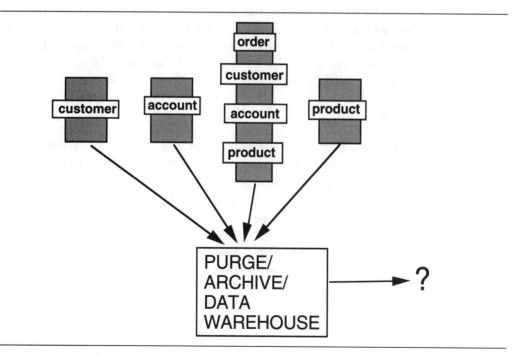

Figure 5.16   Purge criteria for data in the operational data store is an important design decision.

specification. The operational data store holds data that is very fresh—it is usual for it to hold data for about three or four days—up to one month in some cases. If an ODS holds detailed data for much longer, the volume of data starts to mount and other system complexities start to emerge, such as in performance and management of overflow of data. Therefore, it is important that data be purged from the operational data store environment before it starts to become stale.

There are several strategies for purging data from the operational data store. Some of the more common ones are:

- Actual removal and destruction of data
- Movement of data from the operational data store to the data warehouse
- Movement of detailed data to an archival medium
- Creation of rolling summaries of data where data is rolled up into successively higher levels of detail in the data warehouse as it ages

There are as many alternate strategies for purging data from the operational data store as there are types of data; they can be employed in any combination. Whatever the strategy employed, allowing detailed data to remain in the operational data store for any length of time is an architectural mistake.

Turning Off the Log Tape

If, in fact, detailed data is to be stored at the operational data store level and performance is an issue, then under certain circumstances it is possible to turn off the log tape while the ODS is being updated. In doing so, the DBMS operates much more efficiently. Figure 5.17 shows this option.

Turning off the log tape during update processing is a dangerous approach that is applicable only under abnormal conditions. On occasion, the disappearance of one or two updates makes little or no difference to the operational data store end user. In some cases, the transactions that are stored in the ODS can be easily retransacted if need be. In other cases, the transactions themselves are stored in the operational data store after having been performed in the legacy application environment. In this situation, it may not be necessary to have each transaction ex-

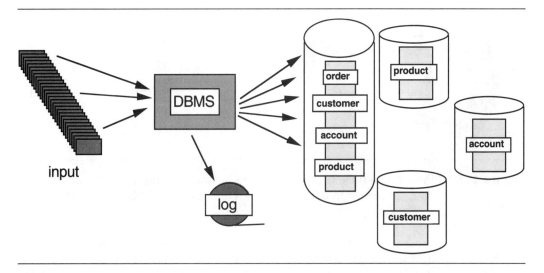

Figure 5.17 Efficiency may be enhanced by turning off the log during online update.

ecuted in the ODS in a high-integrity fashion. If any or all of these circumstances apply, it may be feasible to turn off the log tape during ODS processing and save considerable overhead.

Preprocessing Detailed Transactions

In some cases, it may be possible to enhance operational data store performance by doing a significant amount of preprocessing of detailed transactions before they are allowed to enter the operational data store environment. By preprocessing transactions prior to entry to the operational data store, the operational data store environment is spared the consumption of unnecessary resources, and performance is accordingly enhanced. This alternative of design is illustrated in Figure 5.18 which shows that transactions can be preprocessed by an application before the transactions pass into the operational data store. Typical processing might include:

- Heavy editing, verification of the transaction
- Combination of like transactions into a single composite transaction
- Selection of unique transactions (such as the last transaction of the day) and rejection of other transactions

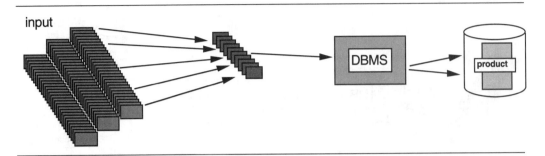

Figure 5.18   Preprocess bulk input data off-line before entering it into the operational data store environment (for Class II and Class III ODS).

By carefully editing and manipulating the detailed transactions prior to entering the transactions into the operational data store job stream, much processing can be saved in the performance-sensitive ODS environment.

Space Management for the Operational Data Store Environment

The issues of performance extend down to as low a level as basic space management in the operational data store environment. Because update is done in the ODS environment, some amount of free space must be left in the physical block where ODS data is stored to avoid conflicts during update. Figure 5.19 shows free space being left in the physical block. The exact percentage of free space that is left is entirely dependent on exactly how much update will occur, whether inserts will be allowed, whether variable-length records will be updated, and so forth. Note that the philosophy for the management of free space in the operational data store environment is the opposite of the philosophy for free space management in the data warehouse environment, where there is no free space allocated upon load-

Figure 5.19   At initial load, some amount of space must be left for future expansion.

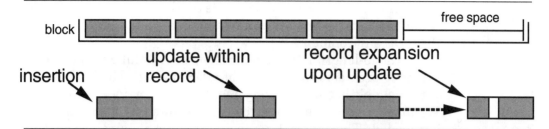

Figure 5.20 The type of update being done has a large impact on the amount of free space that is required.

ing a table. Figure 5.20 illustrates the common kinds of update that can be done and their effect on free space management in the ODS.

In addition to the basic issues of free space management that go hand in hand with ODS updates, there is the issue of managing space in the indexes that point into the ODS. Figure 5.21 shows the need for the management of space at the index level as well as at the data level.

Every time an insert is made to an ODS table, multiple indexes will have to have an entry made to them. And when an indexed field is altered, two index entries must be modified—the index entry that points to a now-defunct value must be disabled,

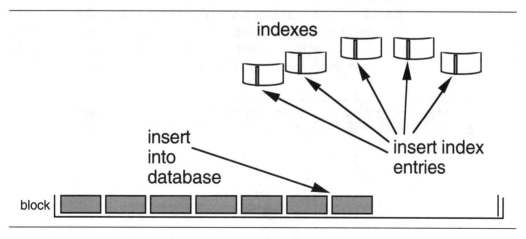

Figure 5.21 Index management is a performance issue as well.

and a new index entry must be made for the newly defined value. All of the index activities contribute to a performance drag on the ODS environment.

Variable-length records offer their own peculiar space management problems in the face of ODS update. The problem of variable-length space management is shown in Figure 5.22. Variable-length data is packed tightly into its block upon being loaded. Then, at a later point in time it is retrieved and an update is made to the variable-length record. Unfortunately, this update causes the length of the variable-length record to grow. When the variable-length record is returned to its original location, it will no longer fit. At this point, space management can become a nightmare. The specification and management of variable-length records presents its own challenges in the face of ODS update.

SUMMARY

There is a spectrum of development processes that is created by the SDLC and the CLDS. Development for the operational data store fits midway between these two ends of the spectrum. Another development spectrum can be created by the extremities of the data model and the process model. Again, the operational data store fits between these two extremities. In any case, the ODS is best built in an iterative manner, where small, fast, steps of design define it.

Each entity in the data model corresponds to a physical table in the operational data store. In the case of a large number of occurrences of data, an entity may be represented by multiple physical tables in the ODS. The process model shapes the ODS

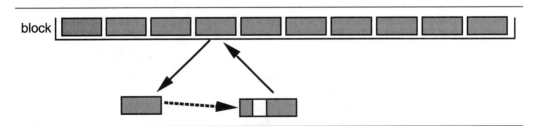

Figure 5.22   Variable-length data can present its own performance considerations.

in the same way that the data model does. The functions and activities defined in the process model result in programs and transactions in the ODS environment.

Once the programs and transactions are identified, they are analyzed with regard to frequency and priority of execution. The most important programs and transactions are identified and the system is physically designed to optimize their performance.

There are several popular design techniques that can enhance system performance:

- Merging of tables
- Proper indexing of data
- Proper purging of old data to keep from cluttering up the ODS environment
- Turning off of the log tape (when circumstances warrant)
- Preprocessing of transactions prior to their entry into the ODS environment
- Proper space management

6

Managing the Operational Data Store Environment

The operational data store environment presents an administrative challenge like no other because it contains so many types of processing. The ODS environment contains high-performance transaction processing, heuristic DSS processing, batch loads, and a host of other processes. In order to successfully run the operational data store environment, *all* of these disparate types of processing must be accommodated. In many cases, design and operational practices that are optimal for one type of processing are not at all optimal for other types. The result is that the ongoing administration of the ODS environment is no simple matter.

MONITORING SYSTEM UTILIZATION

There are many facets to the ongoing administration of the operational data store environment. Perhaps the most important activity of ODS administration is the continual monitoring of its hardware and software activities. The ODS environment requires constant monitoring because it is like a finely-tuned car that can easily get out of balance.

The systems environment of the operational data store is constantly changing. Data is being added; more users start to run programs; the system of record needs to be altered, and so forth. Each change in the operational data store environment requires some adjustment to be made. Only through careful and consistent monitoring will the ODS architect be aware of the changes that are occurring and be able to respond.

One of the telltale measurements that the operational data store administrator needs to look at is the profile of hardware utilization that is created by monitoring hardware activity, as seen in Figure 6.1. The pattern of usage of hardware utilization reveals many things, such as:

- When the hardware is starting to become overwhelmed
- When the hardware is not tuned properly
- When the usage patterns of the end user are changing
- Where spare machine resources are
- At what rate usage is growing

The pattern of hardware utilization is one of the most important measurements that can be captured by the operational data store architect.

Contrasting Utilization Profiles

Continuously monitoring hardware utilization is a resource-intensive activity. Turning the hardware monitor on requires its own significant set of resources. Because resources are required

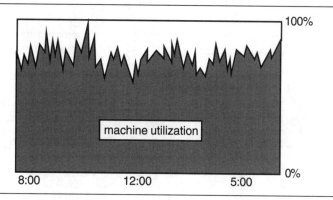

Figure 6.1   Looking at the profile of hardware utilization periodically can enhance system performance.

for measuring hardware utilization, most organizations turn on the hardware monitor only sporadically. A common practice is to monitor hardware utilization at selected periods or intervals. Those intervals are collected and compiled to form a profile of "average" utilization. Then, when the ODS environment experiences performance difficulties, the profile of hardware utilization during the period of difficulty is compared with the profile representing average utilization. Figure 6.2 illustrates the practice of contrasting patterns of hardware utilization.

There can be several causes for poor performance in the operational data store environment. There may be an anomaly occurring in system utilization. If there are 200 end users it is possible that 195 of them hit the ENTER key at precisely the same moment. Or there may be a system problem: Buffers may have overflowed, or an update function may have neglected to take checkpoints periodically. There may be a design problem resulting in one table suddenly becoming a bottleneck. Whatever the problem is, the contrast between the pattern of hardware utilization when things are running properly versus when things are not running properly tips off the ODS administrator as to how to solve the problem.

Another important ongoing measurement that the ODS administrator needs to track is the growth in the number of users and their rate of system utilization and activity. Figure 6.3 shows a simple graph that tracks the number of end users of the operational data store.

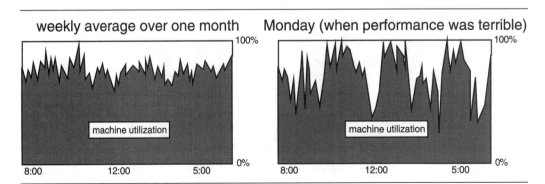

Figure 6.2   Comparing problem days with normal days is a good way to spot performance difficulties.

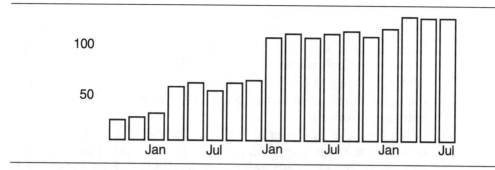

Figure 6.3   Measuring the growth of the number of users over time.

There are several important reasons why the number of end users should be monitored. The most obvious reason is that the growth of hardware can be tracked along with growth in utilization. But there is another important reason why the number of end users should be tracked. Occasionally the operational data store administrator is called upon to justify the expenditures made on its behalf. Having the exact number of end users and a profile of their activity is a first line of defense in justifying resource expenditures for the ODS.

Another important parameter that should be measured over time is that of the growth of storage within the operational data store environment, as suggested by Figure 6.4. Like the

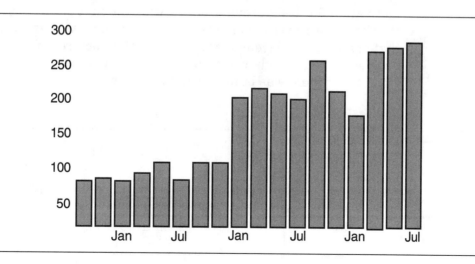

Figure 6.4   Measuring the growth of storage in gb over time.

data warehouse, the operational data store has a tendency to accumulate volumes of data over time. These volumes of data, if unmanaged, can clog things up and cause all sorts of system and application problems. Therefore, it is important for the ODS administrator to keep a close watch on the growth of data within the operational data store to ensure that it is anticipated and managed properly.

In fact, the management of the growth of data is so important that managing growth at a wholesale level is probably not adequate. The ODS administrator should be advised that managing growth by individual table is probably in order. Figure 6.5 shows growth being tracked on an individual table basis. When growth is tracked by tables, the ODS administrator develops a feel for what data is being used the most and where the advances in the volumes of data are coming from. When it comes time to make decisions about purging data from the ODS environment and moving the data off to archival and data warehouse environments, the administrator knows exactly where to consider pruning.

DESIGN REVIEW IN THE OPERATIONAL DATA STORE ENVIRONMENT

Design review is the practice of carefully reviewing the design of an application before the first line of code is struck. The motivation for design review began with the first online system that had to be rewritten because of poor design. It was discovered that many more development and maintenance resources are needlessly consumed trying to repair a system after the fact when the system was built poorly to begin with.

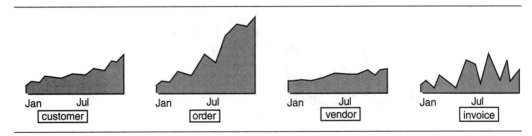

Figure 6.5   Managing the growth of data by individual table.

The notion behind design review is that the system already being managed would have been built quite differently had the right question been asked at the right time. Design review attempts to ask the right question at the right time, *before* the system is built, thereby potentially saving huge amounts of rework in design and development.

Design review has always been especially relevant to online high-performance systems, and in that regard the operational data store environment admirably qualifies. Indeed, the diversity of processing that occurs in the ODS environment makes it a prime candidate for the ongoing practice of design review as new parts are added to it. It is in the best interest of the ODS administrator to make design review a regular and normal part of operational data store administration.

Design review is best done early in the operational data store development process. As soon as the new development in the operational data store environment is formalized, it is time to do design review. Design review is almost always best conducted by an outsider—someone who is not connected with the operational data store development effort. If it is conducted by an insider, the review process can turn into an exercise of politics and personal criticism. The more political and personal a design review becomes, the less effective it is. Having an outsider conduct a design review is the best tactic to ensure that the review process is apolitical and impersonal.

Preparation for the operational data store design review process is minimal. The designer simply takes what design documents have been created and uses them as the basis for review. If there is a massive preparation effort done on behalf of a design review, then the review is being conducted improperly.

The operational data store design review typically takes two or three days, depending on the size and complexity of the development being reviewed. If it takes fewer than two or three days, then the review is probably superficial. If a review takes longer than two or three days, then it becomes tedious and loses much of its value.

The actual procedure of an ODS design review is conducted from a standard checklist, such as that suggested by Figure 6.6. All the participants in the ODS design review are allowed to view in advance the questions and issues that will be discussed. The participants in the review include anyone who has a stake

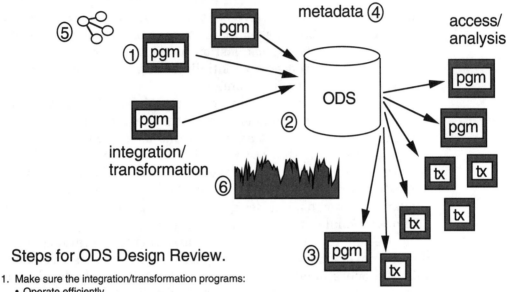

Steps for ODS Design Review.

1. Make sure the integration/transformation programs:
   • Operate efficiently.
   • Operate from changed data rather than against the database.
   • Accomplish the integration that is needed.
2. The structure of the ODS:
   • Make sure it is able to be efficiently accessed.
   • Make sure it conforms to the corporate data model.
   • Make sure that future additions will fit.
   • Make sure indexes are available and efficient.
3. Access/analysis transactions:
   • Make sure that access programs are operating efficiently.
   • Make sure that data is being purged efficiently.
   • Make sure that analysis is effective.
   • Make sure that new analysis that is stabilizing is being considered.
   • Make sure that the processing window is not being squeezed.
4. Metadata:
   • Make sure metadata is available, accurate, and being tracked automatically.
5. Data model:
   • Make sure that current development is synchronized with the corporate data model.
   • Make sure that future development is in synch with the corporate data model.
6. Ongoing monitoring of the ODS:
   • Make sure that current activity levels are being monitored.
   • Monitor response time levels.
   • Monitor number of users.
   • Monitor time of day of usage.
   • Monitor overnight batch window.

Figure 6.6   Design review in the operational data store environment.

in the success of the ODS development and operation. Typically these participants include:

- The ODS developer
- The data modeller
- The end user
- The DSS analyst
- Systems programmers
- Database administrators
- Programmers
- Auditors
- Management

Of the participants, the end user and the DSS analyst are easily the most important; their input is invaluable.

In many cases, having the end user and the DSS analyst in the same room as the developers inspires direct communication that otherwise would not have happened. This direct conversation can be an extremely important by-product of doing a design review.

The topics of conversation for the operational data store include *any* topic relevant to the success of the ODS development. The more controversial the topic, the more appropriate it is for discussion.

As the ODS design review is occurring, notes are taken. At the end of the review the notes are reviewed and form the basis of the formal findings of the review. Generally speaking, the notes are divided into several categories:

- general observations
- action items
- red flags

The bottom line of design review in the operational data store development environment is where expectations are met with no untoward surprises.

CAPACITY PLANNING IN THE OPERATIONAL DATA STORE ENVIRONMENT

In addition to design review, the operational data store architect should institute the ongoing practice of capacity planning for ODS administration. Figure 6.7 shows some of the activi-

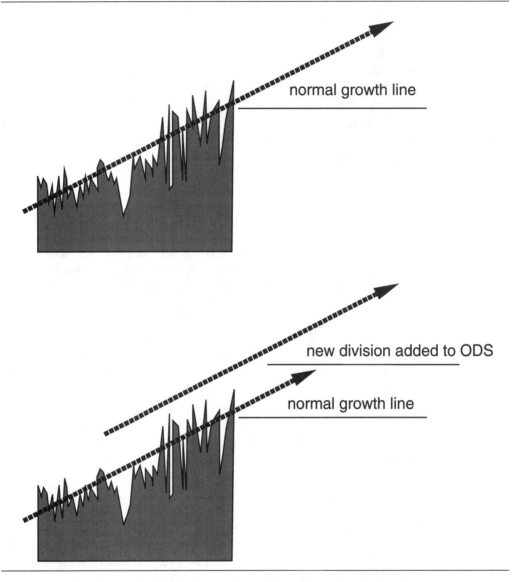

Figure 6.7   Capacity planning in the ODS environment.

ties of ODS measurement and monitoring in which the ODS architect engages. In addition to other measurements, the ODS architect has an ongoing interest in the growth of hardware (CPU, memory), DASD and other forms of storage, and end-user activity.

Once the ODS architect starts to develop the measurements that reflect current system activity, he or she can then start to project those measurements to predict future growth. There are two simple ways that growth is projected:

- Current growth is linearly extrapolated
- Known future expansion not yet factored into current growth is added to the extrapolation

The net of these two considerations is an expectation of how much capacity will be needed in the future and when.

VERIFYING THE SYSTEM OF RECORD

Although the operational data store designer tries very hard to identify and properly use the system of record at the outset of the design effort for the ODS environment, the system of record has a habit of changing over time. One of the ongoing activities of the ODS administrator is to periodically review the system of record to see if changes need to be made. There are many reasons why the system of record may have changed, for instance:

- The nature of the business has changed.
- Legacy systems have changed.
- The DSS analyst has pointed out a new opportunity.

The changes that need to be made to the operational data store environment show up in the modification of the system of record itself, the transformation and integration interface into the ODS, and the actual definition and content of the ODS itself.

Figure 6.8 shows the system of record periodically being reviewed. The ODS administrator looks for such things as the following:

- Has the application underlying the system of record changed?
- Has a new application been added that will make a better system of record?
- Has the interpretation of the operational data store data changed so that under today's conditions there is a better system of record?
- Has the end user or the DSS analyst requested a change?

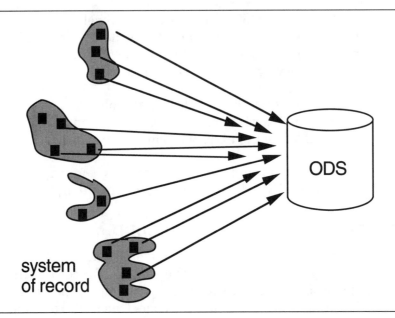

Figure 6.8   Alignment of the ODS and the system of record needs to be periodically checked.

The operational data store administrator must not assume that once the ODS is built and has been populated the system of record will remain permanently cast as originally defined.

THE METADATA INFRASTRUCTURE

As with the system of record, the metadata structure of the operational data store also undergoes change. Figure 6.9 illustrates the metadata infrastructure of the ODS environment. The metadata infrastructure in the operational data store environment encompasses four venues:

- Definition of the system of record
- Transformation of the system of record into the operational data store
- Contents of the operational data store
- Availability of the metadata to the end user

New requirements and changes to existing requirements for the ODS environment are usually generated in one of two places, as seen in Figure 6.10. Changes in requirements will occur in

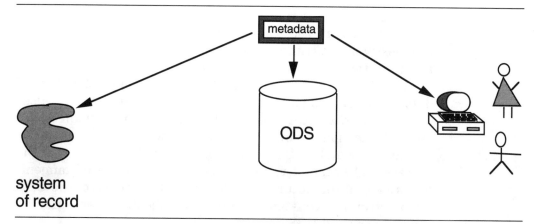

Figure 6.9 Periodically reviewing the metadata infrastructure.

the integration and transformation of the legacy data to the ODS environment.

Typically, the requirements generated here are part of the iterative development process in which the DSS part of the operational data store participates. On occasion, there is the need

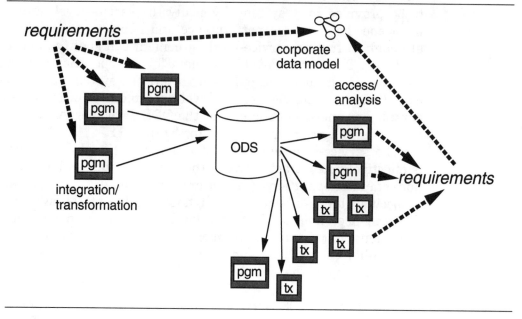

Figure 6.10 Integrating external requirements into the ODS and internally generating new requirements.

to change the transformation and integration programs because of the changes in the legacy environment itself. The size and complexity of the transformation and integration programs are a natural target for changes in requirements.

The other type of changes that often occur in the operational data store environment are those that are picked up as end-user feedback at the access and analysis level. These changes are often a reflection of new opportunities and discoveries made by the end user and DSS analyst. Changes here are a sign of the success and usage of the operational data store environment. Regardless of the nature of the change, it is the job of the ODS administrator to constantly monitor the feedback generated by the end user and DSS analyst.

SERVICE-LEVEL AGREEMENTS

Because there is an important online component of the operational data store environment, service-level agreements are a standard part of the ODS environment. A service-level agreement is a statement of the expected (quantified) level of service to be provided by a system. Typically the service-level agreement specifies levels of performance and hours of availability, although in truth a service-level agreement can specify almost anything. The service-level agreement for the operational data store is agreed upon and published before the system goes into execution. As such, the service-level agreement provides measurable parameters of success for the ODS developer. A sample service-level agreement is shown in Figure 6.11.

The service-level agreement for the operational data store is effectively a contract between the end user and DSS analyst and computer operations. Computer operations agrees to provide a specified level of service throughout the life of the system. The end user knows what that level of service is before the operational data store environment is built. If the service level is not high enough, the end user is free to raise the level of service as long as the end user is willing to pay for the enhanced service.

Periodically, ODS service is measured and benchmarked against the published service-level agreement. Because of the

Service-level agreements:

Performance:
Mon – Fri — 8:00 am to 5:00 pm
class A transaction - 3-second response time
class B transaction - 30-second response time
class C transaction - 5-minute response time
90% of the time

Availability:
Mon – Fri — 8:00 am to 5:00 pm
system available 95% of the time
no more than 2 outages a week
outage to last no longer than 10 minutes

Figure 6.11   First establish and then manage within the confines of a service-level agreement.

quantified nature of the service-level agreement, there is never any doubt as to whether the service-level objectives are being met.

LISTENING TO THE END USER / DSS ANALYST

Above everything else the operational data store administrator does, he or she must listen carefully to feedback generated by end users and DSS analysts. Of course, the administrator should filter the requests made by this community. Figure 6.12 illustrates this ongoing task.

SUMMARY

The administration of the operational data store environment begins with the ongoing monitoring of system activities, such as hardware utilization, end-user growth, and growth in the volume of data. Both "average" and "problem" utilization profiles are created. The difference between these two types of profiles creates a basis of solving performance problems.

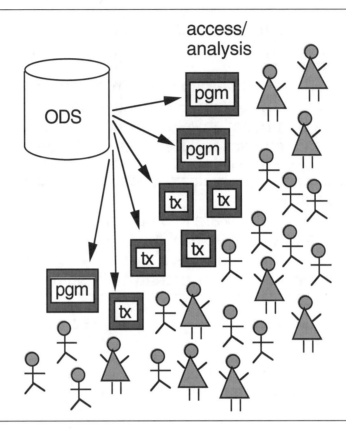

Figure 6.12   The ongoing task of the administrator is to listen to the end user/DSS analyst community—on any subject relevant to the success of the operational data store.

Design review is the process of carefully interrogating an operational data store design before the design is coded. Design review is especially important for the high-performance portion of the ODS environment. Reviewing a system properly can save huge amounts in redevelopment costs.

Capacity planning is another ongoing activity of the operational data store environment. Both normal growth and planned expansion should be taken into consideration.

The system of record and the metadata infrastructure must be periodically reviewed. Service-level agreements need to be specified before the operational data store environment is established.

7

Technology and the Operational Data Store

Technology required to support the operational data store falls into a number of categories. Since an operational data store (like a data warehouse) is a solution made up of numerous components, each component should be looked at separately. An overall picture of the operational data store looks something like Figure 7.1. Notice that the major components required are the transformation layer, the hardware and software platform that will support the operational data store, and the middleware that will be used to access it.

TRANSFORMATION SOFTWARE

The first component of the operational data store that will be examined is the transformation software. It is here that data is transformed, scrubbed, and propagated from the legacy environment into the ODS. Various tools are available in the market that support this function either directly or by generating the necessary code to implement these functions. This type of support often proves to be critical to the success of an operational data store (or a data warehouse), since it permits the flexibility required to iteratively implement a solution.

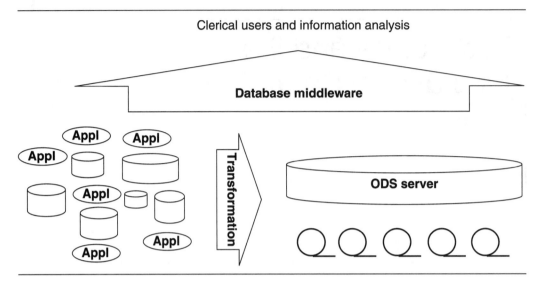

Figure 7.1   An operational data store is made up of three core technologies: middleware, transformation software, and the operational data store Server environment.

In this discussion, transformation will be considered to be a logical layer that extends from the legacy data to the point of insertion into the operational data store. Various components of this software may exist on the source platform or on the target ODS platform. Indeed, transformation software often runs on a third platform, such as a workstation, and generates the functions needed onto the source and target platform, as shown in Figure 7.2. This discussion does not differentiate between these approaches.

Support for Numerous Source and Target Platforms

An obvious requirement of a transformation tool is that it can deal with all of the source data stores that will be used to populate the proposed environment. This includes an understanding of the data types and the conversions necessary to populate the operational data store platform. Conversely, the transformation tool should target a wide variety of ODS platforms with the flexibility to add new ones as they become available. The transformation tool is the first line of defense against vendor lock-in

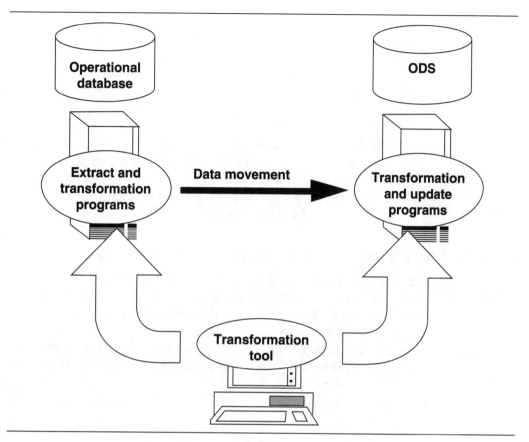

Figure 7.2   Some tools that automate the transformation layer actually reside on a third platform and generate the code necessary to do transformations.

within the operational data store, since it can provide portability to new technologies as they become available.

Ability to Capture Change

The key to maintaining synchronization in the operational data store is the ability to quickly and efficiently capture change in the operational environment. Facilities that automatically capture change can dramatically impact the complexity of an operational data store project by negating the need to modify decades of legacy code in order to write application exits for capturing change. As mentioned earlier, reading journal tapes is an effective way to implement a Class III operational data store, since it allows for the processing of tapes away from the production environment. It requires that the tool perform the complex task of understanding the images on the tape and relating them to the database design. The downside is that near-synchronous propagation of data is not possible since tapes must be filled and dismounted. In certain environments, such as when data is time sensitive (a Class I ODS) or when the operational data store is being used as a platform for reengineering, this may not be sufficient. In those cases, it may be necessary to capture transactions as they happen and feed them directly to the transformation logic as shown in Figure 7.3.

Ability to Support Multiple Types of Transformations

An important technological requirement is that the tools being used can support most of the transformations needed in the operational data store. These transformations are similar to the types of things that would be done in a data warehouse, since they include integration, decoding, aggregation, and so on. The difference is that the tools must update data that is in place and

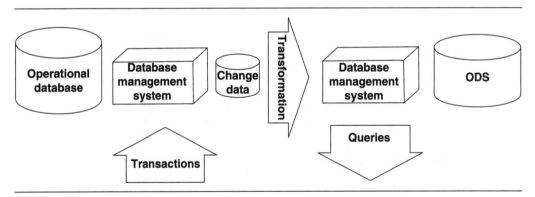

Figure 7.3   In cases where data is very time sensitive or the operational data store will be used as a basis for reengineering, near-synchronous propagation may be required. This is often done by having the DBMS in the legacy environment (DB2, IMS, etc.) generate a record of changes made to the operational database. This change is often in the form of log tapes that are then read by the transformation layer and applied by the DBMS in the query environment to the ODS.

may be required to trickle information in a near-synchronous manner. If this is the case, the tools must be able to receive data from the change capture facility and pass it directly into the target operational data store. (Note: Few tools today are designed with this capability, and as a result this type of activity is often custom coded.) In addition, a tool must be able to integrate custom transformation logic written by the enterprise to support unique requirements.

Ability to Quickly and Easily Adapt to Design Changes

In an operational data store, as in a data warehouse, change is the order of the day. Because operational data stores are built in an iterative fashion, it is often necessary to change the design and therefore the transformation layer. Clearly one of the benefits of transformation tools is a reduction of effort required to modify and add new transformations by automating this process. Transformation tools often generate software to do the transformations or use a rules engine to allow changes to be made. The ease of use of this tool in modifying the transformation layer is extremely important.

Ability to Assure Delivery of Data

It is important that the transformation layer assure the delivery of the data to the operational data store. If the operational data store is unavailable for any reason, change must be applied to it when it comes back online, otherwise the data in it will grow to be inconsistent with the operational environment. This means that some method of store and forward should be present for operational data store outages. Likewise, the transformation layer must have the ability to assure proper completion of the updates and inserts to be applied against the target operational data store. This implies that the transformation layer must have control over transaction boundaries such that it can assure the completion of inserts, updates, and deletes from the ODS. It is desirable to be able to vary the size of the groups of changes that are committed together for performance and locking reasons. In some cases, it is advantageous to have the ability to group changes based on their business implication such that a consistent view of the business is presented. In Figure 7.4, the

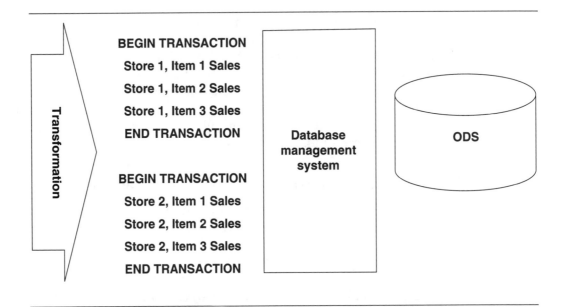

BEGIN TRANSACTION

Store 1, Item 1 Sales

Store 1, Item 2 Sales

Store 1, Item 3 Sales

END TRANSACTION

BEGIN TRANSACTION

Store 2, Item 1 Sales

Store 2, Item 2 Sales

Store 2, Item 3 Sales

END TRANSACTION

Transformation

Database management system

ODS

Figure 7.4   Updates to the operational data store may be group committed to provide a consistent view based on the users' requirements. In this example, all updates relevant to a particular store are committed by the DBMS as a single transaction.

implication is that users will tolerate an inconsistent view of item sales across stores but not within a store.

Metadata Support

The transformation layer of the operational data store environment has a great deal of responsibility in the maintenance of the metadata in an operational data store. The transformation layer is where knowledge of the current state of the ODS and the rules used to create it reside. This information is invaluable to the users of the operational data store, since it provides a sense of the timeliness and origin of the data being used. The transformation tool should store metadata in an open and accessible way for users.

THE OPERATIONAL DATA STORE PLATFORM

The hardware and software platform that supports the operational data store has a number of requirements placed on it.

These requirements vary depending on the class of ODS implemented. The most demanding is a Class I ODS, since this requires the combination of the characteristics of an online transaction processor (OLTP) system and a high-performance query system. Specifically, the platform must be at a unique intersection of systems that have the ability to manage large volumes of data, perform transactional updates, perform large-scale query, and manage large populations of clerical users, as shown in Figure 7.5. The following are the key areas of interest for implementing a Class I ODS. Many will carry over into a Class II and Class III implementation.

Scalability

Due to the nature of a DSS system's growth, the operational data store platform must be capable of cost-effective, incremen-

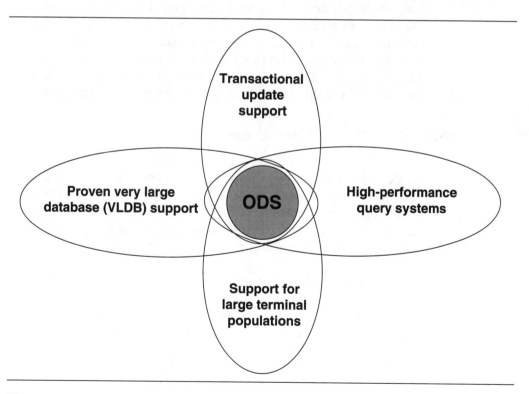

Figure 7.5   The computing platform used to support an operational data store lies at the intersection of four diverse requirements.

tal growth. This allows the platform to support a small initial implementation and to grow seamlessly as subject areas and users are added over time. In addition, the range of scalability must be extreme in order to support a potentially demanding implementation. One approach to this is to build the ODS on a software environment that will allow it to be ported over a wide range of computer systems. If the operational data store outgrew the platform that supported it, the platform could be replaced with a more powerful one. Many DBMS environments today are capable of running on multiple computer platforms that would allow the entire ODS to be ported if needed. The downside of this is that a "box swap" would be required rather than growing the existing investment; there is, as well, the potential to become tied to the vendor who sells the portable environment.

Another approach is to provide scalability through the use of parallel processing. In this scenario, individual tasks are spread over multiple processors and disk and I/O devices to enable growth through addition. Parallel processing has only reached maturity with a few vendors but in those cases it has demonstrated the ability to handle large volumes of data and complex query loads. It also has the advantage of allowing incremental scalability in small units of growth as workloads increase.

A Word About Parallel Processing

Some of the discussion in this book refers to parallel processing. While this is not a requirement for support of an operational data store, there are a number of reasons why it is a useful technology. Two commercial flavors of parallel processing computers are used today: symmetrical multiprocessing (SMP) and massively parallel processing (MPP). This is shown in Figure 7.6.

SMP systems are characterized by multiple processors having access to a common pool of memory. This is the most popular method due to its relative ease of implementation. One copy of the operating system and database software resides in memory as it would in monolithic systems and it has been taught to schedule multiple threads of execution across all of the processors. This approach will provide scalability until memory becomes a bottleneck for communications, and then will exhibit a decrease in processing speed for each processor that is added.

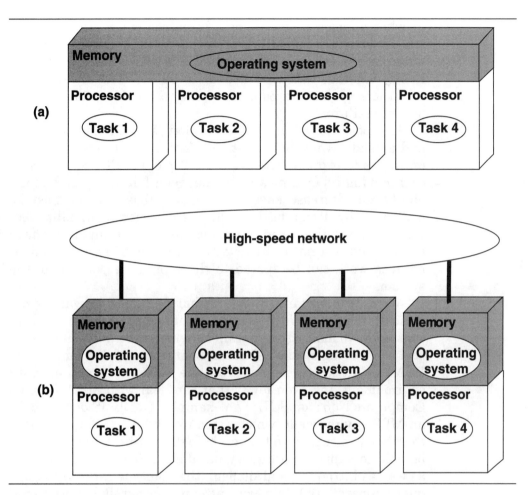

Figure 7.6 (a) Shared memory implementations such as SMP have a single instance of the operating system, which schedules work across many processing resources. (b) Shared nothing implementations, known as MPP, have an instance of the operating system in every processor, which must work together to present a single system image.

MPP systems are characterized by nonshared memory. The concept is similar to a distributed network of computers, each with its own operating system and DBMS. The difference is that in an MPP system, these "computers" are aware of each other and can work on a common task. Due to the speed of the interconnect and the peer-to-peer nature of the system software, the distinction between processors is blurred in an MPP, resulting in what appears to be a single large computer. An MPP system is relatively difficult for a vendor to build, since it implies multiple copies of the operating system and DBMS working so closely together that they appear to be one. The advantage is that there are no shared components to provide bottlenecks or produce failure.

It is possible to build a system that is much more scaleable and available than SMP systems. A side effect of parallel processing is that due to the use of multiple, parallel components, each having its own mean time between failure, system availability can decrease as system size increases. This must be addressed by designing into the system such availability features as the ability to continue execution when components have failed. This is a natural thing to do in a parallel environment because work can be spread to the remaining portions of the system.

What is important to note is that parallel hardware is not difficult to build for an operational data store. It is the software that is key to making the parallel environment work and that is still an evolving market. There are only a handful of commercial DBMSs that were designed from the start to work in an SMP environment and even fewer that can deal with MPP. Tandem Computers NonStop SQL is an example of a DBMS designed for an MPP environment, which explains why it has demonstrated the ability to scale into the terabyte databases. DBMSs need to be able to support interquery parallelism (concurrent queries) as well as intraquery parallelism (the ability to execute a single query in parallel). While early attempts at parallel query would simply decompose a query into subqueries for each processor to handle, newer designs are allowing the entire query to be optimized in a parallel fashion, as shown in Figure 7.7. This can dramatically enhance performance.

In addition, all of the system utilities used should be able to work in parallel. If a computer has 100 processors and any job or utility cannot be run in parallel, the job will operate in 1/100th of the system, which may be less than optimal. This applies to loading, inserting, index creation and maintenance, data reorganization, sorting, scanning, joining, and so on. It is important to remember that scalability, the implied benefit of parallel processing, can be mitigated by the inability to manage large, commercial databases if unproven technology is applied.

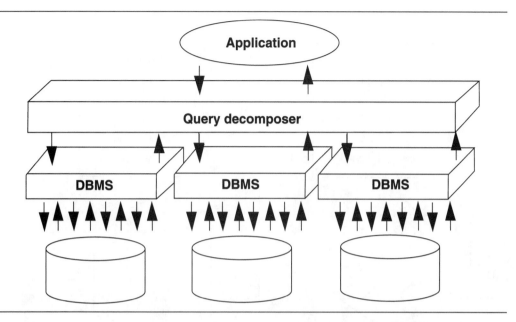

Figure 7.7　Simple parallel query can be achieved by external parallelization, which allows a large query to be broken into subqueries that are executed separately. Newer implementations use internal parallelization for better efficiency.

Support for Large, Diverse, and Demanding Networking

An operational data store has two sets of networking requirements: one that puts data into the system and one that allows it to be taken out. On the inbound side, high bandwidth communications are required to allow data to be moved into the operational data store. The need is often for legacy interoperability using proprietary mainframe protocols, but more and more can be achieved using open communications protocols such as asynchronous transfer mode (ATM) and fiber distributed data interface (FDDI). Because cost rises exponentially with bandwidth, it is important that the ability to parallelize this type of communications over numerous low-cost lines be available (Figure 7.8).

On the outbound side of an operational data store it is necessary to support both legacy connections to allow terminal en-

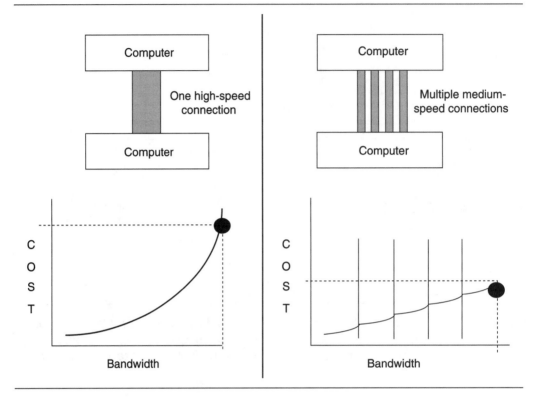

Figure 7.8   Multiple parallel connections between systems provide a more cost-effective solution for moving data but the system software must make this transparent.

vironments to access the operational data store and high speed open connections for local area networks (LANs) and wide area networks (WANs). Because of the potential for a large clerical user population using prebuilt query applications, support for legacy system access will prove useful. In order to allow access to the widest variety of workstation tools, mainstream LAN and WAN connectivity, such as TCP/IP and Xerox Network System (XNS) will be needed.

In addition, communications facilities capable of high-speed data transfers might be needed if the operational data store must snapshot data into a data warehouse residing on a separate physical platform.

High Availability

It is often assumed that, because DSS systems are query only, they can fail with minimal impact. This is not always true. Both data warehouses and operational data stores can have a major impact on the enterprise when they become unavailable since they service many important decision makers. The owners of the world's largest DSS systems in retail, telecommunications, and transportation will typically list system availability as one of the largest challenges they face. In an operational data store this is paramount, since the data is often very timely and since it supports tactical, short-term decision making by senior management and large numbers of clerical workers. If an operational data store supports 400 operators in a call center, for instance, an hour of unavailability could cause havoc (as well as a great deal of career planning for the IS department).

The platform supporting the operational data store should provide the ability to survive component outages wherever possible without interruption of service to the users. This should include disk, processor, or software failures. Availability goes well beyond component failures. Operations (backup, reorganization, restructuring, etc.) that are performed on a regular basis should be able to run in an online fashion with full user access. With many companies moving to international operations, it is increasingly difficult to dedicate batch windows for system unavailability.

Ability to Perform High-performance Inserts, Updates, and Deletes

Central to the concept of an operational data store is the fact that it is not appending new snapshots of data like a data warehouse. It is a moving snapshot of the operational systems and as such requires insert, update, and delete capabilities. Contrary to popular belief, these added capabilities do not inherently cause a DBMS to perform more slowly on queries (query pathlength does not grow because a DBMS can perform audited updates), but they do generally raise the cost of the product. One reason for the increased cost is that full-function DBMSs generally have to support mission-critical environments. These DBMSs must be built to rigorous standards with heavy quality assurance. This is a curse or a blessing depending on the degree of cost consciousness versus risk aversion that is required.

In an operational data store it is imperative that inserts, updates, and deletes can be applied to the database. In a Class I ODS, this activity must be performed with absolute integrity. Otherwise, the operational data store can fall out of synch with the operational systems. As will be mentioned later, the availability of a well-hosted transaction processing monitor can improve the performance, integrity, and manageability of this function. The DBMS must be able to deal with random as well as sequential changes to the database. This requires an efficient lock management system, which should include row-level locking and the ability to detect a deadly embrace (two transactions locking each other out of completion). In addition, it is important that the system can either read through locks or provide a consistent image of changing data, depending on users' requirements. Designs that provide a before snapshot of changing data may be preferable unless update volume is large, in which case the before images can overrun the system.

In order to handle random and sequential insertions as well as the deletion of aged records and update of variable-length fields, the operational data store platform must have an efficient way of dealing with block splits. Block splits occur when records are deleted from and inserted to a sequentially organized data structure, causing fragmentation of the blocks. If block splits are not minimized or make inefficient use of space, database fragmentation will cause performance to be reduced due to the data losing its sequential nature. Failing to minimize block splits can cause the database to need frequent physical reorganization.

Transaction Processor Monitor Functionality

A transaction processor (TP) monitor is loosely defined as containing process management, link management, and transaction management, as shown in Figure 7.9. These functions have traditionally been provided by a TP monitor. Recently, some of these functions are being provided by DBMS vendors. These capabilities are often more important in the operational data store than in a data warehouse. The reason is because a data warehouse might have a profile of 50 users running queries of difficulty 10 while an operational data store might have 500

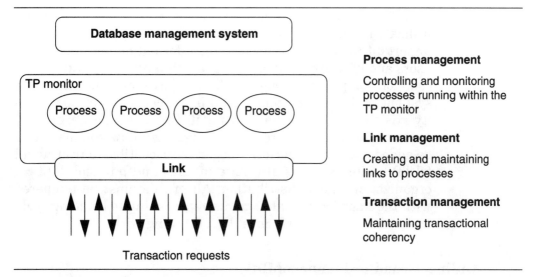

Process management

Controlling and monitoring processes running within the TP monitor

Link management

Creating and maintaining links to processes

Transaction management

Maintaining transactional coherency

Figure 7.9   A TP monitor provides three primary functions.

users running queries with a relative difficulty of 1 and 30 users with a relative difficulty of 10. Due to the larger user population and shorter query profile, the ability to provide multithreaded access to the database can dramatically reduce memory requirements in an operational data store. Traditional TP monitors provide such features as load balancing and recoverability, which make the implementation much easier to manage. In addition, a well-implemented TP monitor can actually increase performance for updating and inserting by performing such techniques as deferred writes and group commits. Prioritization capabilities provided by a well-implemented TP monitor will often prove invaluable for the task of mixing workloads as needed by an operational data store.

Availability of a Performance Monitoring/Tuning Infrastructure

It is critical in an operational data store as well as a data warehouse that the supporting platform be instrumented for performance monitoring and tuning. Otherwise, management can become overwhelming due to the mixed workload and complexity of the operational data store. This means that the major subsystems are instrumented in such a way that they provide meaningful information on system performance, CPU utilization, cache utilization, data access patterns, and query optimization. It is important to be able to capture this information and relate it to users and user groups in order to understand usage patterns. A common complaint among people who have implemented these systems is that the system is running at capacity but no visibility exists into who or what is using it. Unlike a data warehouse, an operational data store does not readily allow summaries to be added to enhance performance; it is susceptible to traditional OLTP tuning, such as alternate indexes and physical data reorganization and redistribution. All of this must be tempered with the knowledge that some users are going to be doing truly ad-hoc queries that defy most OLTP tuning tricks.

Online, Granular Manageability

In order to manage large volatile databases such as an operational data store, two key capabilities are needed. First, the database utilities should be able to be operated while users access the database. If this is not possible, users must be taken off of the system for maintenance. DBMSs exist today that allow activities such as index creation, backup, repartitioning, redistribution, and reorganization to be performed while users have full read, write, and update capability. The last of these, reorganization, is particularly important since data is being inserted and updated, causing block splits to occur.

Second, in addition to being online, database operations should be able to be performed at a very granular level. This is to say that work should be performed only on the piece of the database that is to be affected without impacting the rest of the system. If, for instance, a reorganization needs to be performed it should be able to be targeted at a specific segment of a specific table and run at a low priority while online operations are performed to that partition at a high priority. Reorganization should be able to be throttled, paused, and restarted.

Database Administration/System Programmer and System-controlled Placement of Data

Placement of data in a query processing system is very important. As shown in Figure 7.10, sometimes it is beneficial to have

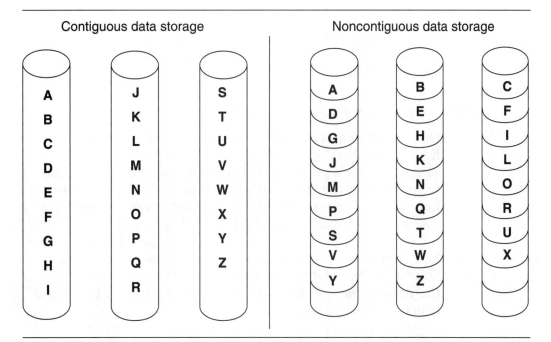

Contiguous data storage   Noncontiguous data storage

Figure 7.10   Much of the query processing is range based; thus sequential storage of data is helpful while other workloads benefit from a random distribution of data.

data spread randomly over many disk volumes and sometimes it is best to have data in sequential order. Many DSS queries, for instance, have an element of time in them (how many widgets were shipped last Tuesday) that might imply a range of sequential data. It might be beneficial for the data to be placed in contiguous disk space. In other circumstances, it might be best to have contiguous data spread over many disk volumes to reduce hot spots or areas of high activity.

It is important for the Database Administrator (DBA) to have control over the placement of data, including tables and indexes, such that he or she can select a method of data distribution that is optimal for the environment. Ideally, data which is very active could be specifically placed by range in certain locations. This is especially important in some parallel processing environments, since data placement can affect allocation of processing power. In other situations, uniformly spreading data using hashing or striping is very useful. Methods such as these can attempt to evenly spread data over a large group of disks automatically.

System-managed storage is of value as long as it is open to operator intervention. In fact, for managing temporary space, such as sort space and temporary or intermediate tables, it is almost mandatory.

Ability to Perform Massive Queries

One aspect of an operational data store that makes it very difficult to support with current technology is the multiple personalities that a platform is required to support. While there is technology on the market that is good at transaction processing, and systems optimized for complex query processing and systems capable of supporting large amounts of data, the intersection of these three capabilities is fairly limited. In particular, high-performance query processing presents a few challenges. One example is retrieving the data from disk. Assuming that the data cannot be accessed via an index, it must be scanned, which is very costly.

Once the data has been retrieved, it must be joined with other data, which often implies sorts. Since sorting is a logarithmic function, time to complete grows exponentially with sort size, making traditional sort/merge join techniques costly for large databases. One clever approach to solving this is heavy use of indexing. Technology exists that allows a table to be heavily indexed with minimal storage overhead, thus reducing scans and sorts. However, the creation and maintenance of indexes is costly from a CPU standpoint. The tradeoff between indexes and insert/update performance is shown in Figure 7.11. It is for these reasons that high-performance parallel processing is currently a leading technology for operational data store implementation. It has a proven capability to deal with high-performance scanning and a few implementations have a track record for supporting large amounts of data in a high-performance query environment.

The platform supporting the operational data store must therefore be able to perform extremely high-speed scans of data for environments where analysis requires access without indexes. The platform must be able to perform large joins, unions, and aggregations. More advanced DBMSs have implemented hashing techniques for joining and aggregation, which scale far better than traditional methods due to their elimination of sorting. The platform must still be able to sort large amounts of

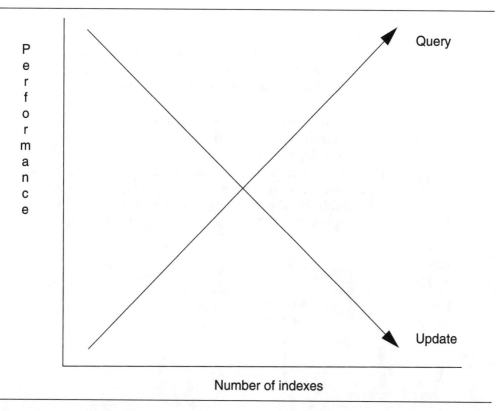

Figure 7.11 While adding indexes can benefit query performance, it has a negative impact on update workloads typical of an operational data store.

data. Although these hashing techniques can eliminate most sorting done in queries (a requirement to eliminate the logarithmic effect mentioned earlier), sort utilities will still be needed for normal operations and management of the system.

Ability to Perform Mixed Workloads

There are multiple types of workloads present in an ODS:

- Short queries designed to support the clerical community and the EIS users. These are often simple selections of data with the need to find next/find previous within a sequence of data.
- Long and complex queries designed to support the analytical community. These often involve reading millions if not bil-

lions of records and performing large joins and aggregations of tables.

- Inserts, updates, and deletes involved in keeping the operational data store in synch with the operational systems. In a Class I ODS, these can be extremely demanding.

It is important that the operational data store platform be able to mix these workloads; otherwise, the users would have to be relegated to certain times of the day and the near-synchronous updating of a Class I ODS would not be possible. Long-running queries need to run at a lower priority and be interruptable by shorter high-priority queries and updates, as seen in Figure 7.12. The system should also be able to schedule

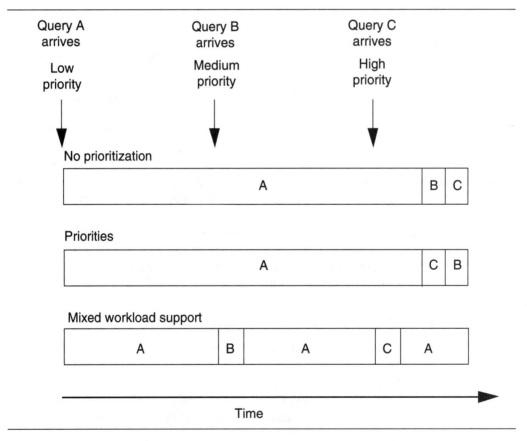

Figure 7.12 The ability to support mixed workloads effectively will allow the large queries to be interrupted by high-priority clerical users.

queries such that large non-time-critical queries can be scheduled for overnight execution. Some query environments today can deal with this issue and even detect large queries prior to execution and suggest to the user that they be deferred. It is also important that these types of rules be defined at the user and/or user-group level.

Efficient Index Support

Based on the tradeoff mentioned earlier, it is important to have as efficient an indexing mechanism as possible. Since an operational data store is built in an iterative fashion, one of the things that may become necessary is to add alternate indexes to the database for performance reasons. Assuming that the management infrastructure mentioned earlier is available, the DBA will begin to see patterns of usage appear primarily from the clerical and EIS users due to the repetitive nature of their activity. When this happens, alternate indexes must be able to be built quickly and maintained by the DBMS using minimal storage. If it is a parallel processing environment, the creation, deletion, and maintenance of the indexes must be done in parallel to provide minimal impact on daily operations. In addition, the DBMS should be able to perform index-only scans when the data requested is contained entirely within an index.

Single-image Distribution of Data

One way to mitigate the decision of centralization versus distribution is to base the operational data store on a technology that provides transparent distribution of data. There are two challenges here: transparency and bandwidth. Transparent distribution has been evolving into DBMS technology for some time. Some DBMSs today allow multiple physical sites to appear as a single database. The best implementations allow a single table to be partitioned across multiple sites. In this case, the optimizer will recognize queries that can be satisfied from local ranges of data and will not impact remote locations. If queries are launched that encompass the entire database, the multiple sites return their result sets to the user as a single answer.

The drawback to this is in the area of bandwidth. If a DBMS is asked to join two 100GB tables across a traditional Ethernet, the query might outlive the user. For this reason, the question of centralization vs. distribution is based on the requirement for internode queries and the profile they may have. This is not true in some parallel processing environments, however, because users can own sections of the computer and yet it can operate as a whole for enterprise questions.

Logging and Journaling

For a platform to be capable of supporting an operational data store, transaction logging will be a key function. How well and how fast the platform provides this function can define the limit to growth and timeliness of an operational data store implementation. Specifically, high-performance locking should be available and will be characterized by the ability to do group commits and deferred writes, and support multiple, configurable logs. Group commits allow transactions to be written to the log in batches, which increases performance due to the boxcar effect. The boxcar effect is the ability to improve performance by taking many units of work and performing them in an organized sequence, such as grouping transactions and committing them in a sequential pass of the heads over a disk. By lining up the commits like cars of a train and committing them sequentially, performance can actually improve as the system comes under load. Deferred writes allow the transactions to be logged but not immediately written to the base tables and indexes. In this way, the system can write a large number of changes to the database in a single pass over the disk yet maintain transaction integrity. The ability to have multiple parallel logs is important to be able to deal with the potentially large number of changes that might be applied to an operational data store as it is refreshed. In the interest of reducing log space, audit compression should be supported, which will allow change to be logged at the field level rather than the row level. This is important in an operational data store, since fields are often modified within an otherwise unchanged row. It is also important that logging can be configured for individual tables and indexes.

MIDDLEWARE

The network middleware is an important part of an operational data store. Middleware provides the glue between users' applications and the data contained in the ODS as well as in the data warehouse and operational systems, as seen in Figure 7.13. In some cases, it is valuable to relate information in the ODS to information in a data warehouse. If, for instance, the requirement is to isolate a group of customers who are candidates for a new sales program, it might be beneficial to determine their historical buying habits as well as their current account status. In these situations it is the middleware that can provide a common access method for numerous data stores (given that the data stores are not already within a common distributed DBMS). It is also the middleware that often determines which platforms, tools, and network protocols will be available for our use. Following is a discussion of important considerations for the middleware in an ODS implementation.

Support for a Wide Variety of Client Interfaces

Clearly, the middleware used in an operational data store needs to be versatile in its support of tools and applications. This is

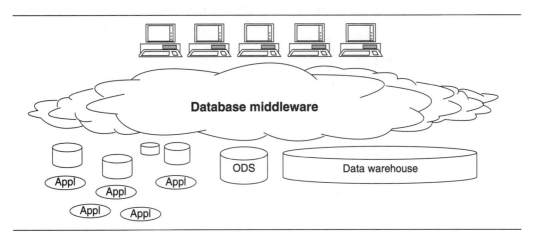

Figure 7.13 Database middleware provides the glue between users and the various sources of data in the enterprise.

best achieved by having support for multiple-client machines and multiple programming interfaces. The most common clients are PCs and Macintoshes, but others need to be considered. In the implementation of three-tiered client-server systems it is common for the operational data store to be accessed by mid-tier servers running a flavor of UNIX. This can allow relatively small PC clients to be used by offloading analytical processing to a mid-tier server. It is also important in an operational data store to consider the large number of clerical users who may still be attached via terminal to legacy systems. In this case, the current operational platform acts as a client to the operational data store and must be supported. All require support for common data-access programming interfaces. The interfaces described are manifested in the form of formats and protocols (FAPs), application programming interfaces (APIs) and dialects, as shown in Figure 7.14. All are important since the most robust middleware product would be of little value if it required a massive investment to replace thousands of terminals or a large network environment.

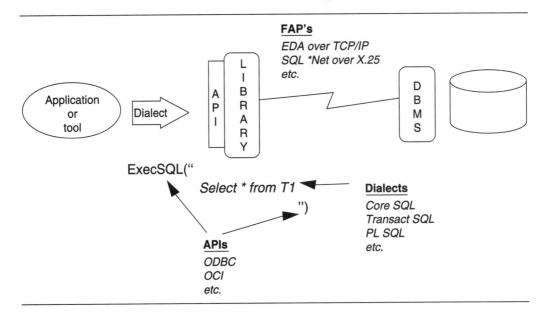

Figure 7.14   The difference between formats and protocols (FAPs), application programming interfaces (APIs), and dialects.

Compatibility with Many Relational and Nonrelational DBMSs

Since middleware is the glue that connects users to data, it is equally important that a middleware product connect to a variety of data management systems. Since data may be contained in a legacy environment with mere pointers in the operational data store, it is important that the middleware be able to access the production systems as well as the operational data store. This is not to say that one could use middleware to negate the need for a data warehouse or ODS, since most of the benefits of data rearchitecting would be lost. Used together, middleware and an operational data store make a powerful combination. This implies that the middleware must understand and deal with modern relational structures as well as older flat file or network databases, and perhaps over time, object data stores as well.

Distributed Schema Awareness and Routing

One of the more valuable things that middleware can provide to an operational data store is an overall awareness of the schemas of the various data sources. If the middleware is intelligent enough to work at the schema level, it then has the ability to present a single integrated catalog to the user's application that masks the physical location of the data. This implies that the middleware is capable of decomposing a query that might access multiple physical platforms, allowing each to retrieve a partial result set that is returned to the user in an integrated fashion. Database integration is typically done by requiring that the various platforms return data sorted in the same order and then merging this data, as shown in Figure 7.15. It is not easy to do this well, since it implies that much of the intelligence of a DBMS should reside in the middleware.

Monitoring and Statistics Gathering

Because the middleware is the common software through which all query activity will pass, it is in the unique position to assist in the administration of the operational data store environment. If the middleware gathers enough meaningful data about usage of the ODS environment, a foundation will be provided for un-

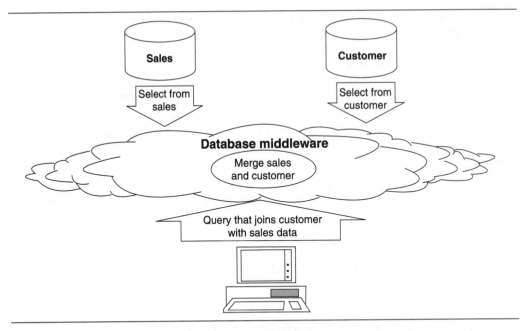

Figure 7.15   Database middleware decomposing a query to be executed on two
databases and merging the results for the user. These databases could
reside in different database management systems or even on different
physical computer systems.

derstanding the entire decision-making environment in a way
that the ODS platform cannot. Middleware will have a view of
which users launched queries, at what times of day, and what
data elements they touched. If, for instance, it was clear that operational data store users were repetitively retrieving data from
the operational system, the DBA might decide that it would be
advantageous to propagate that data to the ODS periodically. If a
data warehouse is present, the middleware can provide valuable
information about the need for certain summary views, which
would enhance performance.

Queuing and Scheduling

One of the often-overlooked benefits of middleware is in the
task of overall query management. A user might want to issue
a query or report that runs every Monday morning at 8:00 A.M.
Middleware exists today that will allow the user to insert this

query into a schedule for regular execution. Likewise, this type of middleware can precost the query and, if over a certain threshold, suggest to the user that it be run in off-peak hours or even mandate it. Since most query platforms see diminishing returns as the number of concurrent queries rises (due to thrashing for memory or disk contention), some middleware can track the number of submitted queries and queue them if need be for delayed execution. If the middleware is to provide deferred or batch execution of queries, it is implied that it must be able to store and forward the results. The ability to store and forward is particularly valuable if the client is not always available, as is the case for a retail buyer who works on the road with a portable computer.

SUMMARY

Technology to support an operational data store can be complex. Technology is required to support functions that are not often found on a common platform. Compared with a Class I ODS, implementing a Class II or III ODS will be technologically less demanding. The technology required to support an operational data store falls into three areas: transformation software, the ODS platform, and middleware. The transformation software must be able to effectively link legacy environments to the operational data store, potentially in a near-synchronous mode. Using vendor-supplied transformation software as a base can accelerate the deployment of the operational data store by reducing the effort to build this layer from scratch.

The operational data store platform may require a great deal of the functionality needed to support OLTP, such as logging, updating, and online manageability as well as the high-performance query associated with some query-only environments. Parallel processing is a suitable technology for the operational data store and is currently maturing in the market. The middleware used in an operational data store will be responsible for interfacing the various user populations to the operational data store as well as allowing them to retrieve data from the operational systems.

8

The Role of Standards

Much of the activity in today's computer environment is driven by standards and the open systems movement. Standardization is of keen interest for the builder of an operational data store, because it can provide the interoperability needed to access legacy environments and to deliver information to end users. It also is important due to the portability that standards bring. Because an operational data store is developed iteratively, it will tend to grow over time. Portability at the server level allows the operational data store to be retargeted to new platforms to take advantage of new price/performance levels as time goes by. While retargeting an operational data store is not something that is typically desirable, it is often necessary as it outgrows the performance and function of the platform it is on. If, for instance, an operational data store started as a Class III and grew into a Class I, a different platform may be needed to support the increase in function.

AN OPEN WORLD?

In the beginning of data processing, standards were needed only to allow for the transfer of data from one computer system to another. Applications were batch and mostly standalone. Standard tape formats permitted data to be shared between applications, systems, and, on rare occasions, companies. As technology evolved, there was a growing need to be able to share data, applications, and people throughout the environment. Standards came relatively easily at first because there was one dominant vendor who could drive the process.

In the late 1980s, the world began to change as people migrated away from a single-vendor model. It was the promise of standards that were used to promote this approach. As the computing world changes, it is natural to wonder what is next. While it seems that the leading edge of the industry is unlike anything seen before, it is actually not unique.

The computer industry is repeating a process seen in many other forms of technology. Stereos and other consumer electronics have taken the same path and it is in this context that the current state of standards becomes clear. When video recording was first undertaken, it was a very expensive commercial venture. Entire studios were built by a single vendor with numerous components linked together by proprietary interconnections. As time went by, the interfaces between various types of equipment were standardized by bodies such as the IEEE. Much of the standards work evolved from existing implementations, which made it easy for some vendors to support them. In the same way that computers have now been defined to be a collection of components such as disk, tape, and memory, video production was made up of cameras, recorders, character generators, and so on. Standardization led to specialization such that vendors would build a single component and, by thus focusing their core competency, would build superior products to those who tried to do everything.

In the early 1980s, the consumer video market blossomed. Home video recorders and cameras became popular and, as volumes rose, prices came down. Even though this equipment was not suitable for much of the commercial marketplace, there were many jobs that could be downsized to organizations using subprofessional equipment. This combined with the reduced cost of components, such as integrated circuits and tubeless cameras, drove costs down for commercial production facilities. Today, professional video equipment is still superior to consumer gear; therefore commercial production facilities still need to use it. Fortunately, the cost of professional equipment has come down since standardization has lead to an open market where specialization has reduced cost and improved quality.

Clearly the computer industry has taken a similar tack with standards and the emergence of a consumer market driving component costs, such as chips and disks, lower but with products still being differentiated in the commercial world. PCs have reached toaster status, but the commercial IS shops will continue to have needs for reliability, operability, and scale that cannot be satisfied with consumer-grade equipment. Open standards promise the ability for an organization to off-load work that is less than mission critical to lower-cost platforms and still present an integrated computing environment. Although standards are paying off in many environments, the promise of "open" is in many ways oversold.

A Simple Example

Assume that an organization has a new application to build. The organization wants to evaluate platforms that might host this application. The organization might come to the conclusion that the application should be built in a client-server fashion using PC clients and a UNIX server as platforms. This conclusion seems logical, since UNIX is known to be an open operating system due to the fact that it runs on many hardware platforms and adheres to published interfaces. In order to have complete portability, a relational DBMS is chosen that runs on many platforms and will allow the application to be built in a portable development environment.

Under this model a sizable application is developed that supports the business very well. As the years pass, a problem arises; the application needs to grow in some way that the chosen platform cannot support. For instance, the organization may be going to a seven-day, twenty-four-hour environment and the DBMS environment requires nightly downtime for maintenance. In addition, there is a list of other enhancements that the users need that cannot be met by the current software platform.

While the organization has built in the ability to change hardware platforms, it is locked into a software environment. It might turn out that the organization has written thousands of lines of code in a development environment that only targets one DBMS or has used proprietary features of the DBMS that pose an obstacle to porting. In effect, the organization would have to trade hardware dependence for software dependence at a time when the price of software is skyrocketing and the price of hardware is dropping.

The point of this is twofold: First, "open" is not something you buy; it is something you do. It is very possible to become locked into an environment that conforms to every standard available because vendors will add features to make themselves unique in the marketplace. Users may find that these features are so powerful that they must use them, but they should do so knowing the impact on portability. Second, the open market is still maturing. While it is well defined at the lower levels of a computer system, it is still being defined at the higher levels, as shown in Figure 8.1. From this picture it is interesting to note that where standards are in place and working, prices have been driven down dramatically, but at the higher levels vendors can still demand high margins.

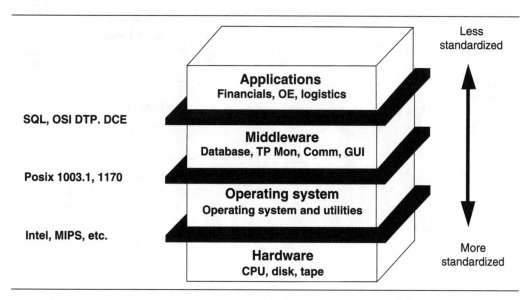

Figure 8.1   Standards are evolving from the lower layers of a computer to the applications.

PORTABILITY OF AN OPERATIONAL DATA STORE

With the above example in mind, we will next focus on what is required to maintain both hardware and software portability when building an operational data store. It turns out that this is not very difficult when compared with the challenge of making an operational application portable. This is because today's standards for accessing data are more defined than those used to update it. In an operational data store, updating is the responsibility of the transformation software, rather than being embedded into every application as it is in an operational application.

Portability in an operational data store should be thought of as a definition of interfaces rather than implementation. As shown in Figure 8.2, choosing to standardize on an implementa-

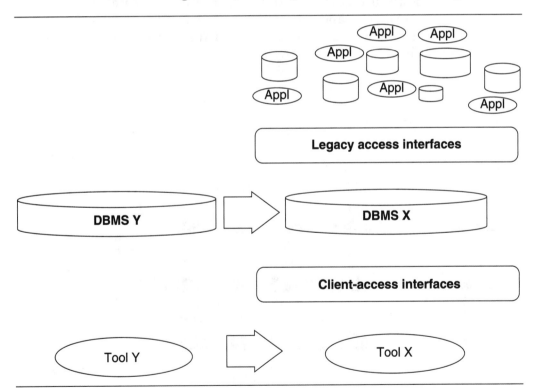

Figure 8.2   The key points where standards are applied to an operational data store are the interfaces rather than the implementations. This allows implementations to be changed.

tion rather than an interface will restrict the available solution. Instead, an approach where the interfaces between the major components of an operational data store are defined will allow various implementations of technology to be used. In an ODS, these interfaces happen at two points, as shown in the figure.

CLIENT ACCESS

End users typically access an operational data store from a client platform running an application or tool. This client could be a traditional PC or it could be mainframe-based software. In the latter case, the networking environment and geography of the users could dictate that the mainframe be used as a client, as shown in Figure 8.3. Mainframe clients are sometimes the only feasible solution for the clerical users.

If the client is a workstation or departmental server, there are a number of database access standards available. Middleware products often support numerous DBMSs but in the past provided their own APIs, so tools and applications had to be ported to them. This led to the larger database vendors having the widest support. In recent years, standards such as those cre-

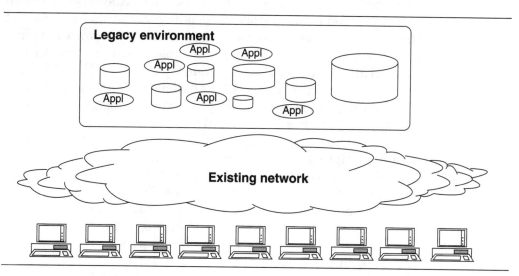

Figure 8.3   Existing networks and terminal devices may dictate that the operational data store applications and tools reside in the legacy environment.

ated by the SQL Access Group (SAG) have been implemented by the workstation software vendors. Soon it will be difficult to buy a workstation operating system without an installed database driver such as DAL (Macintosh) or ODBC (Windows). These interfaces are being offered now for virtually all middleware and DBMSs. Using the native call-level interface of an operating system typically gives access to the widest variety of tools and applications.

If the client is the legacy host environment, standards may be more difficult to find. In this case, the most common call-level interface may be the dynamic query facility of the legacy platform. Indeed, some middleware products such as IBI's Enterprise Data Access emulate this interface to allow host-based software to issue queries to the operational data store. The other alternative to this issue is to build the ODS on the same platform with the legacy environment. Although this may not align with many organizations' strategic plans, it can simplify access from older terminals and terminal emulators.

LEGACY DATA ACCESS

The legacy interconnect is often a dedicated high-speed connection used to propagate data from the current system of record to the operational data store. Depending on the size and class of the ODS, this connection may be a simple communications line or may require a proprietary interconnect such as a mainframe channel attach or Enterprise System Connections (ESCON) link. This interconnect will be the foundation for the transformation layer, so dependence on a proprietary technology may mean trading performance for portability.

In order to apply updates to the operational data store, both a data manipulation and a transaction control interface will be needed. The data manipulation interface will most likely be the native interface to the DBMS and the TP interface will likely belong to a TP monitor. Both of these will be accessed by the transformation layer, as seen in Figure 8.4. This arrangement will allow the database to maintain integrity by either locking or presenting consistent before images to the user until groups of updates are committed. Database standards defined by ANSI are helpful but not as implementation specific as the workstation

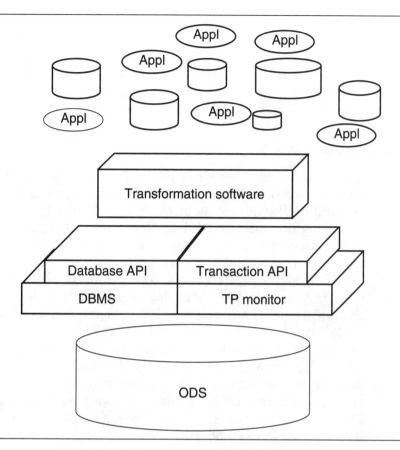

Figure 8.4   The transformation layer will access the operational data store through database and transactional interfaces.

call-level interfaces mentioned earlier. Adhering to standards such as these can minimize the effort to port transformation code to a new DBMS, but not eliminate it. In addition, standards for transaction control are still being defined. Currently, the standards body governing this area has agreed to include three different APIs in the standard and is considering adding more. This combined with the budding open TP monitor market makes standardization difficult.

The lack of standards definition is not tragic so long as this is taken into account in the design of the transformation layer. Calls to the DBMS and TP environments on the operational data store platform should be kept in a minimum of locations.

Isolating this logic to a single module of software with an internally developed API is one approach that accomplishes this. The other approach that can mitigate this issue is to use a tool for transformation that supports numerous ODS platforms. Doing this shifts the burden of portability to the tools provider but can result in a dependency on a third party.

The Process of Portability

Achieving a high degree of portability requires planning and process. It is desirable to put a process in place that will ensure portability. Portability requires that guidelines be set when architecting the operational data store that will suggest the standards and practices to be used. An approach that some have undertaken is to create a portability plan. This is a document that defines the steps required to port from the selected environment to a new platform. This document should include plans for the replacement of all relevant components including hardware, DBMS, communications, and so forth. It is a wise practice to ask the vendor of any selected product to provide this plan an example. For instance, vendors of DBMSs can be asked to deliver documents detailing how the operational data store might be ported to different DBMS technology as a part of their proposal. This practice leverages the knowledge of the vendors and assists in the selection of standards.

Once a plan is made, someone must watch over it. While it is possible to designate someone as the gatekeeper of standards, it is often adequate to integrate the concept into the process of building the operational data store. Standards are governed by reviewing new development for portability in regular status meetings and design reviews. In smaller projects, this is often favorable to designating people to act as standards police.

SUMMARY

Building an operational data store that conforms to standards can provide the ability to continually move to new technology. This is particularly important to the operational data store since it is an entity that evolves over time and is likely to grow and have changing requirements. In many ways, the computer industry is still evolving through a process of standardization that other industries have already been through. From this it is clear that although standards will not allow us to run our businesses on consumer technology, they will drive down the cost of commercial computing equipment.

It is possible to build an operational data store on a platform that supports open standards and not achieve portability if standards are not adhered to. With this in mind, there are two major areas that require attention to standards in an operational data store. One is client access standards that typically reside on a workstation or on the legacy environment. The other is the set of standards that affect legacy data access.

Putting a process in place that defines standards for an operational data store implementation is key to a good design effort. Once this is done, it is important to designate an ongoing process for ensuring conformance to standards as the operational data store evolves.

9

Reengineering and the Operational Data Store

Many companies are finding that they must reengineer their systems to better support the current business process. It is a daunting task to architect and engineer systems that not only match the company's new business processes but are flexible enough to deal with change. Much has been written about this task and how best to achieve it. As difficult as this is, it is nowhere near as difficult as implementing this change in an existing mission-critical environment without missing a beat. Someone has said that the reason that God could create the world in seven days was because He had no installed base. Reengineering produces a similar situation. Most organizations are too large to simply rebuild to a new plan, then flash cut over. It turns out that taking a current inventory and designing the way it should be is minimal next to the task of actually migrating. The process of migrating from old to new is lengthy and requires the maintenance of a dual infrastructure. This has proven to be too challenging for some organizations.

SHORT-TERM RELIEF

The role that an operational data store plays in reengineering is similar to that of an aspirin—it can quickly relieve some of the pain of change but does not solve the underlying problem.

One of the symptoms of the need to reengineer is that users are trying to deal with the changed business model and find that they cannot get the information they need for proper decision making or to support daily activities.

As an example, ten years ago many financial institutions were very account-centric, as shown in Figure 9.1. This resulted from growing up in an environment where they offered a narrowly defined service, such as long-term loans. Over the last ten years, many of these organizations have changed their business model and now offer a wider range of financial products. As a result, financial institutions are finding that the account-centric view of the world is no longer sufficient since they have customers with numerous accounts of different types. If systems were built over the years for each new business, by now they might have long-term loan systems, card services systems, and consumer savings systems that are perfectly suited to their respective functions but are not integrated. Since the various systems evolved over many years, they are probably on different technology bases. As the organizations move to a customer-centric view of the world they are not equipped to compete. If the new business model calls for an account manager who services a customer in every way, this person might end up with three terminals on his or her desk.

In the same way that a data warehouse can help an organization to get an integrated view of their customers for strategic objectives, an operational data store can help in tactical ways. In an operational data store, a customer's current status could be integrated into a common view that would show all current balances, recent history, demographics, and so on to support various operations in the new model. In this way, a customer wishing to open a new line of credit but delinquent on a mortgage and having bounced nine checks would be identifiable on the spot.

From a technology standpoint, building an operational data store and a data warehouse can be helpful to the reengineering effort in a number of ways. It can provide an opportunity to deal with many of the challenges that will be encountered during reengineering in a less mission-critical environment. Much of the process and technology for each are the same but an operational data store implementation can often be more forgiving

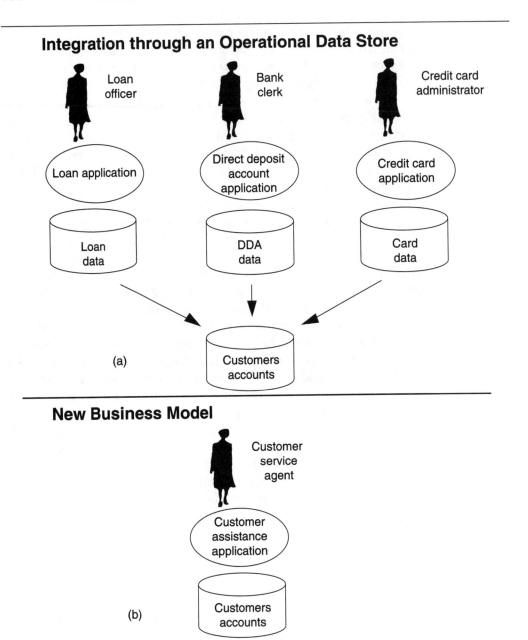

Figure 9.1 A comparison of the results of (a) integrating data with an operational data store and (b) actually reengineering the business.

than a reengineering effort. Reengineering and building an operational data store both require the following:

- The organization must assess its data. The system of record must be identified by finding the best source for each and every data element in the enterprise. When data exists in multiple locations, rules must be defined to reconcile it.
- A new data design must be made. The organization must cast its legacy environment in an integrated, subject-oriented design that reflects the new business model. A reengineered operational environment and an operational data store will have some differences (to be discussed later) but the process of design is quite reusable.
- A mapping must be made of the old data model as it applies to the new. Transformations must be defined that will apply technology changes as well as business rules to create the new data store from the old. This involves dealing with platform differences and decoding as well as changes that will require the new rules of the business to calculate new data from old.
- The infrastructure must be built that will maintain a level of synchronization between the operational and query environments. As is often the case, the technology is a minor part of this effort. What is often most challenging is building the skills and practices that must be in place to make synchronization work.
- New technology must be encountered. Moving to a reengineered environment as well as building an operational data store will often take advantage of new technology. While this is not a requirement, many organizations are using distributed computing, object-oriented programming, and so on, in their operational data store implementations and would likely do the same in an operational reengineering effort.

By building an operational data store, an IS organization can overcome many of these challenges in an environment that is less mission-critical than a reengineered production environment. In doing so, they will be better equipped to deal with reengineering. This is an indirect benefit of an operational data store but there is a direct benefit as well: The operational data store and the data warehouse will relieve the legacy environment of a great deal of data and processes. As shown in Figure 9.2, most legacy environments have already implemented a number of query support systems in the form of extracts, data propagations, and operational queries. Query support systems add to the overall complexity of reengineering. By removing data and query processing from the legacy environment the task of reengineering can thus be reduced.

THE OPERATIONAL DATA STORE AND THE IDEAL SYSTEM OF RECORD

So far this chapter has dealt with the relationship between the operational data store and the current system of record. Discussion has centered around the need for change in the existing environment to enable better decision making. Indeed, the operational data store was conceived to help deal with many of the shortcomings in today's legacy environment, such as the lack of integration and the process-oriented nature of many systems. If reengineering is to be considered, a look at the relationship of the operational data store to an ideal system of record is needed. This will help us understand the role of an operational data store in a true reengineering effort.

The operational data store has much in common with a well-reengineered environment, since both are intended to address many of the same issues. This holds true at the logical level, but

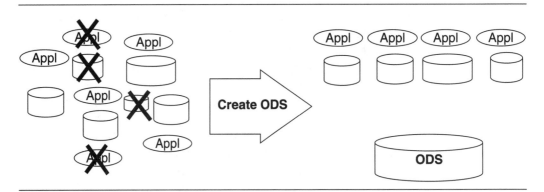

Figure 9.2   Often the legacy environment will contain data extracted for query processing. By building a structured DSS environment, much of this can be eliminated, leaving a smaller, more manageable reengineering project.

Similarities	**Differences**
• Integrated data	• Level of normalization
• Subject oriented	• Data content
• Periodicity	• Methodology
• User community	
• Technology base	

Figure 9.3 Similarities and differences between an operational data store and the ideal system of record.

there are some differences at the physical level that one should be aware of. These similarities and differences are shown in Figure 9.3.

Integration

Most reengineering efforts involve an effort to better integrate lines of business or functional systems that may have been designed at different times on different technology bases. One of the early steps in most reengineering efforts is to develop a corporate data model that can be used as a foundation for new applications. This is a commonality with an operational data store, which also seeks to interpret the current environment in an integrated fashion.

Subject Orientation

Many systems are process oriented and therefore do not support the enterprise's way of viewing the various subjects it deals with. Both reengineering and an operational data store typically express the current data in a manner that is grouped around the major subjects of the enterprise. Subject-oriented data goes hand in hand with integration.

Periodicity of Data

Periodicity is defined as the time range of data that is maintained. Periodicity is measured in two ways. The first is the degree to which the data is in synch with the real world. Throughout most of the 1980s, organizations have worked to move from batch processing to online transaction processing. This movement was fueled by lower-cost technology and an explosion in data capture capability. Today, most organizations can capture data at the moment events occur and often cannot use the data as well as they can capture it. This occurs for two reasons: capture technology, such as point-of-sale and bar-code devices, has progressed much faster than query processing technology, and cost-justifying query processing systems can be challenging. This implies that the ideal operational database will have a close level of synchronization with the real world such that at the moment an item is purchased or a part manufactured, the corporation's data stores will represent it. A Class I ODS works in a similar way. Data is propagated from the operational environment in a near-synchronous method.

The second measure of periodicity of data is the length of time that it remains in the data store before being archived to off-line or near-online media. In both an ideal system of record and an operational data store, the data is maintained as long as it serves an operational purpose. This may be 30 days for some industries or much longer or shorter for others. Neither the operational data store nor the reengineered data stores should be designed to store long-term data as in a data warehouse.

User Community

The user community for the operational data store is typically made up of clerical users and a smaller number of information analysts. The clerical community has a profile similar to the users of a system of record. There may be a relatively large number of users doing short transactions. The users may also be distributed geographically. The users of an operational data store are usually a subset of the current users of a system of record and are sometimes moved from the system of record to the operational data store to gain its benefits.

Technology Base

Comparing underlying technology needed to support an operational data store and a system of record, we find they can be very similar when the ODS in question is Class I in nature. A Class II or Class III ODS is substantially less demanding of technology. The ODS platform may be a slight superset in functionality of the one needed to support a system of record. Both need to be able to perform all of the OLTP functions mentioned in a previous chapter while the ODS also needs to have the ability to perform high-performance query. Today they are often hosted on a relational database capable of performing both OLTP and DSS. They have similar availability profiles and need to support similar workloads and numbers of users.

Normalization

Normalization represents the first difference between the operational data store and an ideal system of record. OLTP systems are often highly normalized into a third normal form (3NF). DSS is often best performed on a relatively denormalized structure called a *star schema*. Star schemas are a structure pioneered by Ralph Kimball where the majority of the data in a subject area is contained in a single fact table that is surrounded by numerous small supporting tables. Organizing data this way provides a structure that can be much easier for the user to understand and access. There are also a number of reasons that relational DBMS technology will perform well in this environment, particularly for the large "lunking" queries typical of ad hoc analytical users.

Data Store Content

The second potential difference between the operational data store and an ideal system of record is the content of the data stores. It can be seen in Figure 9.4 that the ODS may use pointers to data currently in the operational systems and therefore it may not have the level of detail that lies in a system of record. Often, the operational data store is designed using the current system of record as a starting point. One of the first modifications that is made is to jettison data that is not required to support integrated decision making. This activity leads to a more sparsely populated model than that of an operational database.

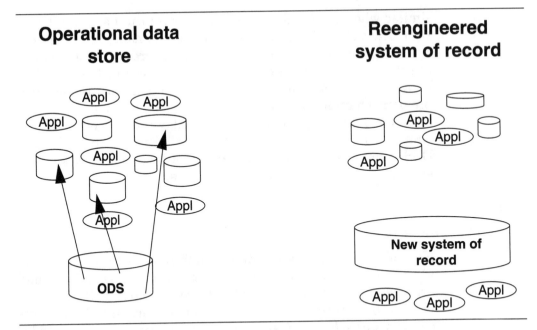

Figure 9.4   While an operational data store is a minimalist implementation that references some data still in the legacy environment, reengineering will require the detail to be moved to the new database.

Methodology

There is a fundamental difference in the methodology used to create an operational data store versus a new system of record. The ODS is grown iteratively as subject areas are added to it. Flexibility is a key benefit of an ODS. As described in Chapter 5, the methodology used to develop an operational data store lies somewhere between the SDLC model used for operational systems and the CLDS model used for data warehouses. A dual methodology is needed to support both the DSS analyst and the clerical users who access the operational data store (See Chapter 11 for ODS Development Methodology).

MIGRATING THE SYSTEM OF RECORD

When thinking about the relationship between building an operational data store and building a new system of record the obvious thought is to migrate the current system of record over time to the operational data store. Application migration is possible, but requires an ODS design that is conducive to migration. The movement of the system of record dictates certain things be considered in the design of the ODS. With careful planning, migration is feasible and should be considered in situations where major reengineering is imminent due to changing business processes. Combining a short-term operational data store strategy with a long-term reengineering effort can offer a valuable mix of instant gratification and long-term change. This multistep approach is shown in Figure 9.5, where data elements B and C are eventually moved to the ODS platforms along with certain applications.

The first assumption is that the starting point is a Class I operational data store. This assumption provides the design criteria that more closely matches a reengineering effort. The Class I ODS will share many of the platform requirements since the online propagation of data drives the need for an OLTP-capable platform and trickle-capable transformation software.

The database design of an operational data store tends to be more normalized if it is destined to be a system of record at some time. Since this can have a negative impact on the large queries typical of information analysts, it is important to consider who the primary user of the operational data store will be. If the information analyst is the primary user, then it is not a good candidate for eventual reengineering due to the level of normalization that will have to occur to support the operational environment. If the operational data store will support mostly clerical queries, it will be more conducive. This is often the case in a reengineering effort since clerical query processing will be offloaded from the legacy environment.

The operational data store used to support reengineering could eventually contain an enormous amount of detailed data that is not needed for pure ODS function. Much of the data that will be left behind in most ODS implementations will eventually find its way to the system to support a new system of record. This is a blessing as well as a curse, since it can have a very positive impact on response time due to the locality of the data but will no doubt make the migration more challenging.

One of the keys to making this work is data synchronization. It is fundamental to understand that the legacy systems will be

Day 1—Build Class I ODS.

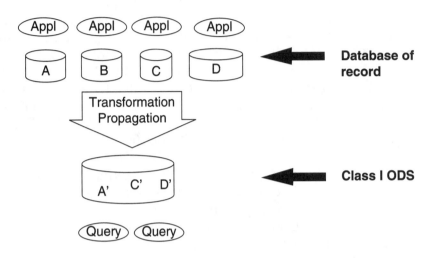

Day *n* — Migrate applications and part of the database of record.

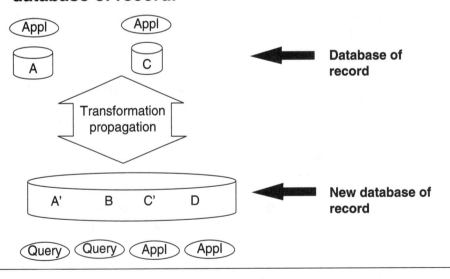

Figure 9.5   Evolving an operational data store into a new system of record.

in place for some time. It is likely that they will never go away entirely since there will be existing applications and databases that serve their purpose and do not need to change. This results in a requirement to deal with a system of record that has data elements spread over more than one platform, as shown in Figure 9.6. Synchronizing these data sources with integrity is necessary for success.

CASE STUDY: THE DATA MIGRATION ENGINE

Some time ago a major telecommunications company came to the realization that they needed to migrate from their legacy environment to a newer client-server environment. This started a project that led to the creation of a concept known as the *data migration engine* (DME). (Unfortunately, at about the same time, the Open Software Foundation coined the same acronym to mean *distributed management environment*, but these two terms have no relationship and in this text DME will refer to the *data migration engine*).

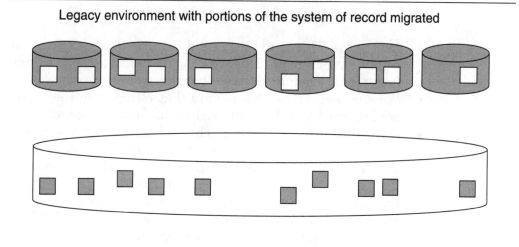

Figure 9.6 Reengineering requires the ability to deal with a system of record that is partially migrated to new technology. Elements of data exist in both environments.

Conceptually, DME is an architecture that deals with the issue of living with a system of record split across old and new platforms for the purpose of reengineering. A goal of DME is to blur the distinction between the old and new databases, allowing them to appear as one virtual database. It was implemented as a successful pilot using a framework of products from a virtual corporation formed by Information Builders, Tandem Computers, Apertus Technologies, Potomac Scheduling, and Computer Network Technologies (CNT) for the purpose of this project. The essence of this concept is to create an operational data store with applications being reengineered onto it. It provides a graceful way to implement the changes driven by business process reengineering while continuing to support existing business systems.

A fundamental guideline of this project was that the new environment would be implemented in a client-server fashion. New application logic would reside on mid-tier departmental servers and desktop PCs. Data was migrated to a parallel processing SQL engine attached to the legacy environment as shown in Figure 9.7.

Conceptually, there are three types of data maintained by the transformation layer in the architecture:

- *New data*—This is data that did not previously exist in the legacy environment. This data is created as a result of new functionality being added to the current environment.
- *Passthrough data*—This is data that remains on the legacy environment and does not exist on the new platform.
- *Controlled redundant data*—This is data that resides on both platforms and is synchronized by the transformation layer, which in this case was known as the scrubber/propagator. The term *redundant* here should not be construed to mean that the data is merely copied, since it is transformed into an integrated, subject-oriented data store on the fly. This immediate transformation and propagation designates this as a Class I ODS.

The definition of new data should be self-evident and passthrough data is relatively simple. For this project, traditional database middleware was modified to provide a high-

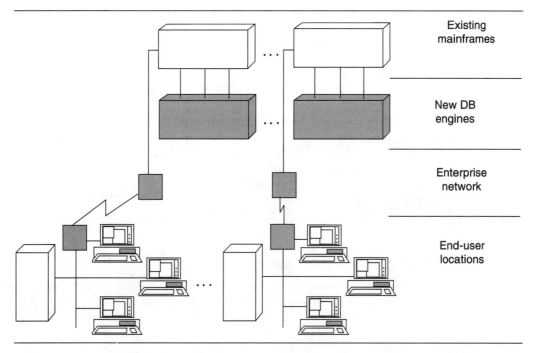

Figure 9.7 The architecture of the data migration project was built around a client-server model with new database engines being implemented in front of the system of record.

performance link to the legacy databases. The implementation required access to mainframe-based IMS, DB2, and VSAM data. New application logic was able to access the named legacy environments when needed due to the middleware's distributed schema awareness and routing capabilities. This is illustrated in Figure 9.8.

The bulk of the work done was required to build a robust yet high-performance transformation layer. This software was implemented to capture change made to the system of record by capturing audit as it was created and reformatting it into a database of change. As this change was captured it was fed directly through the scrubber/propagator, which used a rules-based system to determine the required change on the non-system-of-record database, as shown in Figure 9.9. These transformations deal with the differences in the physical storage between the platforms as well as the logical database design

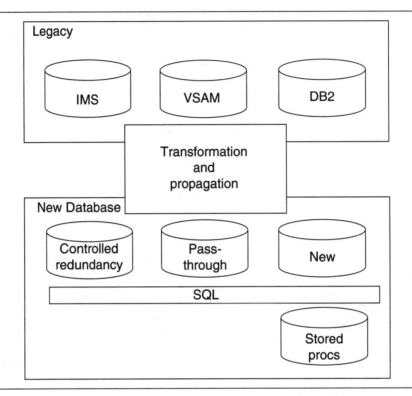

Figure 9.8   The data migration engine project defined three types of data that interoperated with the legacy environment.

differences. The change was then applied to the second database using the middleware mentioned earlier. In order to achieve performance that could support a large production environment (this company had numerous large mainframes), elements of the transformation layer were written as low-level communications programs called *sockets*.

The effect of this was that the ability to synchronize a Class I ODS with a database design radically different from the legacy environment was achieved. The relationship between the legacy and the operational data store can be expressed as rules in the transformation layer and implemented in near real time. In addition, the transformation layer was designed in such a way that would enable two-way propagation of data. New applications could be built to use the new database, and any data elements

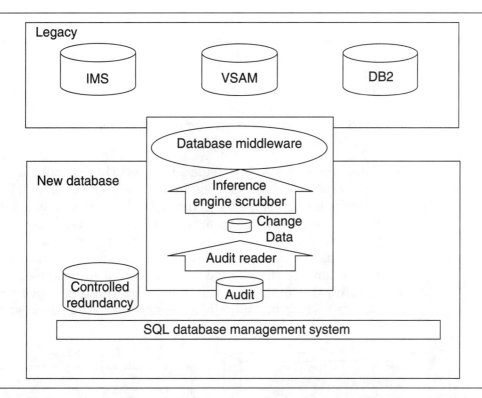

Figure 9.9   Controlled redundant data was near-synchronously fed through the transformation layer. As changes are applied to the new database of record, any
impact on legacy data is automatically applied. This feedback to the legacy
environment is the key difference between the operational data store and
the data migration project.

needing to be shared between the legacy and the new platform
would be synchronized. Data synchronization is one of the reasons that a rules engine was used for transformation. In order
to make the environment work, one must be able to deal with
collisions where users simultaneously update the same data element on both platforms. While collisions are infrequent in the
real world, it is a possibility and must be dealt with. Clearly
collisions are not a trivial issue and careful consideration must
be given to whether they will be allowed. In the DME pilot, collisions were detected and written to a log file, but automated
resolution of those conflicts was not implemented. This is slated
for a follow-on implementation.

This project was a proof of concept and to date has been tested for both performance and functionality. Overall the results were exceptional. Performance was better than expected and proved that adding a new layer of processing to the environment in the form of the operational data store and associated middleware actually caused a performance improvement. The transformation layer was extremely effective. Two key results were as follows:

- Passthrough data was tested by executing concurrent inserts, updates, and reads against the legacy databases, first directly and then passing through the target operational data store platform, as shown in Figure 9.10. The result was that the average response time was significantly better when passing through due to better efficiency in the network utilization and the general "boxcarring" of transactions.
- Controlled redundancy was tested by running concurrent inserts and updates against the new relational data struc-

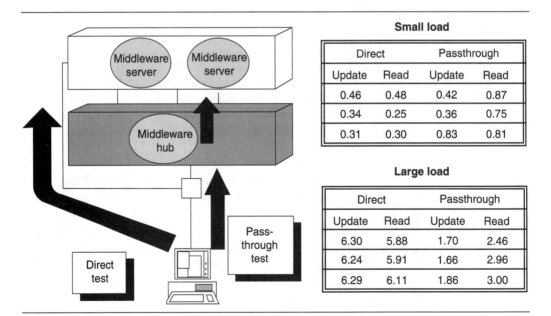

Small load

Direct		Passthrough	
Update	Read	Update	Read
0.46	0.48	0.42	0.87
0.34	0.25	0.36	0.75
0.31	0.30	0.83	0.81

Large load

Direct		Passthrough	
Update	Read	Update	Read
6.30	5.88	1.70	2.46
6.24	5.91	1.66	2.96
6.29	6.11	1.86	3.00

Figure 9.10 Shown is the response time in seconds measured for transactions that read and update the legacy databases. When testing access directly to host legacy data compared to passthrough, the direct access was actually slower once the system was under load.

tures on the DME platform, which were then interpreted by the translation software and applied against a legacy IMS data structure on the mainframe. Propagation was set to near-synchronous and the result was that all updates to the new system of record were translated and propagated to the legacy system of record within two seconds. Also tested was the ability to capture collisions by having the translation layer compare before images.

SUMMARY

Many organizations are now finding a need to reengineer their legacy environment. This is often in an effort to create systems that support a business environment that has changed since the current systems were built. While the design of new systems is possible, migrating a system of record while continuing to support the enterprise can be very difficult.

An exploration of the relationship between an operational data store and a reengineered environment shows that there are a number of similarities. The similarities lead to the idea of using an operational data store as a basis for reengineering. In this scenario, after a Class I ODS has been populated, applications would be migrated from the legacy environment to the operational data store.

There are three potential differences that must be addressed before this can happen. The database design may have to be more normalized than if the operational data store were not going to be used as a system of record. This may impact strategic query processing by the information analyst. More data will have to be moved to the operational data store rather than using pointers to legacy data and a different methodology must be used. A careful balance of CLDS in the early operational data store development with a concurrent SDLC for OLTP functionality must be used.

The key component required to make a migration of the system of record work is robust and efficient translation software. This software must be able to deal with the synchronization of the old and new system of record and deal with exceptions such as collisions that occur when both databases are updated simultaneously.

10

Case Studies

The following case studies demonstrate the various uses of the operational data store. There are four different scenarios that depict suggested purposes for the ODS. These case studies show how the operational data store can:

- Facilitate completeness of operational data
- Foster data synergy due to the integration of operational data
- Improve accessibility of critical operational data
- Shorten the path of data warehouse construction

The cases demonstrating these uses are given in order and are combinations of several different companies' experiences in building the operational data store. They do not represent any one specific corporation.

CASE 1—FACILITATION OF COMPLETENESS

The Customer:

The customer is a major domestic bank that consists of many branches serving multiple sites. The bank services both commercial and personal checking or savings accounts in addition to other services, such as savings clubs, car and home loans, and safe deposit boxes. However, its most important product and biggest risks are the large commercial loans it makes and processes for various corporations.

The Challenge:

Loan officers are responsible for determining the loan amounts and interest rates on their large commercial loans offered. The amounts and rates are very sensitive to the financial track records of the corporations applying for the loans. The loan officers want to include in their analyses the applying corporation's track record for all of its banking activities occurring in the various bank branches.

Because the bank bought many other banks, merged with others, was not consistent in the development of its own systems, and so on, it has myriad platforms, software, and applications that make integrating the bank's information very difficult to do.

In order to determine the overall activities of their customers in all branches, they would have to examine many systems on a variety of technologies, each one containing some part of the overall customer information. The analysis would take weeks and, in some cases, months to perform. This time frame makes it useless for the loan officers.

The Solution:

The solution is to build an operational data store. A logical data model of the Customer and Account subject areas is created and the operational data store data model is then created from the logical model. Only relevant customer and account transaction data is used in the operational data store model, for example, customer name and addresses; type of bank accounts and their activity; loan information, such as loan amount, interest rates, and payment schedules; and the activity for those loans. The metadata defining the operational data store data and its relationships is kept in a metadata repository easily accessed by ODS users.

Because of the volatility of corporations and their financial situations, the bank determined that extracts of the customer records should be generated from the various systems every hour for their commercial customers. These extracts are integrated into a common customer identifier and combined into one set of records per customer. At that point, various transformations take place, including the following dynamic summarizations or derivations:

- Total outstanding loan amounts
- Total bank account amounts
- Total daily banking transactions

The individual transactions occurring during the day are also integrated and stored in a uniform format in the operational data store.

Through the operational data store, loan officers may now view a corporation's total activity with the bank or, if they wish, look at the individual transactions occurring enterprisewide for a specific customer. The ability to determine proper loan amounts and the appropriate interest rate for those loans has been vastly improved. An additional benefit is the improved ability to determine the risk of loans already made. By tracking all activities made by a specific corporation, the bank is able to project where and when specific loans may be in jeopardy in the near future.

Technological Overview:

Volumes of Data:	400+ gigabytes
Hardware Configuration:	Massively parallel processing
DBMS:	Informix
End User:	Bank Loan Officers and Analysts
Rate of Flow:	One-hour refreshes
Expected Response Time (average):	Less than 20 seconds
Number of Users (average):	50+

CASE 2—FOSTERING DATA SYNERGY

The Customer:

A multi-billion-dollar oil and gas company produces crude oil and natural gas from hundreds of wells in the south central and southeastern United States. From these raw materials, several petroleum-based products are produced, such as Styrofoam, automobile gasoline, and asphalt.

The Challenge:

The majority of the wells operated by the company are partially owned by the company or leased from another party. The tracking of royalty and lease payments on these wells is central to the maintenance of these agreements. These payments are based on the production of gas and oil from the various wells involved. Therefore, the ability to track the specific production transactions from each well is critical to the payments made on the royalties and leases.

The company does not have an easy way to map well production to specific lease or royalty because the production data is kept in several disparate systems, as is the lease and royalty information. The reconciliation of well production to royalty and lease payments takes several weeks of analysts' time and is fraught with potential errors due to the manual effort involved.

The Solution:

The company decided to build an operational data store to integrate the well production data and subsequent royalty and lease payments. They used a data model of the Well and Contract subject areas. In addition, they defined all the metadata for the transformations as well as the attributes and entities contained in the model. This metadata resides in the same database as the operational data store and is accessed by the same data access tool.

The well-production data is gathered from the different systems, integrated into a uniform format, and loaded into the operational data store. Then, the lease and royalty information (e.g., who the partners are in each well, their addresses, interest percentages, etc.) is extracted, transformed to an integrated format, and loaded into the operational data store.

This information along with the metadata is used to generate appropriate payments for each partner or lease agreement for each well. The company is not only able to generate these payments much more quickly but they are able to issue one check for each recipient rather than issuing multiple checks as was required by the previous situation.

Not only is the timeliness of payments improved but the audit trail generated for these payments is greatly enhanced. The company is able to determine at a glance how payments were calculated and to whom these payments were made.

Technological Overview:

Volumes of Data:	100 gigabytes
Hardware Configuration:	IBM Mainframe
DBMS:	Oracle
End User:	Accounts Payable Clerks and Financial Analysts
Rate of Flow:	Daily (24-hour) refreshes
Expected Response Time (average):	Less than 1 minute
Number of Users (average):	15

CASE 3—IMPROVING DATA ACCESSIBILITY

The Customer:

A high-technology company manufactures and sells satellite communications equipment to government agencies and private enterprises. The company either buys or manufactures the parts that go into the construction of satellites.

The Challenge:

Because the communications equipment is very expensive and must perform under harsh conditions for a long period of time, the company must track with great vigor the manufacture and performance of the individual parts making up the satellites.

These parts also have a definite shelf life and must be used within a specified time frame or be retired. Therefore, a great deal of time and effort is spent monitoring and tracking the progression of these parts as they are constructed into bigger and bigger components until they are finally sold to the customer.

Because the information exists in old tapes from systems no longer used and in newer databases from systems that are not integrated, the process of tracking specific parts over time is labor intensive and difficult to perform. Regulations are demanding that better monitoring be performed.

The Solution:

The company developed a data model for the Inventory subject area, specifically the entities and attributes concerned with the equipment construction. The metadata defining the source of the data and transformations performed on the data as it moved into the operational data store is kept in the same database and may be easily accessed by the end user.

Data was extracted once from the old legacy tapes, and transformed, integrated, and loaded into the operational data store. The data is now in a uniform format agreed upon by the company and interested parties and is accessible using a simple end-user access tool.

The data residing in the current systems is extracted on a daily basis. The extracted data is transformed using the same algorithms used for the legacy data. Once transformed, the data is loaded into the operational data store in the same common format and is accessible using the same access mechanism. The metadata for the current data is defined in exactly the same manner as the legacy data where feasible and any differences between the two sources are noted.

End users are now able to track a particular part from its receipt into inventory throughout its productive life as a component of a satellite. In addition, they are able to determine how much of their inventory is assigned to a particular project, how much is scrapped or unaccounted for, how much requires maintenance, and so forth.

An additional benefit due to the improved tracking of components and their parts is the ability to determine more accurately the mean time before failure of specific types of parts. This information, along with the total number of parts that are scrapped, enables the company to look more closely at parts having suspected design flaws.

Technological Overview:

Volumes of Data:	30–40 gigabytes
Hardware Configuration:	RISC Workstations
DBMS:	Sybase
End User:	Inventory Analysts and Managers
Rate of Flow:	Daily (24-hour) refreshes
Expected Response Time (average):	Less than one minute
Number of Users (average):	35

CASE 4—SHORTENING THE PATH TO DATA WAREHOUSE CONSTRUCTION

The Customer:

A company manufactures and sells computers and computer peripherals both domestically and internationally. They have retail stores and distribution centers worldwide. Individual customers may purchase their products from any of the retail stores, and distributor customers may buy in bulk from any of the company's distribution centers.

The Challenge:

The Sales and Marketing department has determined that it must become more customer oriented. One way to become more customer focused is to have detailed sales history immediately available when dealing with a customer.

Armed with this information, the Customer Service Representatives servicing the customers could view recent purchases made by specific customers when they call, and therefore offer more personal service for the customers' requests. In addition, the Marketing and Sales department would like the opportunity to offer other products to that customer based on the customer's particular buying profile.

Because the company has grown rapidly and left much of the technological decisions up to the individual distribution centers and retail stores, they are faced with a difficult situation in which none of their systems interfaces with the others.

In addition, because it is an international company, there is no standard "batch window" when the data can be downloaded and examined.

The Solution:

The company decided to solve the problem in a two-pronged approach. First it decided to implement a client-server environment in which each sales area has its own "node" or client. Day-to-day operations are entered into the existing application within a sales area.

A corporate node is set up as a central repository for all operational data store data. Here, data for the operational data store is collected from the various operational systems used in the service areas. A timetable is set up to accommodate each system's working hours and four-hour extracts of customer activities are performed during an appropriate time frame.

These extracts are sent to the central node for processing, that is, the data is integrated, transformed, and merged with the data already existing in the operational data store. An ODS data model of the Customer, Order, and Product subject areas acts as the road map for the data transformations.

After processing, the data and metadata are segregated or packaged based upon service area requirements. The integrated ODS is returned to the local service areas using the client-server technology. The central node maintains the corporatewide view of customer activity.

The local ODS data allows the customer service representatives (CSR) in each sales area to respond more quickly to customer requests and problems with products by permitting the CSRs to view immediately the specific products the customer recently purchased. The customer does not need to keep product information (model number, serial number, etc.) on hand because it is readily available to the CSR. Specials for peripherals for those products may also be mentioned to the customer as well as enhancements to the existing products already purchased.

The second approach the company used is to build a data warehouse, which would draw its data from the central node's operational data store. The data integration and transformation occurring for the operational data store database makes the implementation of a data warehouse quite simple. The data from the operational data store is summarized, derived, given a time stamp, and so on; it is then loaded into the data warehouse and made available for decision-support analysis.

The data in the data warehouse tracks customer buying habits over long periods, demonstrating the trends in customer purchases. In addition, demographic customer data was brought into the data warehouse to analyze and compare with their customer database. The metadata for the data warehouse is based on the metadata describing the operational data store, but includes any new summarization or derivation algorithms needed for the warehouse.

The data warehouse allows the corporate decision makers to examine the success or failure of specific products in each of the regional sales areas. By using the demographic data, the decision makers are able to come up with lists of products that are likely to be bought by specific customers. This information gives the analysts the ability to determine where and when certain promotions or sales should occur and for what types of customers these activities should be targeted.

Now the CSRs receive information about specific customers' product buying habits on their screens, thus allowing them to suggest additional products to a particular customer when he or she calls. These suggestions are based on the predictive models generated from the demographic data in the data warehouse that has been matched to the specific customer identifier. The list of potential product purchases by specific customers that is generated by the data warehouse is displayed on the CSR screen as soon as the customer calls in.

Technological Overview:

Volumes of Data:	ODS—50–100 gigabytes
	Data Warehouse—150–200 gigabytes
Hardware Configuration:	Client-server
DBMS:	Oracle
End User:	Customer Service Representatives and Marketing Analysts
Rate of Flow:	Four-hour refreshes
Expected Response Time (average):	ODS—subsecond;
	Data Warehouse–one to five minutes
Number of Users (average):	150–200

11

Operational Data Store
Development Methodology

The Operational Data Store Development Methodology[1] is divided into the following sections (see Figure 11.1):

- M1–M6—These steps are for general project planning, sizing and phasing of the project, project evaluation, and operational data store maintenance.
- PREQ1–PREQ3—Steps taken to ensure that the technical environment is established and ready when needed, that capacity has been estimated, and that the first cut at data and application requirements has been made.
- P1–P6—Steps used to develop the operational processing of the operational data store. They include development of a high-level process model, generation of detailed process requirements, analysis of existing operational code for reusability, generation of pseudocode, and the application code itself for the first phase of the ODS project.
- D1–D5—These steps are used to create the operational data store database. They include the creation of the entity-relationship diagram, logical and physical data models,

---

[1]The prefixes are: M = project Management steps; PREQ = PREreQuisite steps; P = Process design steps; D = Data design steps; S = System testing steps; E = End-user environment.

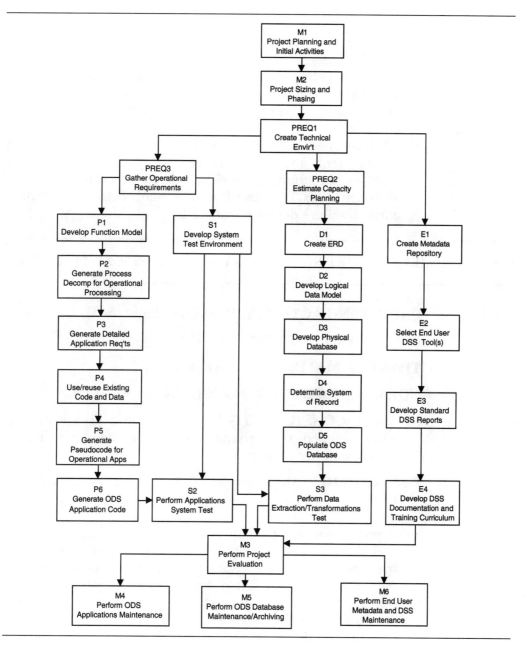

Figure 11.1 Methodology flow chart.

mapping of the source system of record, and population of the operational data store database.

- S1–S3—These are the steps used to test the operational data store applications and database. These include unit, system, acceptance, and stress tests for the operational data store application, and data quality and acceptance tests for the ODS database.
- E1–E4—These steps are used to create the end users' DSS environment and metadata repository. The environment contains the ability to generate ad hoc reports as well as standard DSS reports. The documentation and training curriculum are developed as well.

M1—PROJECT PLANNING AND INITIAL PROJECT ACTIVITIES

PRECEDING ACTIVITY: Decision to build the ODS.

FOLLOWING ACTIVITY: Project Sizing and Phasing.

TIME ESTIMATE: Two and a half weeks.

NORMALLY EXECUTED ONCE OR MANY TIMES: Once.

SPECIAL CONSIDERATIONS: The project plan is continually updated with changes and completed deliverables throughout the project.

DELIVERABLE(S): A project scope document and a project plan.

- A project scope document is written and includes the goals and objectives of the project, executive sponsorship, what is in scope and what is out of scope, initial procurement requirements, and so on. If the company has a strategic business plan, it makes sense to establish how the operational data store requirements relate to the overall strategy by describing this relationship in the scope document. The strategic business plan may help the company struggling with the scope of the first ODS by setting specific goals for it, establishing its business purpose, describing the organizational changes, and so forth.

- The project plan must be developed before the project can go forward. The plan includes the activities, tasks, their deliverables and milestones, resource assignments, and time frames. Once the project plan is established, it is updated with perturbations and/or the actual dates of task performance.
- Other project start activities include reviewing the existing corporate guidelines and standards (e.g., naming and modeling standards, existing methodologies, etc.), establishing the end users and their schedules, developing change control procedures, and identifying any security requirements.
- The project plan, including the milestones, schedule, resources, and so on, and the scope document are reviewed with the executive team for their sign-off.

PARAMETERS OF SUCCESS: When performed correctly, the project start activities reduce the overall ambiguity of the project and establish a clear course of action to deliver the operational data store. The scope is reasonably set defining both what is in scope as well as what is not in scope, specific and measurable goals are determined, and the resources needed for the project are understood. The political as well as the technical components of the project are well defined. The sponsoring organization is identified as well.

M2—PROJECT SIZING AND PHASING

PRECEDING ACTIVITY: Project Planning and Initial Project Activities.

FOLLOWING ACTIVITY: Create Technical Environment.

TIME ESTIMATE: This step is performed quickly, usually no longer than a few days to one week.

NORMALLY EXECUTED ONCE OR MANY TIMES: Once, then revisited for each phase of the development.

DELIVERABLE(S): Identification of the phases of development.

- The general functional requirements are gathered in an informal manner and sized. Generally speaking, the requirements for the operational data store will fall into two areas—the operational area or the DSS area. If the operational data store system to be developed is large, it makes sense to break it up into development phases of manageable size and duration.
- The different development phases must be prioritized and organized into a meaningful sequence, so that the second phase builds upon the first one, and so on.
- The output of this step is the breakup of general requirements into workable, manageable phases.

PARAMETERS FOR SUCCESS: The goal is to continue the operational data store development process in increments that are both economical and workable.

PREQ1—CREATE TECHNICAL ENVIRONMENT

PRECEDING ACTIVITY: Project Sizing and Phasing.

FOLLOWING ACTIVITIES: Estimate Capacity Requirements; Gather ODS Operational Requirements for First Phase; Create Metadata Repository.

TIME ESTIMATE: One and a half weeks (may depend on availability from the vendors).

NORMALLY EXECUTED ONCE OR MANY TIMES: Once.

SPECIAL CONSIDERATIONS: Because technical environments vary from company to company, this step may or may not be needed.

DELIVERABLE(S): Hardware and software contracts, test criteria and schedule.

This step starts with an understanding of the operational data store information cycle. Data enters from the legacy environment, is transformed, and is placed in the operational data store. There the data is used both in a repetitive (operational) manner and in an ad hoc (DSS) manner. The pattern of usage, expected response time, volumes of data, number of users—all of these factors go into the selection of the technology. The technology must also consider peak-period processing and worse-case scenarios.

Technology selection should include the hardware platform, network requirements, middleware, DBMS technology, metadata infrastructure technology, and development tools.

- The technical support resources available to the project should be identified and scheduled. Their role in the construction of the operational data store is critical but is not a full-time position; therefore their availability must be scheduled for the correct point in the project.
- The determination of the hardware, software, and tool requirements will aid in the selection of vendors for these products. A list of required features should be generated before interviewing and evaluating the potential suppliers. Licenses and contracts are negotiated and products are ordered.
- Test criteria (goals of the testing, test tools to be used, other resources needed, etc.) for the operational data store should be established and potential test dates scheduled.

Note: It is recommended that this step be performed early on in the project since delivery times of hardware and software could be lengthy. In addition to this lead time, the "burn-in" time must be accounted for to ensure that proper resources will be in place in time for the operational data store implementation.

PARAMETERS OF SUCCESS: A thoroughly thought-out technical environment will eliminate many problems that could have been avoided. Timely installations and training is crucial to the success of any technical project.

PREQ2—ESTIMATE CAPACITY REQUIREMENTS

PRECEDING ACTIVITY: Create Technical Environment.

FOLLOWING ACTIVITY: Create Entity-relationship Diagram.

TIME ESTIMATE: Depends on the size of the system being built, but usually one week.

NORMALLY EXECUTED ONCE OR MANY TIMES: Once per phase of development.

SPECIAL CONSIDERATIONS: Capacity planning has a history of confusing issues and inclusion of extraneous factors that do not merit special attention. It is important to keep the capacity planning portion of the development process focused and to the point. Otherwise, the exercise can become a roadblock to progress.

DELIVERABLE(S): Storage requirements, hardware platform, DBMS technology, connectivity software, growth patterns, and initial allocations.

The gross amounts of resources consumed by the project need to be determined at this phase of development. In particular, the following need to be considered:

- DASD consumption
- CPU consumption
- I/O utilization
- Main memory requirements
- Network/channel utilization

In addition to these raw requirements, the arrival rate of transactions, peak-period processing, patterns of processing, response time requirements, availability requirements, and mean time to failure requirements are factored in.

The output of this phase of development is the assurance that the required resources are in place. Additionally, both peak-period online processing and off-peak batch loading/monitoring are included. Monitoring plans are developed as well.

PARAMETERS FOR SUCCESS: No surprises when it comes to resources being in place when needed, the lead time needed to acquire resources, and the amount of resources needed.

PREQ3—GATHER ODS OPERATIONAL REQUIREMENTS FOR FIRST PHASE

PRECEDING ACTIVITY: Create Technical Environment.

FOLLOWING ACTIVITY: Develop Process Model; Develop System Test Environment.

TIME ESTIMATE: Three and a half weeks.

NORMALLY EXECUTED ONCE OR MANY TIMES: Once per phase of development.

DELIVERABLE(S): Documented, formal requirements specification.

- The first step in gathering data and process requirements is to hold facilitation sessions with the end users in which the selected subject areas and their processes are discussed. These sessions have multiple purposes:
  - They can be used to educate the end user in what an operational data store is and what it is not.
  - They are used to capture business processes as they should be, not as they are mandated to be by the existing applications' limitations.
  - Testing criteria and goals are gathered.
  - They are used to set end-user expectations and garner their support and participation for the rest of the project.
- The outputs from these sessions are used as inputs into the formal requirements documents. These documents are the actual specifications for the data and functionality of the operational data store. They are reviewed with end users and consensus is reached.

PARAMETERS FOR SUCCESS: Done properly, this stage of analysis transforms all the gathered ideas into workable, formal requirements.

P1—DEVELOP HIGH-LEVEL FUNCTION MODEL

PRECEDING ACTIVITY: Gather ODS Operational Requirements for First Phase.

FOLLOWING ACTIVITY: Generate Process Decomposition for Operational Processing.

TIME ESTIMATE: One week.

NORMALLY EXECUTED ONCE OR MANY TIMES: Once and reviewed for each phase.

DELIVERABLE(S): High-level Function Model.

The first step in developing the operational aspects of the operational data store is to create a high-level function model. If the enterprise has already generated this high-level model, then function(s) to be developed for the operational data store should be selected from that model and further developed in the steps following this one.

- The major functions of the corporation are modeled from the highest level of abstraction. This diagram is equivalent to the entity-relationship diagram (ERD) in data modeling (see D1). Examples of the functions found in the model are Maintain Human Resources, Create Product, Sell Product, Market Product, Support Customers, and so on. Generally, there are between 8 and 12 major functions identified for this model.
- The functions are defined and documented. Enough detail is given to have a firm understanding of the functions but the developer should be careful not to try to go into excruciating detail for each and every one. This level of detail will be achieved when each function is further developed in the later phases of the operational data store cycle. For this project, concentration should be on the function(s) to be developed for this phase only.
- The functions to be further developed for this first phase of the operational data store are selected from the model. The

end users participate in this selection and thereby approve it.

PARAMETERS FOR SUCCESS: All major functions are identified at the highest level of abstraction. Further development efforts will focus exclusively on the selected function(s) for this phase.

P2—GENERATE PROCESS DECOMPOSITION FOR OPERATIONAL PROCESSING

PRECEDING ACTIVITY: Develop Function Model.

FOLLOWING ACTIVITY: Generate Detailed Application Requirements.

TIME ESTIMATE: Depends on the size of the system but, as a rule, this step should not take more than two weeks.

NORMALLY EXECUTED ONCE OR MANY TIMES: Once per function.

SPECIAL CONSIDERATIONS: This is generally an iterative process of developing the decomposition and reviewing it with end users. *Note*: This specification applies only to the operational component of the ODS and not the DSS component.

DELIVERABLE(S): Complete process decomposition of the selected function(s).

If the enterprise has already created a fully decomposed process model, then a review of the selected processes with the end users is all that is required.

- The process decomposition takes the broad function selected for the first phase of the operational data store and breaks it down into a series of successively detailed processes. The processes are further decomposed into primitive activities. The primitive activities constitute the lowest level of detail for the model.

- These lower levels of processes and activities correspond to the logical data model in the data design steps.
- Reviews by end users are critical to validate the accuracy of the processes and activities modeled.
- The output of this step is a large decomposition model describing the various processes and their primitive activities to be performed.

PARAMETERS FOR SUCCESS: The process decomposition reflects entirely and only the processes and activities to be implemented in this phase. Factored into the designs are the considerations of other functions or processes that serve or will serve as building blocks. The document produced here should be understandable, organized, and complete.

P3—GENERATE DETAILED APPLICATION REQUIREMENTS

PRECEDING ACTIVITY: Generate Process Decomposition.

FOLLOWING ACTIVITY: Use/Reuse Existing Code and Data.

TIME ESTIMATE: One hour per activity.

NORMALLY EXECUTED ONCE OR MANY TIMES: Once per activity.

SPECIAL CONSIDERATIONS: This is an iterative step as well and applies only to the operational component of the ODS.

DELIVERABLE(S): Data-flow diagram of each process.

- The detailed process requirements are further documented by process descriptions, data-flow diagrams, structure charts, work flows, and so on.
- For each primitive activity in the process decomposition, a data-flow diagram (DFD) is drawn. The DFD indicates the input to an activity, its output, and the data stores needed to support the activity.
- Structure charts are generated to give more detail of the overall design to the programmers. Work flows show how the activities work together in cohesive units.

- Finally, descriptions are written defining each of the activities being performed.

PARAMETERS FOR SUCCESS: The system or phase of the system is described in thorough detail in terms of inputs, outputs, data stores, structure charts, work flows, and so on. No ambiguity is left to interpretation by the programming staff.

P4—USE/REUSE EXISTING CODE AND DATA

PRECEDING ACTIVITY: Generate Detailed Application Requirements.

FOLLOWING ACTIVITY: Generate Pseudocode for Operational Applications.

TIME ESTIMATE: Done very quickly; usually no more than one week.

NORMALLY EXECUTED ONCE OR MANY TIMES: Once.

SPECIAL CONSIDERATIONS: This step is one of the best ways to ensure code and data reusability. It is crucial to the integration of the environment.

DELIVERABLE(S): Reusable code and data.

- In an architected environment, every project should use as much of the existing code and data as it can.
- This project should prepare for future projects that may use its code and data as well.
- If existing code is to be modified, the modifications are identified as a regular part of the system development requirements. If conversion of the code or data is required, the conversion becomes a component of the development effort as well.

It should be noted that this step applies primarily to the operational aspects of the operational data store. The extract/transformation code may be considered for reuse as well but it generally must be created from scratch.

PARAMETERS FOR SUCCESS: This step should identify any code or data that can be used as a building block for the project and it should identify all code and data that must be built in recognition of future efforts.

P5—GENERATE PSEUDOCODE FOR OPERATIONAL APPLICATIONS

PRECEDING ACTIVITY: Use/Reuse Existing Code and Data.

FOLLOWING ACTIVITY: Generate ODS Application Code.

TIME ESTIMATE: Varies, from five minutes to two days per activity at the primitive level.

NORMALLY EXECUTED ONCE OR MANY TIMES: Once per activity.

SPECIAL CONSIDERATIONS: If CASE or automated code generators are used, this step may not be necessary.

DELIVERABLE(S): Programmer pseudocode.

- The algorithms and program specifications are further refined into pseudocode. The designer ensures that all needed data for operational processing is available.
- All variables, calculations, derivations, transformations, and so on are identified and defined in detail.
- Performance at the design level is factored in by using the following techniques:
  - Breaking a long-running program into a series of shorter ones
  - Requiring a program to access smaller amounts of data
  - Shortening the time a unit of data is locked
  - Changing a lock from update to access only
  - Using log/journal tapes as input

PARAMETERS FOR SUCCESS: The final step before coding begins includes the following:

- Completeness of designs
- Order of execution of programs
- All cases required
- All contingencies considered (error handling and exception conditions)
- Structure of coding

P6—GENERATE OPERATIONAL DATA STORE APPLICATION CODE

PRECEDING ACTIVITY: Generate Pseudocode for Operational Applications.

FOLLOWING ACTIVITY: Perform Applications System Test.

TIME ESTIMATE: Varies, from one day per activity to two weeks per activity.

NORMALLY EXECUTED ONCE OR MANY TIMES: Once per activity.

DELIVERABLE(S): Source code for the operational applications.

- The pseudocode is translated into source code by the programmers. The source code is compiled and errors corrected.
- The compiled code is thoroughly unit tested by the programmer responsible for the code.

PARAMETERS FOR SUCCESS: The source code is a complete and efficient translation of the pseudocode, including in-line documentation. All operational requirements previously identified are satisfied.

D1—CREATE ENTITY RELATIONSHIP DIAGRAM

PRECEDING ACTIVITY: Estimate Capacity Planning.

FOLLOWING ACTIVITY: Develop Logical Data Model.

TIME ESTIMATE: One week or less.

NORMALLY EXECUTED ONCE OR MANY TIMES: Once for each phase.

SPECIAL CONSIDERATIONS: For even the largest of systems, one week should suffice if the designers are knowledgeable about the corporation. Otherwise, the time could be much longer.

DELIVERABLE(S): Corporate ERD, selected subject area(s) for project.

If an enterprise has already created an ERD, then the subject area(s) to be developed in the first phase of the operational data store should be selected from the model and further developed in the next step.

- The corporation's data needs are distilled down to the essential subject areas. These are typically the highest level of abstraction. Typical subject areas are generally CUSTOMER, PRODUCT, ORDER, and ACTIVITY. This model is at the same level of abstraction as the high-level process model (see P1) and contains the data necessary to support the process model.
- The major relationships between the subject areas are also identified, as well as the cardinality of the relationships. It should be noted that not all relationships are modeled; only those that are of significance at this high level of abstraction are shown in the model.
- The subject area or areas to be implemented for this phase are selected from the entity-relationship diagram. These subject areas will be used to support the operational applications

being developed in P1–P6 as well as the DSS requirements being met in E1–E4.

PARAMETERS FOR SUCCESS: All major subject areas are identified at the highest level of abstraction. Further modeling efforts will focus exclusively on the selected subject areas for this phase. *Note*: Because this is an iterative methodology, the ERD should be reviewed at the beginning of each new phase for validation.

D2—DEVELOP LOGICAL DATA MODEL

PRECEDING ACTIVITY: Create Entity Relationship Diagram.

FOLLOWING ACTIVITY: Develop ODS Physical Database.

TIME ESTIMATE: Four weeks.

NORMALLY EXECUTED ONCE OR MANY TIMES: Once per phase.

DELIVERABLE(S): Logical data model and data specifications document.

- Logical data modeling will concentrate on the selected subject areas only, documenting the gathered data requirements. The logical model contains attributes of data, the grouping of attributes, and keys. Supertypes and subtypes are identified as are associative and characteristic entities.
- The output from this step is a normalized, logical data model for the subject areas containing only the primitive, operational data; derived or summarized data will be identified, stored, and managed elsewhere. Therefore, the logical data model will serve as the basis for both operational processing needs and DSS needs.
- The logical data model will be reviewed with end users for their validation and approval.

Note: The modeling should continue until the ODS-specific data requirements are finished. This concentration on the ODS-specific data requirements allows the developer to determine when the data model is completed for this phase and this phase only. As each phase is completed, more and more of the enterprise data model will be completed.

PARAMETERS FOR SUCCESS: The normalized data model contains all primary, characteristic, associative, and subtype entities for the selected subject area(s). The attributes and keys are identified for each entity. Properly performed, this step produces documents that are understandable, organized, readable, and complete.

D3—DEVELOP PHYSICAL OPERATIONAL DATA STORE DATABASE

PRECEDING ACTIVITY: Develop Logical Data Model.

FOLLOWING ACTIVITY: Determine System of Record.

TIME ESTIMATE: Three and a half weeks.

NORMALLY EXECUTED ONCE OR MANY TIMES: Once per table.

SPECIAL CONSIDERATIONS: If the input to this step is ambiguous or incorrect, the amount of work required here can be much more than what is estimated.

DELIVERABLE(S): ODS data model and physical database schema.

In this step, the addition of some summarized and derived data is incorporated into the logical data model. The removal of data not used in the operational data store occurs and the issue of physical denormalization is addressed. Denormalization techniques are used, such as:

- Merging tables together
- Selective introduction of redundancy
- Creating popular derived and summarized data
- Creating arrays of data
- Separating data according to its probability of access
- Organizing data according to its stability
- Developing fact and dimension tables

The physical design of the database will include:

- Indexing/hashing
- Physical attribution of data
- Partitioning strategies
- Storage (i.e., DASD vs. non-DASD) strategies
- Designation of keys
- Clustering/interleaving
- Management of variable-length data
- Granularity analysis (i.e., the level of detail to be used)
- NULL/NOT NULL specification
- Referential integrity

The output is the actual specification of the database to the DBMS. This database will be used by both the operational applications being developed in P1–P6 and the DSS environment being developed in E1–E4.

PARAMETERS OF SUCCESS: This stage of the analysis produces a design that will be efficient to access and update, both in terms of data and the programs that access and update the data. Performed properly, this step insures efficient resource utilization and a workable database design.

D4—DETERMINE SYSTEM OF RECORD

PRECEDING ACTIVITY: Develop Physical ODS Database.

FOLLOWING ACTIVITY: Populate ODS Database.

TIME ESTIMATE: One and a half weeks per subject area.

NORMALLY EXECUTED ONCE OR MANY TIMES: Once per subject area.

DELIVERABLE(S): Identification of the system of record.

Once the operational data store model has been developed and the physical schema implemented, the next activity is to identify the source data in the existing systems environment. Most of the issues of integration are brought to the fore during this analysis, including:

- Key structure/key resolution as data passes from existing systems into the operational data store
- Attribution
    - What if there are multiple sources to choose from?
    - What if there are no sources to choose from (i.e., default values)?
    - What transformations—encoding/decoding, conversions, etc.—must be made as data passes into the operational data store?
    - How current will data be in the operational data store?
    - How will the operational data store structure differ from the existing systems' structures?

The output of this step is the mapping of the data from the existing systems to the operational data store. The volume of data coming from the legacy environment is estimated. If a journal tape is to serve as a source, that too is specified.

PARAMETERS FOR SUCCESS: When determining the source system of record, the analyst should consider:

- The timeliness of the source data
- The completeness of the source data
- The accuracy of the source data
- How well the source data conforms to the structure of the operational data store
- How near to the source the data is coming from
- How efficient the source data is to access

In addition, the means by which the ODS data will be transformed from the legacy environment technology to the ODS technology is addressed.

D5—POPULATE THE OPERATIONAL DATA STORE DATABASE

PRECEDING ACTIVITY: Determine System of Record.

FOLLOWING ACTIVITY: Perform Data Extraction/ Transformation Test.

TIME ESTIMATE: Four to six weeks.

NORMALLY EXECUTED ONCE OR MANY TIMES: Once per phase of development.

SPECIAL CONSIDERATIONS: If a transformation/extraction tool is not obtained, the time frame for this step must be extended significantly.

DELIVERABLE(S): Transformation/extraction programs, and accompanying metadata, batch software drivers (e.g. JCL/ script), populated ODS.

Once the interface between the existing systems and the operational data store has been outlined, the next step is to formalize the interface in terms of program specifications. The transformation flow plan allows the extraction and integration of data to be programmed efficiently and as simply as possible.

Entry of the transformation and extraction information into the tool will be relatively simple. If entered correctly, verification and preprocessing will go smoothly with minimal problems.

The next step is the execution of the transformation and extraction programs and subsequent loading of the ODS data into the operational data store database. The programs will use the test data created in S1. Any problems with the load or data quality that are uncovered are fixed and the data is loaded again.

PARAMETERS FOR SUCCESS: The code generated from this step should be:

- Efficient
- Documented
- Easily changed
- Accurate
- Complete

The result of executing these programs is an accessible and understandable operational data store database that serves the needs of the operational community. The data will be thoroughly tested in step S3.

S1—DEVELOP SYSTEM TEST ENVIRONMENT

PRECEDING ACTIVITY: Gather ODS Requirements for First Phase.

FOLLOWING ACTIVITY: Perform Applications System Tests; Perform Data Transformations Test.

TIME ESTIMATE: Three weeks.

NORMALLY EXECUTED ONCE OR MANY TIMES: Once per phase.

DELIVERABLE(S): System test plan for operational applications and for the data extraction/transformation programs as well as a test database.

- The scripts used in system testing are developed based on the documented end-user requirements. These scripts will be used to test the operational applications only. Other means of testing will be used to test the quality of the data being loaded into the operational data store database by the extraction/transformation programs.
- The data is developed to support the testing of extraction/transformation programs and is populated into the system test environment. This database should mimic the types of data to be loaded into the operational data store coming from the legacy environment; the data is a small, controllable subset of all the data found in the legacy systems that can

be used over and over to test the extraction/transformation programs.
- The extraction/transformation programs will create the data needed to support the operational applications test scripts (i.e., the integrated, subject-oriented ODS database).

PARAMETERS FOR SUCCESS: The system test script for the operational applications is developed with the philosophy that it will test the most used functions and data fields. The unit test performed by the programmers will test the boundaries and extremes of the functions and data.

The test database will contain real examples of data as described by the end users. However, the test database will only be a small, controlled subset of the actual data to be used in the population of the operational data store database.

S2—PERFORM APPLICATIONS SYSTEM TESTING

PRECEDING ACTIVITY: Develop System Test Environment; Generate ODS Application Code.

FOLLOWING ACTIVITY: Perform Project Evaluation.

TIME ESTIMATE: Varies with complexity of code, but is usually two to four weeks.

NORMALLY EXECUTED ONCE OR MANY TIMES: Once per phase of development.

DELIVERABLE(S): System-tested application code.

- The unit-tested code is moved into the system test environment where the test scripts are run. This testing ensures the integration of the compiled code with other modules.
- The final system tests are run with the entire set of application modules to ensure that the system works as a whole.
- The output of this step is thoroughly tested code, ready for execution.

PARAMETERS FOR SUCCESS: The code that passes system testing has program logic correctly specified. Furthermore, all conditions are tested before the code is implemented including error and exception handling.

S3—PERFORM DATA EXTRACTION/TRANSFORMATIONS TESTING

PRECEDING ACTIVITY: Develop System Test Environment; Populate ODS Database.

FOLLOWING ACTIVITY: Perform Project Evaluation.

ESTIMATE: Two weeks.

NORMALLY EXECUTED ONCE OR MANY TIMES: Once per phase.

DELIVERABLE(S): Thoroughly tested extracted and transformed ODS data.

- Each of the sources of data (created in S1) is tested for the ability of the programs to extract and transform that data into the integrated operational data store database.
- The quality of the data extracted and transformed must be examined. Using the test data, summarization, derivation, code translation, and all other data transformations are to be tested for their accuracy.
- The ability to load the data into the DBMS of choice is tested. The mechanism(s) used to load the data is thoroughly examined for errors and reliability as well as the ability to roll back the data, should a fatal error be encountered.
- Finally, the error handling capability in the extraction/transformation programs is tested. The severity of errors, use of appropriate defaults, error messages logged, and so on are all part of data extraction/transformation testing routines.

PARAMETERS FOR SUCCESS: Fully tested data in the operational data store database and error-handling routines in the extraction/transformation programs.

E1—CREATE METADATA REPOSITORY

PRECEDING ACTIVITY: Create Technical Environment.

FOLLOWING ACTIVITY: Select End-user DSS Tool(s).

TIME ESTIMATE: Two weeks.

NORMALLY EXECUTED ONCE OR MANY TIMES: Once per phase of development.

DELIVERABLE(S): Metadata repository and access.

- A crucial piece of the operational data store architecture is the metadata describing the sources and targets of the ODS data, the transformations, summarizations, and derivations occurring to that data, as well as the definitions, aliases, extract history, and so on of the data found in the operational data store.
- The metadata gathered from the creation of the operational data store database (transformation and extraction information), CASE tool entries, manual entries, and documentation developed for the ODS applications themselves must be organized and compiled into the metadata repository.
- The end user access to this metadata must be built with ease of use and simplicity of access in mind. This access is thoroughly tested and approved by the end user.

PARAMETERS FOR SUCCESS: A robust metadata repository.

E2—SELECT END-USER DSS TOOL(S)

PRECEDING ACTIVITY: Create Metadata Repository.

FOLLOWING ACTIVITY: Develop Standard DSS Reports.

TIME ESTIMATE: Two weeks.

NORMALLY EXECUTED ONCE OR MANY TIMES: Once.

> **SPECIAL CONSIDERATIONS:** The end-user tool(s) for this particular phase may or may not be appropriate for the next group of end users. The corporation may need different tool sets depending on the types of DSS reporting each group performs.
>
> **DELIVERABLE(S):** A suite of appropriate end-user access tools.

- The ODS team and end users should create a list of prioritized requirements to be met by the access tool or suite of tools.

  This list should take into consideration:

  - Amount of ad hoc reporting needed
  - Sophistication of the end users in terms of SQL capability
  - Price
  - DBMSs to be interfaced
  - Interface with other end-user tools (spreadsheets, word processors, etc.)
  - Ease of use (graphical user interface)
  - Hardware platforms to be supported

  The requirements should also consider the types of end users who will use the tools and the types of reporting that they will be performing. These include:

  - Basic reporting—repetitive, rarely changing
  - Variance reporting—relatively routine but slightly more complicated
  - Trend analysis and technical reporting—more complicated and variable
  - Complex reporting—summarized or aggregated data
  - Multidimensional and strategic analysis reporting—quite complicated and heuristic
- An analysis of the tools available for operational data store and metadata access is performed based on the list of requirements generated. A list of potential vendors is created and vendor demos or site visits occur.
- A final set of tools is selected and the contracts placed. The end users should have the final say as to which of the access tools are chosen.

PARAMETERS FOR SUCCESS: A suite of end-user tools selected that permits the end user to have easy access to both the metadata and the operational data store data.

E3—DEVELOP STANDARD DSS REPORTS

PRECEDING ACTIVITY: Select End-user DSS Tool(s).

FOLLOWING ACTIVITY: Develop DSS Documentation and Training Curriculum.

TIME ESTIMATE: Two and a half weeks.

NORMALLY EXECUTED ONCE OR MANY TIMES: Once per phase of development.

DELIVERABLE(S): A set of standard reports generated against the operational data store data.

- A list of standard DSS reports may be created for the end users. The idea is to create a small number of typical DSS reports (10 or less) to show the end user how to generate his or her own reports.
- These reports should be of high priority for the end users, have a standard format, and run at predetermined intervals (e.g., a daily report of the top 10 customers).
- The reports should be as parameter-driven as possible, for example, in the sales report described above, the parameters may be the top x number of customers, based on (dollar amount sold, number of products purchased, YTD dollar amounts, etc.) for the time interval of (this day, another specified day, this week, this month, another week, or another month, etc.).

PARAMETERS FOR SUCCESS: End users have a set of highly useful and flexible reports that they may use as examples to build their own set of specific reports.

E4—DEVELOP DSS DOCUMENTATION AND TRAINING CURRICULUM

PRECEDING ACTIVITY: Develop Standard DSS Reports.

FOLLOWING ACTIVITY: Perform Project Evaluation.

TIME ESTIMATE: Varies depending on system complexity, but usually takes two to three weeks.

NORMALLY EXECUTED ONCE OR MANY TIMES: Once per phase of development.

DELIVERABLE(S): Documentation for the metadata repository, ODS usage, data model in business terms, help function, and fully trained end users.

- From the end users' point of view, this phase of the development is the most important one; icons and menus are generated for end users to navigate the operational data store and the applications.
- End-user documentation is created for all parts of the system. This documentation may be in the form of a manual, online help, and/or some form of help desk function. The documentation must be tested for clarity, ease of use, and correctness.
- As a final step, the training curriculum must be set up and performed. The training includes not only the operational data store applications themselves but also the DSS access tools to the ODS data (outside of the application itself) and the metadata repository.

PARAMETERS FOR SUCCESS: End users trained on both DSS access tools and the applications themselves.

M3—PERFORM PROJECT EVALUATION

PRECEDING ACTIVITY: Perform Applications System Test; Perform Data Extraction/Transformations Test; Develop DSS Documentation and Training Curriculum.

FOLLOWING ACTIVITY: Perform ODS Applications Maintenance; Perform ODS Database Maintenance/Archiving; Perform End-user Metadata and DSS Maintenance.

TIME ESTIMATE: Four to five weeks.

NORMALLY EXECUTED ONCE OR MANY TIMES: Once per phase of development.

DELIVERABLE(S): Implemented system and selected subject areas for next iteration.

- The final step in the project is usage of the operational data store applications, DSS functions, and the metadata repository. End users perform acceptance tests of the resulting system, making the critical Go/No Go decision for future phases.
- To some extent, implementation is an ongoing activity with no end. Some of the activities typical in an implementation are:
  - Loading of programs into the production environment
  - Initial loading of the ODS data into the production database
  - Monitoring utilities established
  - Backup/recovery and reorganization procedures established

The output from these activities is a satisfactorily running system.

- The last set of activities review the project methodology and project plan to determine where steps could have been performed better or more efficiently. The plan and methodology are repeatable processes that will be used in future phases, so a postmortem of the first phase could be quite helpful in the future phases.

PARAMETERS FOR SUCCESS: The result is a happy end user and the go-ahead for future phases.

M4—PERFORM ODS APPLICATIONS MAINTENANCE

PRECEDING ACTIVITY: Perform Project Evaluation.

FOLLOWING ACTIVITY: None.

TIME ESTIMATE: Ongoing.

NORMALLY EXECUTED ONCE OR MANY TIMES: Ongoing.

DELIVERABLE(S): Fully maintained operational applications.

- The procedures for making enhancements or fixing problems within the applications software should be established. These include:
  - Maintaining the development, system test, and production environments
  - Establishing a problem/enhancement reporting and tracking mechanism
  - Setting up version control for the applications
  - Updating all documentation, and training curricula
  - Maintaining the system test scripts to reflect new functionality while allowing for the retesting of unchanged functionality

  All changes to the existing operational software must be reviewed and approved by the end-user community.

- Performance issues may be identified while using the operational applications but are resolved by M5 Perform Operational Data Store Database Maintenance/Archiving process.

PARAMETERS FOR SUCCESS: A smoothly running procedure for identifying, enhancing, and correcting the operational applications of the operational data store.

M5—PERFORM ODS DATABASE MAINTENANCE/ARCHIVING

PRECEDING ACTIVITY: Perform Project Evaluation.

FOLLOWING ACTIVITY: None.

TIME ESTIMATE: Ongoing.

NORMALLY EXECUTED ONCE OR MANY TIMES: Ongoing.

DELIVERABLE(S): A maintained ODS database.

- The procedures for maintaining the operational data store database are established. These include:
  - Updating all data models (ERD, logical, and ODS) with changes
  - Maintaining the metadata and other documentation
  - Performing performance tuning, backup and recovery, and disaster recovery procedures
  - Establishing version control for the ODS databases
  - Establishing problem/enhancement reporting and tracking mechanism
  - Revising testing mechanisms to reflect new changes while verifying no changes to prior database requirements

  All changes to the existing operational data store database must be reviewed and approved by the end-user community.

- Performance tuning will ensure the best response time for the operational application aspects of the operational data store as well as the DSS reporting aspects.
- Version control will take into account the need to keep the database in sync with the enhancement or corrections occurring in the operational applications as well as the changing DSS requirements. Versioning must also maintain the his-

tory of the various versions so that end users may recall data from previous versions.

PARAMETERS FOR SUCCESS: An operational data store database that supports both operational applications and DSS requirements.

M6—PERFORM END-USER METADATA AND DSS MAINTENANCE

PRECEDING ACTIVITY: Perform Project Evaluation.

FOLLOWING ACTIVITY: None.

TIME ESTIMATE: Ongoing.

NORMALLY EXECUTED ONCE OR MANY TIMES: Ongoing.

DELIVERABLE(S): Updated metadata and end-user tool access.

- The metadata repository and DSS functionality are updated with new enhancements or corrections. The procedures to perform this maintenance include:
    - Establishing a problem/enhancement reporting and tracking mechanism
    - Updating all documentation and training curricula to reflect changes
    - Changing the metadata database to reflect new or changed metadata requirements
    - Establishing version control for the metadata repository
    - Creating new or enhancing existing DSS reports based on end-user requests

    All changes to the existing metadata and DSS functionality must be reviewed and approved by the end-user community.

- The metadata repository must keep in sync with the changes occurring within operational applications and DSS reporting mechanisms. It should be versioned while maintaining its history just like the operational data store database is versioned.

- Access to the metadata and the operational data store database must be updated as well to reflect changes. Existing DSS applications or reports must be updated to incorporate these new changes.
- All documentation, such as user manuals, help files, and training materials, must also be maintained.

PARAMETERS FOR SUCCESS: A metadata repository that reflects, in a timely manner, all changes occurring in the operational applications. DSS functionality accurately maintained to support the operational data store database changes that occur.

Appendix: Operational Data Store Project Plan

Methodology Step

	Activity / Task	Days	Dependency	Deliverable	Milestone
M1 - Project Planning and Initial Project Activities					
1.0	**Project Start Activities**				
1.1	Develop project scope document	3.0	None	Project Scope Document	
1.2	Develop project plan	2.0	None	Draft Project Plan	
1.3	Create/review standards and guidelines	2.0	None	Standards & Guidelines	
1.4	Identify user group	0.5	1.2	Distribution List	
1.5	Set up end-user schedule	1.0	1.4	Meeting Schedule	
1.6	Identify security requirements	1.0	None	Security Requirements	
1.7	Review plan & scope document w/ executive team	0.5	1.1, 1.2	Final Project Plan	Approved Project Plan
1.8	Maintain project plan	4.0	1.7	Updated Project Plan	
	Total Days	14.0			
M2 – Sizing and Phasing					
2.0	**Determine General Sizing and Phasing**				
2.1	Gather general system requirements	3.0	1.7	System Requirements	
2.2	Size system requirements	1.0	2.1	Size Requirements	
2.3	Develop project phases	1.0	2.1, 2.2	Draft Project Phases	
2.4	Review phases with end users	0.5	2.3	Final Project Phases	
	Total Days	5.5			

Methodology Step			Days	Dependency	Deliverable	Milestone
	Activity					
		Task				
PREQ1 - Create Technical Environment						
3.0	Document Technical Requirements					
3.1		Identify technical support people	1.0	1.8	Distribution List	
3.2		Document hardware/software/tool requirements	1.0	1.8, 2.1	Technical Requirements	
3.3		Evaluate & Select Vendors	3.0	3.2	Vendor List	
3.4		Negotiate licenses	2.0	3.3	Licenses	
3.5		Order hardware/software/tools	0.5	3.4	H/W, S/W Contract	Order Placed
	Total Days		7.5			
4.0	Construct Technical Environment					
4.1		Install hardware/software/tools	open	3.5	Installed H/W, S/W, Tools	
4.2		Install mainframe communications links	open	3.2, 4.1	M/F Communications	
4.3		Install network communications links	open	3.2, 4.1	Network Communications	
4.4		Construct PC environment	open	3.2, 4.1	PC Environment	
4.5		Test technical environment	open	4.1, 4.2, 4.3, 4.4	Tested Equipment	Development Environment
4.6		Receive training on technology	open	4.5	Trained Team	
	Total Days		open			

227

Methodology Step		Days	Dependency	Deliverable	Milestone
Activity					
Task					
PREQ2 - Estimate Capacity Requirements					
5.0	**Perform Capacity Planning**				
5.1	Determine estimated DASD storage needs	3.0	2.1	DASD Requirements	
5.2	Determine estimated non-DASD storage needs	2.0	2.1	Non-DASD Requirements	
5.3	Order needed storage	0.5	5.1, 5.2	Ordered Storage	Storage Order
	Total Days	5.5			
PREQ3 - Gather ODS Operational Requirements for First Phase					
6.0	**Conduct End-user Operational Requirements Facilitation Sessions**				
6.1	Facilitate sessions for operational requirements	3.0	1.5	Completed Sessions	
6.2	Document operational facilitation sessions	1.0	6.1	Draft Session Notes	
6.3	Review facilitation notes with end users	2.0	6.2	Final Session Notes	
6.4	Analyze notes for operational requirements	6.0	6.3	Operational Req'ts	
6.5	Write formal requirements specification document	3.0	6.4	Draft Req'ts Specification	
6.6	Review with end users	2.0	6.5	Final Req'ts Specifications	Operational Requirements
	Total Days	17.0			

		Task	Days	Dependency	Deliverable	Milestone
Methodology Step						
	Activity					
P1 - Develop High-level Function Model						
7.0		**Document High-level Function Model**				
7.1		Analyze operational requirements for functions	1.0	6.5	Proposed Functions	
7.2		Develop draft functional model	1.0	7.1	Draft Function Model	
7.3		Review with end users	2.0	7.2	Final Function Model	
7.4		Select function(s) for first phase of ODS	1.0	7.3	Selected Functions for ODS	High-level Function Model
		Total Days	5.0			
P2 - Generate Process Decomposition for Operational Processing						
8.0		**Document Operational Process Decomposition**				
8.1		Develop processes for selected function(s)	2.0	7.4	Draft Processes	
8.2		Develop primitive activities for processes	5.0	8.1	Draft Primitive Activities	
8.3		Review diagrams with end users	4.0	8.1, 8.2	Final Process Decomposition	Process Decomposition
		Total Days	11.0			
P3 - Generate Detailed Application Requirements						
9.0		**Identify Detailed Application Requirements**				
9.1		Develop operational data flow diagrams	5.0	6.6, 8.3	Data Flow Diagrams	
9.2		Develop operational dfd descriptions	5.0	6.6,8.3,9.1	Data Flow Descriptions	
9.3		Develop structure charts/work flow diagrams	5.0	6.6, 8.3, 9.1, 9.2	Struct Charts/Work Flows	

Methodology Step		Days	Dependency	Deliverable	Milestone
Activity					
	Task				
9.4	Produce user specifications document	2.0	9.1, 9.2, 9.3	Draft User Specifications	Approved Application Req'ts
9.5	Review application requirements with end users	2.0	9.4	Final User Specifications	
	Total Days	19.0			
P4 - Use/Reuse Existing Code and Data					
10.0	**Determine Usefulness of Existing Code and Data**				
10.1	Analyze existing code & data for reusability	2.0	9.5	Possible Reusable Code/Data	
10.2	Identify modifications needed to code and data	1.0	10.1	Modification Specifications	
10.3	Modify existing code and data	2.0	10.1, 10.2	Reusable Code and Data	
	Total Days	5.0			
P5 - Generate Pseudocode for Operational Applications					
11.0	**Write Pseudocode**				
11.1	Interpret detail designs into application pseudocode	5.0	9.5, 10.3	Draft Pseudocode Designs	
11.2	Document processing cycles	2.0	9.5	Process Cycle Specifications	
11.3	Document performance issues	4.0	9.5	Performance Specifications	
11.4	Review pseudocode with programmers	3.0	11.1, 11.2, 11.3	Final Pseudocode	
	Total Days	14.0			

Methodology Step	Days	Dependency	Deliverable	Milestone
Activity				
Task				
P6 - Generate ODS Application Code				
12.0 **Create ODS Applications**				
12.1 Translate pseudocode into source code	10.0	11.4	Draft Application Code	
12.2 Perform unit tests	5.0	12.1	Unit Test Results	
12.3 Develop application documentation	3.0	12.1, 12.2	Documented Code	Unit Tested Application Code
12.4 Develop application help functions	4.0	12.3	Application Help Files	
Total Days	22.0			
D1 - Create Entity-relationship Diagram				
13.0 **Create Corporate ERD**				
13.1 Develop draft of corporate ERD	2.0	6.6	Draft Corporate ERD	
13.2 Review corporate ERD with end users	1.0	13.1	Final Corporate ERD	
13.3 Select subject areas from model	1.0	6.6, 13.2	Selected Subject Area(s)	Approved Subject Areas
Total Days	4.0			
D2 - Develop Logical Data Model				
14.0 **Document ODS Data Requirements**				
14.1 Map end-user requirements to subject area	5.0	6.5, 8.3, 9.5, 23.2	Mapped Data Requirements	
14.2 Document data archive requirements	1.0	6.5, 8.3, 9.5, 23.2	Archive Requirements	

Methodology Step

	Task	Days	Dependency	Deliverable	Milestone
	Activity				
14.3	Construct draft logical data model	10.0	14.2	Draft Logical Data Model	
14.4	Review logical data model with end users	4.0	14.3	Final Logical Data Model	
	Total Days	20.0			
D3 - Develop Physical ODS Database					
15.0	**Convert Logical Data Model to ODS Data Model**				
15.1	Remove nonessential operational data	2.0	6.6, 9.5, 14.4, 23.2	Draft ODS Data Model	
15.2	Add summarization/derived data attributes	3.0	6.6, 9.5, 14.4, 23.2	Draft ODS Data Model	
15.3	Perform denormalization	3.0	6.6, 9.5, 14.4, 23.2	Draft ODS Data Model	
15.4	Review ODS data model with end users	3.0	10.1, 10.2, 10.3, 10.4	Final ODS Data Model	End User Approval
	Total Days	11.0			
16.0	**Construct Physical ODS Database**				
16.1	Design ODS data model	10.0	15.4	Physical DB Design	
16.2	Create indexes, partitions, keys, etc.	4.0	16.1	Physical DB Design	
16.3	Implement physical database	3.0	16.1, 16.2	Physical DB Schema	Implemented Database
	Total Days	17.0			

Methodology Step					
	Activity				
	Task	Days	Dependency	Deliverable	Milestone
D4 - Determine System of Record					
17.0	**Identify System of Record and Transformation Rules**				
17.1	Map historical data sources to ODS data model	5.0	15.4	Mapped Historical Sources	
17.2	Map ongoing data sources to ODS data model	5.0	15.4	Mapped Ongoing Sources	
17.3	Map future data sources to ODS data model	open	15.4	Mapped Future Sources	
17.4	Develop historical data conversion requirements	open	17.1	Conversion Req'ts	
17.5	Document transformation/extraction rules	2.0	17.1, 17.2, 17.3	Draft Transformation Rules	
17.6	Review rules with end users	1.0	17.5	Final Transformation Rules	Approved Sources of Data
	Total Days	open			
D5 - Populate ODS Database					
18.0	**Create Data Transformation/Extract Programs**				
18.1	Document/Plan Transformation Flow	2.0	15.4, 17.6	Transformation Specs	
18.2	Enter data values into transformation/extract tool	5.0	18.2	Entered Data Values	
18.3	Verify transformation/extract programs	3.0	18.2	Verified Programs	
18.4	Preprocess transformation/extract programs	3.0	18.3	Final ODS Data Programs	ODS Data Programs
	Total Days	13.0			

Methodology Step					
	Activity				
	Task	Days	Dependency	Deliverable	Milestone
19.0	**Incorporate User Exits**				
19.1	Develop user exit modules	3.0	15.4, 17.6, 18.1	Draft User Exit Modules	
19.2	Incorporate user exit routines into tool	2.0	19.1	Draft User Exit Modules	
19.3	Test user exit routines	2.0	19.2	Final User Exit Modules	
	Total Days	7.0			
20.0	**Populate ODS with Data**				
20.1	Generate transformation/extract code	2.0	18.4	Generated Code	
20.2	Generate JCL/Unix-equivalent for code	2.0	18.4	Generated JCL	
20.3	Transfer Code/Drivers to Source Environment	3.0	20.1, 20.2	Executable Code	
20.4	Execute transformation/extract programs	3.0	20.3	Extracted ODS Data	
20.5	Load ODS Data to Target Environment	2.0	20.4	Loaded ODS Data	
	Total Days	12.0			
S1 - Develop System Test Environment					
21.0	**Develop System Test Scripts and Environment**				
21.1	Document test criteria for ODS	1.0	2.1, 6.6	Test Criteria Specs	
21.2	Schedule test dates	0.5	12.4, 16.3, 20.6	Test Schedule	
21.3	Develop system test scripts for applications	5.0	6.6, 9.5	System Test Plan	
21.4	Develop data quality test scripts	3.0	6.6, 17.5	Data Quality Test Scripts	

Methodology Step		Days	Dependency	Deliverable	Milestone
	Activity				
	Task				
21.5	Develop system test database for extract programs	3.0	17.6, 21.1	ODS Test Database	
21.6	Create system test environment	2.0	4.5, 21.4	System Test Environment	System Test Environment
	Total Days	14.5			
S2 - Perform Applications System Testing					
22.0	**Execute System Test Scripts for Applications**				
22.1	Transfer code into system test environment	3.0	12.4	Transferred Applications	
22.2	Execute test scripts	10.0	20.5, 21.3, 21.24	Executed Test Scripts	
22.3	Document system test results	4.0	22.2	System Test Results	System-tested Operational Code
	Total Days	17.0			
S3 - Perform Data Extractions/Transformations Testing					
23.0	**Execute Data Quality Tests**				
23.1	Execute data quality test scripts	7.0	20.5, 21.4	Executed Test Scripts	
23.2	Document data quality test results	3.0	23.1	Data Quality Test Results	Tested ODS
	Total Days	10.0			

Methodology Step			Days	Dependency	Deliverable	Milestone
	Activity					
		Task				
E1 - Create Metadata Repository						
24.0	**Develop Metadata Repository and Access**					
24.1		Develop metadata requirements	2.0	9.4, 10.5, 12.6	Metadata Requirements	
24.2		Design metadata database	1.0	24.1	Metadata Database Design	
24.3		Implement metadata database	1.0	24.2	Physical Metadata Database	
24.4		Load the metadata	2.0	14.4, 15.4, 17.6	Draft Metadata Database	
24.5		Develop metadata access programs	4.0	24.1, 24.3	Draft Metadata Access	
24.6		Test access to metadata	1.0	24.5	Final Metadata Access	
24.7		Review with end users	1.0	24.6	Final Metadata Repository	Metadata Repository
		Total Days	12.0			
E2 - Select End-user DSS Tools						
25.0	**Evaluate End-user DSS Tool Vendors**					
25.1		Develop end-user access requirements	3.0	4.4	End User Access Req'ts	
25.2		Select list of potential vendors	0.5	25.1	Potential Vendor List	
25.3		Conduct demos/site visits	3.0	25.2	Site Visit/Demo Reports	
25.4		Select end-user DSS tool(s)	1.0	25.1, 25.3	Selected End User Tool	
25.5		Place end-user DSS tool order	0.5	25.4	End User Tool Order	
25.6		Receive end-user tool training	3.0	25.5	End User Tool Training	End User Access Tool
		Total Days	11.0			

Methodology Step					
	Activity				
	Task	Days	Dependency	Deliverable	Milestone
E3 - Develop Standard DSS Reports					
26.0	Create Standard Reports				
26.1	Conduct DSS requirements gathering	2.0	15.4, 17.6	Draft DSS Req'ts Specs	
26.2	Review DSS requirements with end users	3.0	26.1	Final DSS Req'ts Specs	
26.3	Prioritize DSS reports	1.0	26.2	Selected DSS Reports	
26.4	Create standard DSS reports	3.0	26.3	Draft DSS Reports	
26.5	Test standard DSS reports	1.0	26.4	Draft DSS Reports	
26.6	Review standard DSS reports with end users	2.0	26.5	Final DSS Reports	DSS Reports
	Total Days	12.0			
E4 - Develop DSS Documentation and Training Curriculum					
27.0	Develop End-user Documentation				
27.1	Develop end-user DSS menus/icons	2.0	23.2	DSS Menus	
27.2	Develop end-user DSS manual	3.0	15.4, 17.6	DSS Manual	
27.3	Develop end-user online DSS help	3.0	15.4, 17.6, 27.2	DSS Help Files	
27.4	Test end-user documentation	1.0	27.1, 27.2, 27.3	DSS Documentation	DSS Documents and Help
	Total Days	9.0			

Methodology Step

	Task	Days	Dependency	Deliverable	Milestone
Activity					
28.0	**Develop Initial Training/Help Desk Function**				
28.1	Develop training schedule	1.0	1.7	Training Schedule	
28.2	Create training curriculum	open	27.4	Draft Training Curriculum	
28.3	Test training curriculum	open	28.2	Final Training Curriculum	
28.4	Perform training	2.0	28.3	Trained End Users	Trained DSS Users
	Total Days	open			
M3 - Perform Project Evaluation					
29.0	**Evaluate ODS and ODS Applications**				
29.1	ODS Applications Acceptance Test	4.0	22.3, 23.2	Acceptance Test Results	
29.2	ODS DSS Acceptance Test	4.0	24.7, 27.4	Acceptance Test Results	
29.3	Perform project post mortum	1.0	29.1, 29.2	Project Post Mortum	
29.4	Document evaluation results	2.0	29.3	Evaluation Report	Go/No Go Decision
	Total Days	11.0			
30.0	**Convert Prototype to Production**				
30.1	Develop conversion plan	2.0	29.4	Conversion Plan	
30.2	Implement conversion plan	3.0	30.1	Implemented Production ODS	
30.3	Implement backup recovery procedures	2.0	30.2	Backup/Recovery Set Up	
30.4	Implement security	2.0	30.2	ODS Security	Production ODS
	Total Days	9.0			

Methodology Step				
Activity				
Task	Days	Dependency	Deliverable	Milestone
31.0	**Plan Next ODS Implementation**			
31.1	Select next subject area(s) to be implemented	2.0	2.4	Draft Selected ODS Phase
31.2	Review with end users	1.0	31.1	Final Selected ODS Phase	Approved Next Phase
30.4	Update project plan for next phase	1.0	1.8, 29.4	Project Plan for Next Phase
	Total Days	4.0		
M4 - Perform ODS Operational Applications Maintenance				
32.0	**Establish ODS Operational Maintenance**			
32.1	Maintain problem/enhancement tracking	open		Problem Tracking Procedures
32.2	Establish version control for applications	open		Version Control Procedure
32.3	Maintain system test scripts and results	open		Updated System Test Results
32.4	Maintain application documentation	open		Updated Application Documentation
	Total Days	open		
M5 - Perform ODS Database Maintenance/Archiving				
33.0	**Establish ODS Database Maintenance**			
33.1	Maintain ODS data models	open		Updated ODS Data Models
33.2	Maintain ODS database	open		Updated ODS Database
33.3	Maintain ODS database performance and tuning	open		Updated ODS Performance
33.4	Maintain problem/enhancement tracking	open		Updated Problem Tracking

Methodology Step				
Activity				
Task	**Days**	**Dependency**	**Deliverable**	**Milestone**
33.5	Perform ODS database backups/versions	open		Backed Up ODS Database	
33.6	Maintain data quality scripts	open		Updated Quality Scripts	
	Total Days	open			
M6 - Perform End-user Metadata and DSS Maintenance				
34.0	**Establish Metadata Maintenance**				
34.1	Maintain documentation and training curriculum	open		Updated Documentation	
34.2	Maintain problem/enhancement tracking	open		Updated Problem Tracking	
34.3	Maintain metadata database	open		Updated Metadata	
34.4	Perform metadata database backups/versions	open		Backed-up Metadata	
34.5	Maintain metadata access	open		Updated Metadata Access	
	Total Days	open			
35.0	**Establish DSS Maintenance**				
35.1	Maintain DSS help and documentation	open		Updated DSS Documentation	
35.2	Maintain standard reports	open		Updated Standard Reports	
35.3	Maintain DSS access and security	open		Updated DSS Access	
	Total Days	open			
	Total for Project (*not* including open items)	335.0			

Glossary

access—the operation of seeking, reading, or writing data on a storage unit.

access method—a technique used to transfer a physical record from or to a mass storage device.

access mode—a technique in which a specific logical record is obtained from or placed onto a file assigned to a mass storage device.

access pattern—the general sequence in which the data structure is accessed (e.g., from tuple to tuple, from record to record, from segment to segment, etc.).

access plan—the control structure produced during program preparation and used by a database manager to process SQL statements during application execution.

access time—the time interval between the instant an instruction initiates a request for data and the instant the first of the data satisfying the request is delivered. Note that there is a difference— sometimes large—between the time data is first delivered and the time when ALL the data is delivered.

active data dictionary—a data dictionary that is the sole source for an application program insofar as metadata is concerned. A data dictionary that is used interactively and on a mandated basis for the development of a system, where all development and all maintenance passes through the dictionary.

ad hoc processing—onetime only, casual access and manipulation of data on parameters never before used and possibly never used again.

address—an identification (eg., number, name, storage location, byte offset, etc.) for a location where data is stored, usually on DASD.

addressing—the means of assigning data to storage to a specific storage location, thereby allowing the data subsequently to be retrieved by checking the location. Addressing is usually done on the basis of the contents of the key of the data.

after image—the snapshot of data placed on a log upon the completion of a transaction.

AIX—Advanced Interactive eXecutive—IBM's version of the UNIX operating system.

algorithm—a set of statements organized to solve a problem in a finite number of steps.

alias—an alternative label used to refer to a data element or entity.

analytical processing—the usage of the computer to produce an analysis for management decision, usually involving trend analysis, drill-down analysis, demographic analysis, profiling, etc. Also called informational processing.

ANSI—American National Standards Institute.

API—application program interface—the common set of parameters needed to connect the communications between programs.

application—a group of algorithms and data interlinked by common code in order to support an organizational requirement.

application blocking of data—grouping into the same physical unit of storage multiple occurrences of data controlled at the application level.

application database—a collection of data organized to support a specific application (almost always an "operational application").

archival database—a collection of data of a historical nature. As a rule, archival data cannot be updated. Each unit of archival data is relevant to a moment in time, now passed.

artifact of a relationship—a design technique used to represent referential integrity in the data warehouse, DSS environment.

atomic—(1) data stored in the current detail level of a data warehouse, (2) the lowest level of process analysis.

atomic database—a database made up of primarily atomic data; current level detail in the data warehouse; a DSS foundation database.

atomic-level data—data with the lowest level of granularity. Atomic-level data sits in a data warehouse at the current level of detail and is time variant (i.e., accurate as of some moment in time, now passed).

attribute—a property that can assume values for entities or relationships. Entities can be assigned several attributes (e.g., a tuple in a relationship consists of values). Some systems also allow relationships to have attributes.

audit trail—data that is available to trace system activity, usually update activity.

availability—a measure of the reliability of a system, indicating the fraction of time when the system is up and available divided by the amount of time the system should be up and available. Note there is a difference between a piece of hardware being available and the systems running on the hardware also being available.

back-end processor—a database machine or an intelligent disk controller.

back up—to restore the database to its state as of some previous moment in time.

backup—a file serving as a basis for the activity of backing up a database. Usually a snapshot of a database as of some previous moment in time.

backward recovery—a recovery technique that restores a database to an earlier state by applying before images.

batch—computer environment in which programs (usually long running, sequentially oriented) access data exclusively, and user interaction is not allowed while the activity is occurring.

batch environment—a sequentially dominated mode of processing; in batch, input is collected and stored for future processing. Once collected, the batch input is transacted sequentially against one or more databases.

batch window—the time at which the online system is available for batch or sequential processing. The batch window typically occurs during nonpeak processing hours.

bill of materials—a listing of the parts used in a manufacturing process along with the relation of one product to another insofar as assembly of the final product is concerned. The bill of materials is a classical recursive structure.

bind—(1) to assign a value to a data element, variable, or parameter, (2) the attachment of a data definition to a program prior to the execution of the program.

binding time—the moment in time when the data description known to the dictionary is assigned to or bound to the procedural code.

bit—*b*inary dig*it*—the lowest level of storage. A bit can be in a 1 state or a 0 state.

bit map—a specialized form of an index indicating the existence or nonexistence of a condition for a group of blocks or records. Bit maps are expensive to build and maintain, but provide very fast comparison and access facilities.

block—(1) a basic unit of structuring storage, (2) the physical unit of transport and storage. A block usually contains one or more records (or contains the space for one or more records). In some DBMSs a block is called a page.

blocking—the combining of two or more physical records so that they are physically colocated together. The result of their physical colocation is that they can be accessed and fetched by a single execution of a machine instruction.

block splitting—the data management activity in which a filled block is written into two unfilled blocks, leaving space for future insertions and updates in the two partially filled blocks.

buffer—an area of storage that holds data temporarily in main memory while data is being transmitted, received, read, or written. A buffer is often used to compensate for the differences in the timing of transmission and execution of devices. Buffers are used in terminals, peripheral devices, storage units, and CPUs.

byte—a basic unit of storage, made up of 8 bits.

C—a programming language.

call—to invoke the execution of a module.

cardinality (of a relation)—the number of tuples (i.e., rows) in a relation. See also **degree of a relation**.

CASE—Computer Aided Software Engineering.

catalog—a directory of all files available to the computer. A form of metadata.

character—a member of the standard set of elements used to represent data in the database.

character type—the characters that can represent the value of an attribute.

checkpoint—an identified snapshot of the database or a point at which the transactions against the database have been frozen or have been quiesced.

checkpoint/restart—a means of restarting a program at some point other than the beginning—for example, when a failure or interruption has occurred. *N* checkpoints may be used at intervals throughout an application program. At each of those points sufficient information is stored to permit the program to be restored to the moment in time the checkpoint was taken.

CICS—Customer Information Control System—an IBM teleprocessing monitor.

CIO—chief information officer—an organizational position managing all of the information processing functions.

"CLDS"—the facetiously named system development life cycle for analytical, DSS systems. CLDS is so named because in fact it is the reverse of the classical systems development life cycle—**SDLC**.

cluster—(1) in Teradata, a group of physical devices controlled by the same AMP, (2) in DB2 and Oracle, the practice of physically colocating data in the same block based on the content of data.

cluster key—the key around which data is clustered in a block (DB2/Oracle).

coalesce—to combine two or more sets of items into any single set.

COBOL—*CO*mmon *B*usiness *O*riented *L*anguage—a computer language for the business world. A very common language.

CODASYL model—a network database model that was originally defined by the Data Base Task Group (DBTG) of the *CO*nference on *DA*ta *SY*stem *L*anguage (CODASYL) organization.

code—(1) to represent data or a computer program in a form that can be accepted by a data processor, (2) to transform data so that it cannot be understood by anyone who does not have the algorithm used to decode the data prior to presentation (sometimes called "encode").

collision—the event that occurs when two or more records of data are assigned the same physical location. Collisions are associated with randomizers or hashers.

column—a vertical table in which values are selected from the same domain. A row is made up of one or more columns.

commit—a condition raised by the programmer signaling to the DBMS that all update activity done by the program be executed against a database. Prior to the commit, all update activity can be rolled back or canceled with no ill effects on the contents of the database.

commit protocol—an algorithm to ensure that a transaction is successfully completed.

communication network—the collection of transmission facilities, network processors, and so on, which provides for data movement among terminals and information processors.

compaction—a technique for reducing the number of bits required to represent data without losing the content of the data. With compaction, repetitive data is represented very concisely.

component—a data item or array of data items whose component type defines a collection of occurrences with the same data type.

compound index—an index over multiple columns.

concatenate—to link or connect two strings of characters, generally for the purpose of using them as a single value.

concurrent operations—activities executed simultaneously, or during the same time interval.

condensation—the process of reducing the volume of data managed without reducing the logical consistency of the data. Condensation is essentially different from compaction.

contention—the condition that occurs when two or more programs try to access the same data at the same time.

continuous time-span data—data organized so that a continuous definition of data over a span of time is represented by one or more records.

control character—a character whose occurrence in a particular context initiates, modifies, or stops an operation.

control database—a utilitarian database containing data not directly related to the application being built. Typical control databases are audit databases, terminal databases, security databases, etc.

CPU—central processing unit.

CPU-bound—the state of processing in which the computer can produce no more output because the CPU portion of the processor is being used at 100 percent capacity. When the computer is CPU-bound, typically the memory and storage processing units are less than 100 percent utilized. With modern DBMSs, it is much more likely that the computer be I/O-bound, rather than CPU-bound.

CSP—Cross System Product—an IBM application generator.

CUA—common user access. Specifies the ways in which the user interface to systems is to be constructed.

current value data—data whose accuracy is valid as of the moment of execution, as opposed to time-variant data.

cursor—(1) an indicator that designates a current position on a screen, (2) a system facility that allows the programmer to thumb from one record to the next when the system has retrieved a set of records.

cylinder—the area of storage of DASD that can be read without the movement of the arm. The term originated with disk files, in which a cylinder consisted of one track on each disk surface so that each of these tracks could have a read/write head positioned over it simultaneously.

DASD—see **direct access storage device**.

data—a recording of facts, concepts, or instructions on a storage medium for communication, retrieval, and processing by automatic means and presentation as information that is understandable by human beings.

data administrator (DA)—the individual or organization responsible for the specification, acquisition, and maintenance of data management software and the design, validation, and security of files or databases. The data models and the data dictionary are classically the charge of the DA.

database—a collection of interrelated data stored (often with controlled, limited redundancy) according to a schema. A database can serve single or multiple applications.

database administrator (DBA)—the organizational function charged with the day-to-day monitoring and care of databases. The

DBA function is more closely associated with physical database design than the DA is.

database key—a unique value that exists for each record in a database. The value is often indexed, although it can be randomized or hashed.

database machine—a dedicated-purpose computer that provides data access and management through total control of the access method, physical storage, and data organization. Often called a **back-end processor**. Data is usually managed in parallel by a database machine.

database management system (DBMS)—a computer-based software system used to establish and manage data.

database record—a physical root and all of its dependents (in IMS).

DatacomDB—a database management system by CA.

data definition—the specification of the data entities, their attributes, and their relationships in a coherent database structure to create a schema.

data definition language (DDL)—also called a **data description language**—the language used to define the database schema and additional data features that allows the DBMS to generate and manage the internal tables, indexes, buffers, and storage necessary for database processing.

data description language—see **data definition language**.

data dictionary—a software tool for recording the definition of data, the relationship of one category of data to another, the attributes and keys of groups of data, and so forth.

data division (COBOL)—the section of a COBOL program that consists of entries used to define the nature and characteristics of the data to be processed by the program.

data-driven development—the approach to development that centers around identifying the commonality of data through a data model and building programs that have a broader scope than the immediate application. Data-driven development differs from classical application-oriented development. The development done for the operational data store is data-driven development.

data-driven process—a process whose resource consumption depends on the data on which it operates. For example, a hierarchical root has a dependent. For one occurrence there are two dependents for the root. For another occurrence of the root there are 1,000 occurrences of the dependent. The same program that accesses the root and all its dependents will use very different amounts of resources when operating against the two roots although the code will be exactly the same.

data element—(1) an attribute of an entity, (2) a uniquely named and well-defined category of data that consists of data items and that is included in a record of an activity.

data item—a discrete representation having the properties that define the data element to which it belongs. See **data element**.

data item set (DIS)—a grouping of data items, each of which directly relates to the key of the grouping of data in which the data items reside. The data item set is found in the midlevel model.

data manipulation language (DML)—(1) a programming language that is supported by a DBMS and used to access a database, (2) language constructs added to a higher-order language (eg., COBOL) for the purpose of database manipulation.

data model—(1) the logical data structures, including operations and constraints provided by a DBMS for effective database processing, (2) the system used for the representation of data (e.g., the ERD or relational model).

data record—an identifiable set of data values treated as a unit, an occurrence of a schema in a database, or a collection of atomic data items describing a specific object, event, or tuple.

data security—the protection of the data in a database against unauthorized disclosure, alteration, or destruction. There are different levels of security.

data set—a named collection of logically related data items, arranged in a prescribed manner, and described by control information to which the programming system has access.

data storage description language (DSDL)—a language to define the organization of stored data in terms of an operating system and device-independent storage environment. See also **device media control language**.

data structure—a logical relationship among data elements that is designed to support specific data manipulation functions (e.g., trees, lists, and tables).

data volatility—the rate of change of the content of data.

data warehouse—a collection of integrated subject-oriented databases designed to support the DSS function, where each unit of data is relevant to some moment in time. The data warehouse contains atomic data and lightly summarized data.

dBase III—a microprocessor DBMS (by Ashton-Tate).

DB2—a database management system by IBM.

DB/DC—database/data communications.

DBMS language interface (DB I/O module)—software that applications invoke in order to access a database. The module in turn has direct access with the DBMS. Standards enforcement and standard error checking are often features of an I/O module.

deadlock—see **deadly embrace**.

deadly embrace—the event that occurs when transaction A desires to access data currently protected by transaction B, while at the same time transaction B desires to access data that is currently being protected by transaction A. The deadly embrace condition is a serious impediment to performance.

decision support system (DSS)—a system used to support managerial decisions. Usually DSS involves the analysis of many units of data in a heuristic fashion. As a rule, DSS processing does not involve the update of data.

decompaction—the opposite of compaction; once data is stored in a compacted form, it must be decompacted to be used.

decryption—the opposite of **encryption**. Once data is stored in an encrypted fashion, it must be decrypted in order to be used.

delimiter—a flag, symbol, or convention used to mark the boundaries of a record, field, or other unit of storage.

denormalization—the technique of placing normalized data in a physical location that optimizes the performance of the system.

derived data—data whose existence depends on two or more occurrences of a major subject of the enterprise.

derived data element—a data element that is not necessarily stored but that can be generated when needed (e.g., age given current date and date of birth).

design review—the quality assurance process in which all aspects of a system are reviewed publicly prior to the striking of code.

device media control language (DMCL)—a language used to define the mapping of the data onto the physical storage media. See **data storage description language**.

direct access—retrieval or storage of data by reference to its location on a volume. The access mechanism goes directly to the data in question, as is generally required with online use of data. Also called **random access** or hashed access.

direct-access storage device (DASD)—a data storage unit on which data can be accessed directly without having to progress through a serial file such as a magnetic tape file. A disk unit is a direct-access storage device.

directory—a table specifying the relationships between items of data. Sometimes a table or index giving the addresses of data.

distributed catalog—a distributed catalog is needed to achieve site autonomy. The catalog at each site maintains information about objects in the local databases. The distributed catalog keeps information on replicated and distributed tables stored at that site and information on remote tables located at another site that cannot be accessed locally.

distributed database—a database controlled by a central DBMS but in which the storage devices are geographically dispersed or not attached to the same processor. See **parallel I/O**.

distributed free space—space left empty at intervals in a data layout to permit insertion of new data.

DL/1—IBM's Data Language One, for describing logical and physical data structures.

domain—the set of legal values from which actual values are derived for an attribute or a data element.

download—the stripping of data from one database to another based on the content of data found in the first database.

drill-down analysis—the type of analysis where examination of a summary number leads to the exploration of the components of the sum.

dual database—the practice of separating high-performance, transaction-oriented data from decision-support data.

dual database management systems—the practice of using multiple database management systems to control different aspects of the database environment

dumb terminal—a device used to interact directly with the end user where all processing is done on a remote computer. A dumb terminal acts as a device that gathers data and displays data only.

dynamic SQL—SQL statements that are prepared and executed within a program while the program is executing. In dynamic SQL, the SQL source is contained in host language variables rather than being coded into the application program.

dynamic storage allocation—a technique in which the storage areas assigned to computer programs are determined during processing.

dynamic summary data—a summarization whose components of calculation are subject to change.

EDI—electronic data interchange.

EIS (executive information systems)—systems designed for the top executive, featuring drill-down analysis and trend analysis.

embedded pointer—a record pointer (i.e., a means of internally linking related records) that is not available to an external index or directory. Embedded pointers are used to reduce search time, but require maintenance overhead.

encoding—a shortening or abbreviation of the physical representation of a data value (e.g., male = "M", female = "F").

encryption—the transformation of data from a recognizable form to a form unrecognizable without the algorithm used for the encryption. Encryption is usually done for the purposes of security.

enterprise—the generic term for the company, corporation, agency, or business unit. Usually associated with data modeling.

entity—a person, place, or thing of interest to the data modeler at the highest level of abstraction.

entity-relationship-attribute (ERA) model—a data model that defines entities, the relationship between the entities, and the attributes that have values to describe the properties of entities and/or relationships.

entity-relationship diagram (ERD)—a high-level data model—the schematic showing all the entities within the scope of integration and the direct relationship between those entities.

event—a signal that an activity of significance has occurred. An event is noted by the information system.

event-discrete data—data relating to the measurement or description of an event.

expert system—a system that captures and automates the usage of human experience and intelligence.

external data—(1) data originating from other than the operational systems of a corporation, (2) data residing outside the central processing complex.

external schema—a logical description of a user's method of organizing and structuring data. Some attributes or relationships can be omitted from the corresponding conceptual schema or can be renamed or otherwise transformed. See **view**.

extract—the process of selecting data from one environment and transporting it to another environment.

(FIFO) first-in-first-out—a fundamental ordering of processing in a queue.

file—a set of related records treated as a unit and stored under a single logical filename.

(FILO) first-in-last-out—a standard order of processing in a stack.

flag—an indicator or character that signals the occurrence of some condition.

flat file—a collection of records containing no data aggregates, nested repeated data items, or groups of data items.

floppy disk—a device for storing data on a personal computer.

foreign key—an attribute that is not a primary key in a relational system, but whose values are the values of the primary key of another relation.

forward recovery—a recovery technique that restores a database by reapplying all transactions using a before image from a specified point in time to a copy of the database taken at that moment in time.

fourth-generation language—language or technology designed to allow the end user unfettered access to data.

functional decomposition—the division of operations into hierarchical functions (i.e., activities) that form the basis for procedures.

granularity—the level of detail contained in a unit of data. The more detail there is, the lower the level of granularity. The less detail there is, the higher the level of granularity.

graphic—a symbol produced on a screen representing an object or a process in the real world.

hash—to convert the value of the key of a record into a location on DASD.

hash total—a total of the values of one or more fields, used for purposes of auditability and control.

heuristic—the mode of analysis in which the next step is determined by the results of the current step of analysis. Used for decision-support processing.

hierarchical model—a data model providing a tree structure for relating data elements or groups of data elements. Each node in the structure represents a group of data elements or a record type. There can be only one root node at the start of the hierarchical structure.

hit—an occurrence of data that satisfies some search criteria.

hit ratio—a measure of the number of records in a file expected to be accessed in a given run. Usually expressed as a percentage: number of input transactions/number of records in the file ×100 = hit ratio.

homonyms—identical names that refer to different attributes.

host—the processor receiving and processing a transaction.

IDMS—a network DBMS from Computer Associates.

IEEE—Institute of Electrical and Electronics Engineers.

image copy—a procedure in which a database is physically copied to another medium for the purposes of backup.

IMS—Information Management System—an operational DBMS by IBM.

index—the portion of the storage structure maintained to provide efficient access to a record when its index key item is known.

index chains—chains of data within an index.

index point—a hardware reference mark on a disk or drum, used for timing purposes.

index sequential access method (ISAM)—a file structure and access method in which records can be processed sequentially (e.g., in order, by key) or by directly looking up their locations on a table, thus making it unnecessary to process previously inserted records.

indirect addressing—any method of specifying or locating a record through calculation (e.g., locating a record through the scan of an index).

information—data that human beings assimilate and evaluate to solve a problem or make a decision.

information center—the organizational unit charged with identifying and accessing information needed in DSS processing.

information engineering (IE)—the discipline of creating a data-driven development environment.

Informix—a Unix-based database management system.

input/output (I/O)—the means by which data is stored and/or retrieved on DASD. I/O is measured in milliseconds (i.e., mechanical speeds) whereas computer processing is measured in nanoseconds (i.e., electronic speeds).

instance—a set of values representing a specific entity belonging to a particular entity type. A single value is also the instance of a data item.

integrity—the property of a database that ensures that the data contained in it is as accurate and consistent as possible.

intelligent database—a database that contains shared logic as well as shared data and automatically invokes that logic when the data is accessed. Logic, constraints, and controls relating to the use of the data are represented in an intelligent data model.

interactive—a mode of processing that combines some of the characteristics of online transaction processing and batch processing. In interactive processing the end user interacts with data over which he or she has exclusive control. In addition, the end user can initiate background activity to be run against the data.

interleaved data—data from different tables mixed into a simple table space where there is commonality of physical colocation based on a common key value.

internal schema—the schema that describes logical structures of the data and the physical media over which physical storage is mapped.

interpretive—a mode of data manipulation in which the commands to the DBMS are translated as the user enters them (as opposed to the programmed mode of process manipulation).

intersection data—data that is associated with the junction of two or more record types or entities, but which has no meaning when disassociated with any records or entities forming the junction.

inverted file—a file structure that uses an inverted index, where entries are grouped according to the content of the key being referenced. Inverted files provide for the fast spontaneous searching of files.

inverted index—an index structure organized by means of a non-unique key to speed the search for data by content.

inverted list—a list organized around a secondary index instead of around a primary key.

I/O—input/output operation. Input/output operations are the key to performance because they operate at mechanical speeds, not at electronic speeds.

I/O bound—the point after which no more processing can be done because the I/O subsystem is saturated.

ISAM—see **indexed sequential access method**.

"is a type of"—an analytical tool used in abstracting data during the process of conceptual database design (e.g., a cocker spaniel is a type of dog).

ISO—International Standards Organization.

item—see **data item**.

item type—a classification of an item according to its domain, generally in a gross sense.

iterative analysis—the mode of processing in which the next step of processing depends on the results obtained by the existing step in execution; heuristic processing.

JAD (joint application design)—an organization of people—usually end users—to create and refine application system requirements.

join—an operation that takes two relations as operands and produces a new relation by concatenating the tuples and matching the corresponding columns when a stated condition holds between the two.

judgment sample—a sample of data where data is accepted or rejected for the sample based on one or more parameters.

junction—from the network environment, an occurrence of data that has two or more parent segments. For example, an order for supplies must have a supplier parent and a part parent.

justify—to adjust the value representation in a character field to the right or to the left, ignoring blanks encountered.

keeplist—a sequence of database keys maintained by the DBMS for the duration of the session.

key—a data item or combination of data items used to identify or locate a record instance (or other similar data groupings).

key, primary—a unique attribute used to identify a single record in a database.

key, secondary—a nonunique attribute used to identify a class of records in a database.

key compression—a technique for reducing the number of bits in keys; used in making indexes occupy less space.

label—a set of symbols used to identify or describe an item, record, message, or file. Occasionally a label may be the same as the address of the record in storage.

language—a set of characters, conventions, and rules used to convey information and consisting of syntax and semantics.

latency—the time taken by a DASD device to position the read arm over the physical storage medium. For general purposes, average latency time is used.

least frequently used (LFU)—a replacement strategy in which new data must replace existing data in an area of storage; the least frequently used items are replaced.

least recently used (LRU)—a replacement strategy in which new data must replace existing data in an area of storage; the least recently used items are replaced.

level of abstraction—the level of abstraction appropriate to a dimension. The level of abstraction that is appropriate is entirely dependent on the ultimate user of the system.

line—the hardware by which data flows to or from the processor. Lines typically go to terminals, printers, and other processors.

line polling—the activity of the teleprocessing monitor in which different lines are queried to determine whether they have data and/or transactions that need to be transmitted.

line time—the length of time required for a transaction to go either from the terminal to the processor or the processor to the terminal. Typically, line time is the single largest component of online response time.

linkage—the ability to relate one unit of data to another.

linked list—set of records in which each record contains a pointer to the next record on the list. See **chain**.

list—an ordered set of data items.

living sample—a representative database typically used for heuristic statistical analytical processing in place of a large database. Periodically, the very large database is selectively stripped of data so that the resulting living sample database represents a cross-section of the very large database as of some moment in time.

load—to insert data values into a database that was previously empty.

local site support—within a distributed unit of work, a local site update allows a process to perform SQL update statements referring to the local site.

local transaction—in a distributed DBMS, a transaction that requires reference only to data that is stored at the site where the transaction originated.

locality of processing—in a distributed database, the design of processing so that remote access of data is eliminated or reduced substantively.

lockup—the event that occurs when update is done against a database record and the transaction has not yet reached a commit point. The online transaction needs to prevent other transactions from accessing the data while update is occurring.

log—a journal of activity.

logging—the automatic recording of data with regard to the access of the data, the updates to the data, and so on.

logical representation—a data view or description that does not depend on a physical storage device or a computer program.

loss of identity—when data is brought in from an external source and the identity of the external source is discarded, loss of identity occurs. A common practice with microprocessor data.

LU6.2—logical unit type 6.2—peer-to-peer data stream with network operating system for program-to-program communication. LU6.2 allows midrange machines to talk to one another without the involvement of the mainframe.

machine learning—the ability of a machine to improve its performance automatically based on past performance.

magnetic tape—(1) the storage medium most closely associated with sequential processing, (2) a large ribbon on which magnetic images are stored and retrieved.

main storage database (MSDB)—a database that resides entirely in main storage. Such databases are very fast to access, but require special handling at the time of update. Another limitation of MSDBs are that they can manage only small amounts of data.

master file—a file that holds the system of record for a given set of data (usually bound by an application).

maximum transaction arrival rate (MTAR)—the rate of arrival of transactions at the moment of peak-period processing.

message—(1) the data input by the user in the online environment that is used to drive a transaction, (2) the output of a transaction.

metadata—(1) data about data, (2) the description of data's structure, content, keys, indexes, and so forth.

metalanguage—a language used to specify other languages.

microprocessor—a small processor serving the needs of a single user.

migration—the process by which frequently used items of data are moved to more readily accessible areas of storage and infrequently used items of data are moved to less readily accessible areas of storage.

mips (million instructions per second)—the standard measurement of processor speed for minicomputers and mainframe computers.

mode of operation—a classification for systems that execute in a similar fashion and share distinctive operational characteristics. Some modes of operation are operational, DSS, online, and interactive.

modulo—an arithmetic term describing the remainder of a division process—10 modulo 7 is 3. Modulo is usually associated with the randomization process.

multilist organization—a chained file organization in which the chains are divided into fragments and each fragment is indexed. This organization of data permits faster access to the data.

multiple-key retrieval—a query that requires searches of data on the basis of the values of several key fields (some or all of which are secondary keys).

MVS—Multiple Virtual Storage—IBM's mainline operating system for mainframe processors. There are several extensions of MVS.

Named Pipes—program-to-program protocol with Microsoft's LAN manager. The Named Pipes API supports intra- and intermachine process-to-process communications.

natural forms—

> **first normal form**—data that has been organized into two-dimensional flat files without repeating groups.
>
> **second normal form**—data that functionally depends on the entire candidate key.
>
> **third normal form**—data that has had all transitive dependencies on data items other than the candidate key removed.
>
> **fourth normal form**—data whose candidate key is related to all data items in the record and that contains no more than one nontrivial multivalued dependency on the candidate key.

natural join—a join in which the redundant logic components generated by the join are removed.

natural language—a language generally spoken, whose rules are based on current usage and not explicitly defined by a grammar.

navigate—to steer a course through a database, from record to record, by means of an algorithm that examines the content of data.

network—a computer network consists of a collection of circuits, data switching elements, and computing systems. The switching devices in the network are called "communication processors." A network provides a configuration for computer systems and communication facilities within which data can be stored and accessed and within which DBMSs can operate.

network model—a data model that provides data relationships on the basis of records, and groups of records (i.e., sets) in which one record is designated as the set owner, and a single member record can belong to one or more sets.

nine's complement—transformation of a numeric field calculated by subtracting the initial value from a field consisting of all nines.

node—a point in the network at which data is switched.

nonprocedural language—syntax that directs the computer as to what to do, not how to do it. Typical nonprocedural languages include RAMIS, FOCUS, NOMAD, and SQL.

normalize—to decompose complex data structures into natural structures.

null—an item or record for which no value currently exists or possibly may ever exist.

numeric—a representation using only numbers and the decimal point.

occurrence—see **instance**.

offset pointer—an indirect pointer. An offset pointer exists inside a block and the index points to the offset. If data must be moved, only the offset pointer in the block must be altered; the index entry remains untouched.

online storage—storage devices and storage media where data can be accessed in a direct fashion.

operating system—software that enables a computer to supervise its own operations and automatically call in programs, routines, languages, and data as needed for continuous operation throughout the execution of different types of jobs.

operational data—data used to support the daily processing a company does.

operational data store (ODS)—the architectural construct where collective integrated operational data is stored. The ODS contains only very current data.

operations—the department charged with the running of the computer.

optical disk—a storage medium using lasers as opposed to magnetic devices. Optical disk is typically write only, is much less expensive per byte than magnetic storage, and is highly reliable.

ORACLE—a DBMS by ORACLE Corp.

order—to place items in an arrangement specified by such rules as numeric or alphabetic order. See **sort**.

OS/2—the operating system for IBM's Personal System / 2.

OSF—Open Software Foundation.

OSI—Open Systems Interconnection.

overflow—(1) the condition in which a record or a segment cannot be stored in its home address because the address is already occupied (in this case, the data is placed in another location referred to as "overflow"), (2) the area of DASD where data is sent when the overflow condition is triggered.

ownership—the responsibility for update for operational data.

padding—a technique used to fill a field, record, or block with default data (e.g., blanks or zeros).

page—(1) a basic unit of data on DASD, (2) a basic unit of storage in main memory.

page fault—a program interruption that occurs when a page that is referred to is not in main memory and must be read in from external storage.

page fixed—the state in which programs or data cannot be removed from main storage. Only a limited amount of storage can be page fixed.

paging—in virtual storage systems, the technique of making memory appear to be larger than it really is by transferring blocks (pages) of data or programs into external memory.

parallel data organization—an arrangement of data in which the data is spread over independent storage devices and is managed independently.

parallel I/O—the process of accessing or storing data on multiple physical data devices.

parallel search storage—a storage device in which one or more parts of all storage locations are queried simultaneously for a certain condition or under certain parameters. See **associative storage**.

parameter—an elementary data value used as a criterion for qualification, usually of searches of data or in the control of modules.

parent—a unit of data in a $1:n$ relationship with another unit of data called a "child," where the parent can exist independently, but the child cannot exist unless there is a parent.

parsing—the algorithm that translates syntax into meaningful machine instructions. Parsing determines the meaning of statements issued in the data manipulation language.

partition—a segmentation technique in which data is divided into physically different units. Partitioning can be done at the application or the system level.

path length—the number of instructions executed for a given program or instruction.

peak period—the time when the most transactions arrive at the computer with the expectation of execution.

performance—the length of time from the moment a request is issued until the first of the results of the request are received.

periodic discrete data—a measurement or description of data taken at a regular time interval.

physical representation—(1) the representation and storage of data on a medium such as magnetic storage, (2) the description of data that depends on such physical factors as length of elements, records, and pointers.

pipes—vehicles for passing data from one application to another.

plex or network structure—a relationship between records or other groupings of data in which a child record can have more than one parent record.

plug-compatible manufacturer (PCM)—a manufacturer of equipment that functionally is identical to that of another manufacturer (usually IBM).

pointer—the address of a record or other groupings of data contained in another record so that a program may access the former record when it has retrieved the latter record. The address can be absolute, relative, or symbolic, and hence the pointer is referred to as absolute, relative, or symbolic.

pools—the buffers made available to the online controller.

populate—to place occurrences of data values in a previously empty database. See **load**.

precision—the degree of discrimination with which a quantity is stated. For example, a three-digit numeral discriminates among 1,000 possibilities, from 000 to 999.

precompilation—the processing of source text prior to compilation. In an SQL environment, SQL statements are replaced with statements that will be recognized by the host language compiler.

prefix data—data in a segment or a record used exclusively for system control, usually unavailable to the user.

primary key—an attribute that contains values that uniquely identify the record in which the key exists.

primitive data—data whose existence depends on only a single occurrence of a major subject area of the enterprise.

privacy—the prevention of unauthorized access and manipulation of data.

privilege descriptor—a persistent object used by a DBMS to enforce constraints on operations.

problems database—the component of a DSS application where previously defined decision parameters are stored. A problems database is consulted to review characteristics of past decisions and to determine ways to meet current decision-making needs.

processor—the hardware at the center of execution of computer programs. Generally speaking, processors are divided into three categories—mainframes, minicomputers, and microcomputers.

processor cycles—the hardware's internal cycles that drive the computer (e.g., initiate I/O, perform logic, move data, perform arithmetic functions, etc.).

production environment—the environment where operational, high-performance processing is run.

program area—the portion of main memory in which application programs are executed.

progressive overflow—a method of handling overflow in a randomly organized file that does not require the use of pointers. An overflow record is stored in the first available space and is retrieved by a forward serial search from the home address.

projection—an operation that takes one relation as an operand and returns a second relation that consists of only the selected attributes or columns, with duplicate rows eliminated.

proposition—a statement about entities that asserts or denies that some condition holds for those entities.

protocol—the call format used by a teleprocessing monitor.

punched cards—an early storage medium on which data and input were stored. Today punched cards are rare.

purge date—the date on or after which a storage area may be overwritten. Used in conjunction with a file label, it is a means of protecting file data until an agreed-upon release date is reached.

query language—a language that enables a user to interact directly with a DBMS to retrieve and possibly modify its data.

queue time—the amount of time a transaction spends after being transmitted to the processor and before going into execution. Queue time is dependent on many factors: the system load, the level of integrity of processing required, the priority of the transaction, and so on. Queue time can become the largest factor in poor online response time.

random access—to obtain data directly from any storage location regardless of its position with respect to the previously referenced information.

random access storage—a storage technique in which the time required to obtain information is independent of the physical location of the information most recently obtained or accessed. This strict definition must be qualified by the observation that we usually mean relatively random. The magnetic drum storage devices are relatively nonrandom access in nature when compared with magnetic cores for main memory, but relatively random access when compared with magnetic tapes for file storage.

record—an aggregation of values of data items or elements.

record-at-time processing—access of data a unit at a time (i.e., sequential processing).

record type—the category to which an instance of a record belongs, as defined by the record format in the database schema.

recovery—the restoration of a database to its status at a previous moment in time, where transactions can be rerun against the database.

recursion—the definition of something in terms of itself, such as a bill of materials or an organization chart.

reorganization—the process of unloading data in one state and reloading the data in a proper and organized state.

repeating group—a collection of data that can occur multiple times within a given record.

response time (user)—the amount of time the user has to wait from the time a transaction is entered until the first of the response comes back to the originator of the transaction. Response time is a result of many factors such as line time, I/O time, queue time, buffer time, and execution time.

rolling summarization—the practice of compacting details of data based on the age of the data. The more current the data, the more details there are.

row—a nonempty sequence of values in a table. The smallest unit of data that can be physically stored in a table.

scope of integration—a statement of the boundaries of the data model.

SDLC—the classical *system development life cycle*, where requirements are gathered and where system implementation results.

secondary index—an index on other than the primary key of the table or database.

secondary key—the column of data on which a secondary index is based.

secondary storage—storage facilities not forming an integral part of the computer facilities.

security—protection provided to prevent unauthorized or accidental access/manipulation of a database.

set-at-a-time processing—the access and manipulation of data by groups of data having a commonly identifiable characteristic.

snapshot—a database dump or archiving of data as of some past moment in time.

sort—to sequence data according to some set of criteria.

static summary data—summary data whose variables will not be subject to change.

stress test—a test to determine how many resources are consumed during different levels of input processing.

subject database—a database organized around the major entities of the corporation.

system of record—the final authority as to the accuracy of any given occurrence of data.

table—a relation that consists of a set of columns with a heading and a set of rows.

time-variant data—data whose content is accurate as of some moment in time. The common forms of time-variant data are continuous, discrete, and periodic discrete.

transaction—a command, message, or input record that explicitly or implicitly calls for a processing action. A transaction is atomic with respect to recovery and concurrency.

transition data—data exhibiting both primitive and derived characteristics.

"type of" relationship—the grouping of attributes according to subsets of data.

update—the process of altering the contents of a database.

variable field—a field that may or may not occur.

variable-length field—a field whose length may vary.

view—an external relation that consists of attributes retrieved or derived from one or more base relations joined and projected as given in the view definition.

Books and Articles of Interest on Data Warehousing and the Operational Data Store

Books

Inmon, W. H., *Building the Data Warehouse*, New York: Wiley, QED, 1993.

Inmon, W. H., *Data Architecture: The Information Paradigm*, New York: Wiley, 1989.

Inmon, W. H. and Hackathorn, R. D., *Using the Data Warehouse*, New York: Wiley, 1994.

Inmon, W. H. and Osterfelt, Sue, *Data Pattern Processing: The Key to Competitive Advantage*, New York: Wiley, 1990.

Kelly, Sean, *Data Warehousing: The Route to Mass Customization*, New York: Wiley, 1993.

Love, Bruce, *Enterprise Information Technologies*, New York: Van Nostrand Reinhold, 1990.

Articles

"Providing customized decision support capabilities: Defining architectures," Auerbach Publications, 1990, by J. D. Welch—*decision-support systems and architecture (based on the PacTel Cellular DSS architecture)*.

"A case study: Implementing and operating an atomic data base," *Data Resource Management Journal*, Auerbach Publications, April 1992, by Dan Wahl and Duane Hufford—*a description of U.S. ARMY DSS data architecture*.

"The need for reporting," *Data Base Programming/Design*, July 1992, by W. H. Inmon—*the various kinds of reports found throughout the different parts of the architecture.*

"Building the data bridge," *Data Base Programming/Design*, April 1992, by W. H. Inmon—*ten critical success factors in building the data warehouse.*

"Data warehouse—A perspective of data over time," *370/390 Data Base Management*, Feb. 1992, by W. H. Inmon—*a description of the relationship of data warehouse and the management of data over time.*

"Data structures in the information warehouse," *Enterprise Systems Journal*, Jan. 1992, by W. H. Inmon—*a description of the common data structures found in the data warehouse.*

"Winds of change," *Data Base Programming/Design*, Jan. 1992, by W. H. Inmon—*data administration and the data warehouse—a description of how data administration evolved to where it is today.*

"The cabinet effect," *Data Base Programming/Design*, May 1991, by W. H. Inmon—*a description of why the data-warehouse-centered architecture does not degenerate into the spider web environment.*

"Going against the grain," *Data Base Programming/Design*, July 1990, by W. H. Inmon—*a description of the granularity issue and how it relates to the data warehouse.*

"At the heart of the matter," *Data Base Programming/Design*, July 1988, by W. H. Inmon—*primitive and derived data and what the differences are.*

"Neat little packages," *Data Base Programming/Design*, Aug. 1992, by W. H. Inmon—*a description of how data relationships are treated in the data warehouse.*

"Metadata: A checkered past, a bright future," *370/390 Data Management Review*, July 1992, by W. H. Inmon—*a conversation about metadata and how metadata relates to data warehouse.*

"Guidelines for defining requirements for decision support systems," *Data Resource Management Journal*, Oct. 1991, Auerbach Publications, by Paula Goldberg, Robert Lambert, and Katherine Powell—*a good description of how to define end-user requirements before building the data warehouse.*

"EIS and the data warehouse," *Data Base Programming/Design*, Nov. 1992, by W. H. Inmon—*the relationship between EIS and data warehouse.*

"Chargeback in the information warehouse," *Data Management Review*, March 1993—*charge back in the data warehouse can be both a blessing and a curse. This article addresses both sides of the issue.*

"Now which is data, which is information," *Data Base Programming/Design*, May 1993—*the difference between data and information.*

Data Administration Support for Business Process Improvement, Duane Hufford, AMS, Washington, DC,—*a discussion of the data warehouse and data administration.*

A Conceptual Model for Documenting Data Synchronization Requirements, Duane Hufford, AMS, Washington, DC,—*data synchronization and data warehouse.*

"The Unified Data Architecture: A Systems Integration Solution," Auerbach Publications, 1992, by W. H. Inmon, Michael Loper—*the original paper (republished in a revised state) suggesting that a data architecture was in order for future systems development.*

"An architecture for a business and information system," *IBM Systems Journal*, 17 (1), 1988—*a description of IBM's understanding of the data warehouse.*

"Data patterns day the darndest things," *Computerworld*, Feb. 3, 1992, by W. H. Inmon and Sue Osterfelt—*a description of the usage of the data warehouse in the DSS community and how informational processing can be derived from a warehouse.*

"Information management for competitive advantage," *Strategic Systems Journal*, ACR, June 1993, by Jon Geiger—*a discussion of how the data warehouse and the Zachman framework have advanced the state of the art.*

"Information preservation," *CIO Magazine*, July 1993, by Jim Ashbrook—*an executive's view of the data warehouse.*

"An Information Architecture for the Global Manufacturing Enterprise," Auerbach Publications, 1993, by Robert Sloan and Hal Green—*a description of information architecture in the large-scale manufacturing environment.*

"Retail Technology Charges Up at KMart," by *Discount Store News*, Feb. 17, 1992—*a description of the technology employed by KMart for their data warehouse, ODS environment.*

"Smoking out the elusive smoker," *Business Week*, March 16, 1992, by Walecia Konrad—*a description of database marketing in the advertising-restricted marketing environment.*

"Building a data warehouse," *INFOWORLD*, Feb. 21, 1994, by Peggy Wallace—*a description of the data warehouse marketplace.*

"Data warehouse lays foundation for bringing data investment forward," *Application Development Trends*, Jan. 1994, by W. H. Inmon—*a description of data warehouse and the relation to legacy systems.*

"Liberate your data," *Forbes*, March 7, 1994—*an interesting but naive article about the data warehouse as viewed by the businessperson who has very little insight into the issues. A superficial treatment of data warehousing.*

"The 12 rules of data warehouse," *Data Management Review*, May 1994, by W. H. Inmon and Chuck Kelley—*a description of the defining characteristics of data warehouse.*

"The structure of the information warehouse," *Data Management Review*, Aug. 1993, by W. H. Inmon—*this article addresses the different levels of data found within the data warehouse.*

"Untangling the web," *Data Base Programming and Design*, May 1993, by W. H. Inmon—*exploring the factors that turn data into useful information.*

"The data warehouse—all your data at your fingertips," *Communications Week*, Aug. 29, 1994, by W. H. Inmon—*an overview of data warehouse.*

"Commandeering mainframe database for data warehouse use," *Application Development Trends*, Aug. 1994, by W. H. Inmon and Phyliss Koslow—*a discussion of optimal data warehouse use inside the mainframe.*

"The doctor of DSS," DBMS interview, *DBMS magazine*, July 1994—an interview with Ralph Kimball.

"Why decision support fails and how to fix it," *Datamation*, June 1994, by Ralph Kimball and Kevin Strehlo—*a good description of fact tables and star joins, with a lengthy discussion about Ralph's approach to data warehouse and decision support.*

"Proving the data warehouse to management and customers: Where are the savings?"—*a presentation by Mark Thiessen, Hughes Aircraft, 1994 Data Warehouse Conference, foils and handouts, 714-732-9059.*

Prism Solutions Tech Topics

WHAT IS A DATA WAREHOUSE? vol. 1, no. 1—*This Tech Topic defines what a data warehouse is and what its structure looks like. This is a basic discussion appropriate to anyone investigating the world of data warehouse.*

CREATING THE DATA WAREHOUSE DATA MODEL FROM THE CORPORATE DATA MODEL vol. 1, no. 2—*These are the steps you need to take to create the data warehouse data model from the corporate data model.*

DEFINING THE SYSTEM OF RECORD vol. 1, no. 3—*These are the design considerations of identifying and defining the system of record.*

SNAPSHOTS OF DATA IN THE WAREHOUSE vol. 1, no. 4—*This is a description of the different types of snapshots and the advantages and disadvantages of each.*

DATA RELATIONSHIPS IN THE DATA WAREHOUSE: ARTIFACTS OF DATA vol. 1, no. 5—*These are design issues for the building of data relationships in the data warehouse.*

METADATA IN THE DATA WAREHOUSE vol. 1, no. 6—*Metadata is an important component of the data warehouse. This Tech Topic discusses why, and what the different components of metadata are for the data warehouse.*

PARALLEL PROCESSING IN THE DATA WAREHOUSE vol. 1, no. 7—*The management of volumes of data is the first and major challenge facing the data architect. Parallel technology offers the possibility of managing much data. This Tech Topic is on the issues of parallel technology in the data warehouse environment.*

OPERATIONAL AND DSS PROCESSING ON A SINGLE DATABASE: SEPARATING FACT AND FICTION vol. 1, no. 8—*An early notion was that a single database should serve as the basis for both operational processing and DSS analytical processing. This Tech Topic explores the issues and describes why data warehouse is the appropriate foundation for DSS informational processing.*

TIME-VARIANT DATA STRUCTURES vol. 1, no. 9—*This is a discussion of the different types of data structures and their advantages and disadvantages.*

CAPACITY PLANNING FOR THE DATA WAREHOUSE vol. 1, no. 10—*This Tech Topic discusses the issue of capacity planning and projection for both disk storage and processor resources for the data warehouse environment.*

LOADING THE DATA WAREHOUSE vol. 1, no. 11—*At first glance, loading data into the data warehouse seems to be an easy task. It is not. This discussion is on the many different considerations of loading data from the operational environment into the data warehouse.*

ACCESSING DATA WAREHOUSE DATA FROM THE OPERATIONAL ENVIRONMENT vol. 1, no. 12—*Most flow of data is from the operational environment to the data warehouse environment, but not all. This Tech Topic discusses the "backward" flow of data.*

INFORMATION ARCHITECTURE FOR THE 90'S: LEGACY SYSTEMS, OPERATIONAL DATA STORES, DATA WAREHOUSES vol. 1, no. 13—*This Tech Topic describes the role of operational data stores and a description of them, along with a description of the architecture that results when you mix an operational data store and a data warehouse.*

DATA WAREHOUSE AND CLIENT-SERVER vol. 1, no. 14—*Client-server processing is quite able to support data warehouse processing. This Tech Topic addresses the issues of architecture and design.*

INFORMATION ENGINEERING AND THE DATA WAREHOUSE vol. 1, no. 15—*The data warehouse architecture is extremely compatible with the design and modeling practices of information engineering. This Tech Topic describes that relationship.*

REENGINEERING AND THE DATA WAREHOUSE vol. 1, no. 16—*Many organizations are not aware of the very strong and very positive relationship between re-engineering and the data warehouse. This topic identifies the relationship and discusses the ramifications.*

THE OPERATIONAL DATA STORE vol. 1, no. 17—*The operational counterpoint of the data warehouse is the operational data store. The ODS is defined and described in detail in this Tech Topic.*

DATA WAREHOUSE AND SECURITY vol. 1, no. 18—*Security takes on a very different dimension in the data warehouse from the way it is in other data processing environments. This Tech Topic describes these issues.*

USING THE GENERIC DATA MODEL vol. 1, no. 19—*Some corporations have a data model as a point of departure for the design of their data warehouse; others do not. The generic data model "jump starts" the data warehouse design and development effort.*

SERVICE LEVEL AGREEMENTS IN THE DATA WAREHOUSE ENVIRONMENT vol. 1, no. 20—*One of the cornerstones of online operations is the service-level agreement. Service-level agreements are applicable to the data warehouse but are implemented quite differently.*

BUILDING THE DATA WAREHOUSE: GETTING STARTED vol. 1, no. 21—*The data warehouse is built iteratively. This Tech Topic describes the first steps, in a detailed manner, you need to take.*

SEPARATING OPERATIONAL AND DSS PROCESSING: SOME CRITERIA, vol. 1, no. 22—*In every shop the issue arises—what is operational and what is DSS? This Tech Topic tells you how to tell the difference between the two environments.*

MANAGING MULTIPLE DATA WAREHOUSE DEVELOPMENT vol. 1, no. 23—*When the organization starts to build multiple data warehouse efforts simultaneously, a new set of design and development issues arise. This Tech Topic identifies and addresses those issues.*

SUMMARY DATA IN THE DATA WAREHOUSE/OPERATIONAL DATA STORE ENVIRONMENT vol. 1, no. 24—*Summary data has its own set of unique considerations. For example, there is dynamic summary data and static summary data. Both types of summary data require very different treatment. This topic goes into a taxonomy of summary data and how it relates to both the data warehouse and the ODS.*

MANAGING DETAILED SALES DATA IN THE FACE OF A CHANGING ORGANIZATION CHART, vol. 1, no. 25—*Analysis of sales data is complicated by the ever-changing organizational structure. This Tech Topic addresses this issue.*

EXPLAINING METADATA TO THE END USER vol. 1, no. 26—*When the layperson first encounters metadata, the reaction usually is, "what in the world is metadata and why would I ever need it?" This Tech Topic addresses this issue in plain, straightforward terms.*

THE DATA WAREHOUSE BUDGET vol. 1, no. 27—*This Tech Topic addresses the different patterns of spending and the rate at which the expenses are spent. In addition, some suggestions for minimizing expenses are discussed.*

DSS AND DATA WAREHOUSE HARDWARE: CHANGING THE AMDAHL RATIOS vol. 1, no. 28, by Tim Bridges—*Dr. Amdahl suggested that there was a constant ratio of memory to CPU to I/O rates. Dr. Amdahl's ratios held true as long as people were doing operational processing. But in a world of DSS the ratios change.*

DATA WAREHOUSE AND SOFTWARE DEVELOPMENT vol. 1, no. 29—*Data warehouse has had a profound effect on software development. This Tech Topic outlines what that effect has been.*

Prism Solutions Executive Briefings

EIS AND DATA WAREHOUSE—*EIS under a foundation of legacy systems is very shaky, but EIS under a data warehouse foundation is very solid, as detailed in this executive topic.*

DATA WAREHOUSE AND COST JUSTIFICATION—*A priori cost justification is a difficult thing for a data warehouse to do. This topic discusses the issues.*

CHANGED DATA CAPTURE—*The resources required for repeatedly scanning the operational environment for the purpose of refreshing the data warehouse can be enormous. This briefing addresses an alternative way to accomplish the same thing—changed data capture.*

Tech Topics and Executive Briefings can be obtained from:
PRISM Solutions
1-800-995-2928

Index